Indian Prairie Library
401 Plainfield Road
Darien, IL 60561

MAY 2 1 2018

W9-AND-568

COOL SMOKE

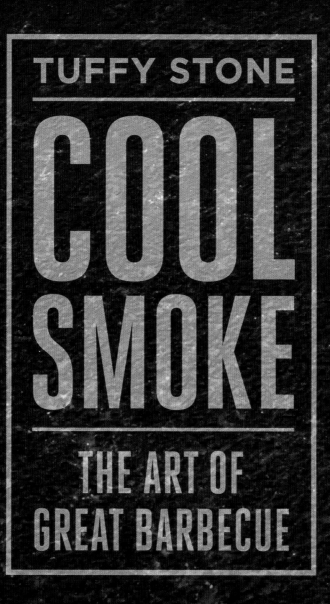

TUFFY STONE

COOL SMOKE

THE ART OF GREAT BARBECUE

PHOTOGRAPHS BY KEN GOODMAN

ST. MARTIN'S GRIFFIN
NEW YORK

COOL SMOKE. Copyright © 2018 by Tuffy Stone.
Photographs copyright © 2018 by Ken Goodman.
All rights reserved. Printed in China.
For information, address St. Martin's Press,
175 Fifth Avenue, New York, N.Y. 10010.

www.stmartins.com

Recipe writing and testing: Danielle Goodreau
Manuscript and recipe editor: Janice Shay
Food and Prop Stylist: Libbie Summers
Additional photographs on pages 32, 39, and 41
  copyright © Robert Jacob Lerma
Illustrations on pages 7, 10, 14, and 19
  copyright © Kelly Alder
Photograph on page 41 (lower right-hand corner)
  copyright © Heather Anne Thomas
Designer: Jan Derevjanik
Production Editor: Eric C. Meyer
Production Manager: Cheryl Mamaril
Editor: BJ Berti

The Library of Congress Cataloging-in-
Publication Data is available upon request.

ISBN 978-1-250-13784-5 (paper-over-board)
ISBN 978-1-250-13785-2 (ebook)

Our books may be purchased in bulk for
promotional, educational, or business use. Please
contact your local bookseller or the Macmillan
Corporate and Premium Sales Department at
1-800-221-7945, extension 5442, or by email
at MacmillanSpecialMarkets@macmillan.com.

First Edition: May 2018

10 9 8 7 6 5 4 3 2 1

To my wife, Leslie, and my son, Sam

CONTENTS

FOREWORD BY STEVEN RAICHLEN

Many people write books. Many people compete in barbecue competitions. Few do either with the sheer bravura of pit master turned reality TV star Tuffy Stone. In the thirteen years since Tuffy founded the Cool Smoke Barbecue, his team has won more than forty Grand Championships and five World Championships. In 2012, he joined the *BBQ Pitmasters* TV show, catapulting the former Marine to international barbecue stardom.

It turns out that Tuffy and I have a lot in common. We both came to barbecue through a highly unlikely port of entry: classical French cuisine. I got my start in the food world at the La Varenne cooking school in Paris. Tuffy trained with French chef Alain Vincey and eventually became his partner at the celebrated French restaurant, La Maisonette in Richmond. Maybe that's why his recipes are so thoughtfully organized and precise.

The book you now hold in your hand is the result of a lifetime of cooking experience, more than a decade of that spent in barbecue. The evocative photos will inspire you as much as the recipes. But make no mistake, this isn't just another pretty-face cookbook. It's loaded with practical information and solid common sense on everything from buying and operating your dream smoker to sourcing your gear to competing on the barbecue competition circuit.

As for the recipes, you'll certainly want to learn the secrets of Tuffy's Competition Brisket Cool Smoke style (hint: spray it with apple juice, wrap it in foil, and let it rest for 2 hours before serving). His Coffee-Rubbed Cowboy Steaks made my mouth water and his Grilled Goose Breast gave me goose bumps—and that was just from reading the recipe. Tuffy is equally at home brining pork loins (to be smoked and served with peanut–brown butter vinaigrette) as he is with grilling oysters, blackening rockfish, and smoking venison (dished up stroganoff style). If you're still hungry (and even if you're not), I'm sure you'll find room for Tuffy's Chocolate Whiskey Balls and Spiced Pecan Pie with Bourbon Whipped Cream.

Cool Smoke sits on an honored shelf in my barbecue library; it certainly belongs in yours.

Steven Raichlen
Miami, Florida

INTRODUCTION

A LITTLE MAGIC

Over the years, I've learned a lot about cooking good barbecue, and part of what I learned is that it takes a load of stamina and plain hard work to keep up a competition barbecue schedule. I've pulled my pit across parts of this country over 150 times for barbecue, and have traveled to several other countries to attend competitions, cook for our troops, or teach barbecue classes as well. It can be a rugged lifestyle, and on top of this, I am busy with restaurants, a cooking school, and a catering company.

Don't get me wrong, I'm not complaining. These past years have provided me with not only challenges and opportunities that have fed my knowledge of how to create better bbq, but the wonderful gift of endearing friendships and wonderful memories. It has been, and still is, fun to create a little magic with fire and smoke—taking that tough cut of meat and coaxing something great from it. I hope to share my enthusiasm for cooking barbecue with you in this book, sharing the tips, tricks, and lessons I've learned through trial and error, smoking and grilling in various regions and in all types of weather.

We all love barbecue in our own way. Whether you are grilling for family and friends, or thinking of competing on the barbecue competition circuit, the love of creating wonderful food in an outdoor setting is a shared inspiration. Many of us are bitten by the 'cue bug when we're young, watching our fathers tend a backyard grill in the summer; or wistfully wishing we could join the adults who keep an eye on the whole hog pit through the night.

My path to barbecue was a bit more circuitous.

HOW I HAPPENED TO GET HERE

I've always had an interest in cooking. In college, my roommate and I would prepare gourmet meals in our small apartment. We had a decent collection of cookbooks and were pretty adventurous with our meal planning. I made sourdough bread three times a week using sourdough starter from my grandmother Florence.

Like many college students, I worked to support myself by tending bar and waiting tables. After a while, I began to realize how much I liked cooking at home, and decided it would be more fun to work in the kitchen of a restaurant instead of in the dining room. My thinking was that I might simply learn a little more about cooking and make enough money to pay my bills. At this point, I never really thought about a career in food service. I just figured I could develop some great cooking skills to use in a future domestic setting.

After coming to this decision, I researched all the chefs in Richmond, Virginia, where I was attending college. I made a prioritized list of the best local chefs I wanted to work under. At the top of my list was a French chef named Alain Vincey, who owned a very small, fifty-five-seat restaurant, La Maisonette. He had been the daytime sous chef at Lutèce, a famous New York City restaurant; worked at a couple of Michelin 3-star restaurants in France; and had also been the chef for Jacques Cousteau on his research boat, *Calypso*. I made an appointment to meet with him.

Being fresh out of the Marine Corps, I dressed sharply for our meeting and arrived on time, résumé in hand. Entering the kitchen, I noticed everything was immaculate. Alain and his sous chef both wore clean white chef jackets and toques. Stocks were simmering, and fresh fish were being trimmed. He worked as we talked, and I explained that I wanted to work for him and learn how to cook. He continued to work, listening, then said he would call me. I got the impression he would not.

I went home thinking about what I had seen in that kitchen, and I knew this was the place I wanted to be. I stayed awake all night wondering how I could get my foot in the door of La Maisonette. By the next morning, I had come up with an idea I thought Chef couldn't refuse.

The next day I knocked on the back door of the kitchen. When Chef opened the door, I told him I would work free on Wednesdays and Saturdays from eight a.m. to noon; that I would do whatever was needed—wash dishes, prepare lettuce, clean floors—anything. Alain thought about it . . . and agreed—and this was how I started cooking in a fine French restaurant. The year was 1987.

Over time I moved up to sous chef, and was made a partner in the restaurant. La Maisonette was a very disciplined kitchen, and I found myself eventually working full-time, eighty to one hundred hours a week, making perfect food. Once Chef Alain made me a partner, there was no looking back: cooking had become my career and my passion. The cooking was exhausting, but the rules and rigor of French cooking fit my personality perfectly, and I loved it.

Later I met and married my wife, Leslie, and we opened our catering company, A Sharper Palate. Our dream was to bring the best in quality food to off-premise catering in Richmond, Virginia. We grew the company, and by 2004 we employed fifty full-time and up to one hundred part-time staff. I was managing the company with Leslie, but not cooking anymore, and I began to really miss it. I knew that I needed a new culinary challenge, something that would reconnect me to the food.

In the back of my mind, I had always wanted to try cooking barbecue over a wood fire. I began to research barbecue, reading every cookbook I could find. In the spring of 2004, I purchased my first barbecue pit: a reverse-flow offset pit. When it arrived, I got some hickory wood, a couple of pork butts, made a rub, lit a fire . . . and ruined a big ol' bunch of meat. But it was awesome! Here I was, a chef who could cook all these hard-to-pronounce French dishes, and barbecue had kicked my butt. It was a great challenge, but I was hooked. So off the deep end I went, headfirst, to try to figure out everything about making good barbecue. It wasn't easy; it took research, lots of time, generous advice from pit-masters on the competition circuit, and my own scientific method of trial-and-error cooking to get to where I am. I eventually realized it wasn't just basic ingredients and fire that made for good 'cue—not by a long shot.

Since that first backyard barbecue failure, I've learned the importance of good smoke, a little moisture, a lot of patience, a boundless curiosity, rolling with the weather, which cuts of meat to choose, how spices work, and a whole batch of other things that I want to share in this book. But most of all, I hope to share the excitement and magic of making and enjoying good barbecue.

SMOKE, FUEL, AND FIRE PRIMER

EQUIPMENT

There are many elements to take into account in order to achieve good barbecue: fuel, fire, smoke, moisture, weather, equipment, tools, product, and tenderness or doneness. The two most important of these factors are smoke and tenderness, but first things first: let's start with choosing your equipment, specifically your barbecue cooker.

There are many choices available, and before you make a purchase you will want to take a few important things into consideration so you can choose the right cooker for your plans and needs.

How much meat will you prepare at one time? If you are cooking for a small number of people, you can use a smaller cooker or grill, such as a bullet-style smoker. If you want to cook for larger groups of people, then you will need a cooker or grill that holds more meat, like a large offset smoker or gravity-fed cooker.

Consider what you want to cook. If you like to cook steaks, chops, burgers, and seafood, then a grill will do, but if you want to cook bigger cuts of meat like a brisket, then you will need a pit, such as an offset cooker, to handle that job.

Determine where you will use your cooker—tailgate parties, catering events, or solely in your own backyard? Does it need to be portable? Some cookers are easily transported, such as a trailer offset cooker, or smaller bullet-style cooker that can be hauled in a truck. If you are interested in activities such as tailgating, picnics, or even catering, choose a cooker that can easily be placed in a vehicle, or towed behind your vehicle.

How much work and time do you want to put into the cooking process? Some cookers can operate for a long time without any tending—gravity-fed cookers and pellet cookers, for example—but others, such as an offset cooker, require more fire maintenance. If you are very busy, you may want a pit that requires less work; or if you enjoy tending a fire, you should pick a cooker that allows you to do so. If you cook in a very cold region, it may be beneficial to buy an insulated cooker, a gravity-fed cooker, a ceramic cooker, or a pit made from a heavier-gauge metal. This will enable you to control the heat (and therefore your time) better. Some pits can run or burn a long time without assistance or refueling. Others need frequent attention. There are also temperature-control devices available that can make your time at the grill easier. BBQ Guru (see Source Guide, page 279) is an example of a product that makes cooking easier by controlling the air flow to maintain a consistent cooking temperature. Wood-burning offset cookers like the one I use on the barbecue competition circuit require more attention, but the effort can be worth it because of the rich smokey flavors produced by a properly managed fire.

If you live in an area where it is difficult to get wood, you may prefer a small offset driven by charcoal, or a bullet-style cooker, gravity-fed cooker, drum smoker, water cooker, or ceramic cooker. These are all fueled by charcoal, or some other source of fuel besides wood.

Budget is another big consideration, so my best advice is to buy the best-quality cooker or grill that you can afford. There are many well-made options at affordable prices. Here are types of cookers to consider:

OFFSET COOKERS

These cookers have two separate chambers: one to place the meat in, and a firebox for the wood and charcoal. The exhaust stack is at the opposite side of the cooking chamber from the firebox. These pits/cookers use indirect heat to cook the meat and are great for cooking meats like ribs, pork shoulders, and briskets. They come in varying sizes from small ones found in hardware stores to big, beautiful Jambo Pits like the ones I use on the competition barbecue circuit. (See Source Guide, page 279, and the illustration, below.) On most offset smokers, the fire exhaust stack is located at the opposite end from the firebox and the cooking chamber is in the middle. There is also what is called a Reverse-Flow Offset Cooker. What makes these cookers different is there's a metal plate that runs the length of the cooking chamber and the fire exhaust stack is located at the same end as the firebox. The heat travels from the firebox into the cooking chamber, then underneath the steel plate to the other end of the cooking chamber, where it rises up though a small opening and travels across the meat (placed on a metal rack above the plate), then exits the fire exhaust stack.

OFFSET COOKER

Cooking Chamber— Grate

Smoke Stack— Exhaust

Firebox

Firebox Door— Intake

BULLET-STYLE SMOKERS

These are one of the most common cookers available, and are very affordable. They are an excellent type of cooker for any level of expertise. My grandmother Florence had two, and I can remember her smoking turkeys right outside the kitchen door for holidays; I also have a friend, Jeff Hayes, who uses them in competition and wins prizes for his barbecue. The shape is oval—or shaped like a bullet—with a rounded bottom and top, intake vents in the bottom, and exhaust vents in the top. They are easy to use and are fueled mostly by charcoal with wood chunks or chips added for more smoke flavor. Because the meat is placed above the fire, they are able to cook using direct heat; but they can also serve somewhat as indirect cookers because they have a pan that can be filled with water and placed between the meat and the fire. In the bottom of the cooker is a metal charcoal ring that sits on a metal grate. This is filled with charcoal and wood chunks/chips. A metal pan sits on a rack above the charcoal ring, and can be filled with water or sand, or not used at all. The pan is designed to be a heat sink and help lower the cooking temperature. There is a removable lid on top. One bullet smoker that I recommend is the Weber Smokey Mountain, which comes in both 18.5- and 22.5-inch sizes.

GRAVITY-FED COOKERS

These cookers are very popular indirect cookers because they can burn for long periods of time without having to tend or fuel the fire, and they run at a preset desired temperature. These cookers are shaped like small refrigerators with the door on the front, which swings open, allowing access to wire racks on which meats are placed. The exhaust vent is located on the top of the pit, and on the side of the pit is a charcoal shoot with a small door at the top where the charcoal is loaded. At the bottom of the charcoal shoot is another small door, which allows access to the firebox. Inside the top of the firebox is a heavy-gauge metal grate, which allows the charcoal to be suspended inside the shoot. As the fire burns, gravity continues to pull more charcoal down and feed the fire as needed. By adjusting the size of the intake, you control the cooking temperature by how much air the fire gets. The heat travels from the firebox, into the cooking chamber, and up to the exhaust vent at the top of the cooking chamber. Some gravity-fed cookers require electronic draft/temperature-control devices in order to operate. Others use a simple ball valve to adjust the airflow, which adjusts the temperature.

Gravity-fed cookers are a bit more expensive because of the materials needed and the difficulty of construction. Most are insulated, which helps retain the heat, making them more fuel efficient, and also means they can cook in all types of weather. They range in size, but for the most part have a large cooking capacity, making them a great choice for feeding larger groups. They are also an excellent choice for the competition barbecue circuit because they allow the cook to rest while cooking large cuts of meat like brisket and pork shoulders. A rested cook will do a better job than a cook who gets no sleep.

GAS GRILLS

Gas grills are another popular choice because of their ease of use and how quickly they heat up. They are most often used for grilling steaks, chops, and other quick-cook items directly over the fire. If a gas grill has two or more control knobs for multiple burners, you can cook using the 2-Zone Method, which is good for big cuts of meat such as pork shoulders and beef brisket. Gas grills range greatly in size.

PELLET COOKERS

Pellet cookers are fueled by wood pellets and come in a multitude of varieties. They require electricity and are popular because of their ease of use. They have a temperature-adjustment control that you can set for precise cooking, and it will maintain the temperature for the duration of your cooking time. There is a range in size, but most pellet cookers handle a larger quantity of meat.

DRUM SMOKERS

These kinds of smokers have been around for a very long time, but have really grown in popularity on the competition barbecue circuit. They are very affordable to make or buy, and even though they are direct cookers, they can accommodate a variety of different cuts of meat. When cooking big meats like brisket, keep in mind that you will be actively tending the meat by flipping and rotating it so the meat doesn't sear too much as it sits over the fire. The distinctive smoky flavor of meat cooked in a drum smoker is created by the juices of the meat dripping onto the coals. My friend Tim Scheer, a great competition barbecue cook, makes Gateway Drum Smokers, which are very well-made cookers. In drum smokers, the charcoal basket, with chunks of wood added for more smoke flavor, is placed in the bottom of the drum and the meat is placed on racks directly above. A lid with an exhaust vent comprises the top of the barrel, and there are intake valves at the bottom of the barrel—the cooking temperature is controlled by adjusting these vents. The more air allowed into the fire, the hotter the cooking temperature will be. Drum smokers tend to cook meat in less time than indirect cookers, so although they keep you active, the process is shorter.

WATER COOKERS

These are fueled by wood, charcoal, or a combination of both, and feature a heavy-duty water pan that sits directly above the fire. As the fire burns, it boils the water in the pan, producing steam. This steam assists in creating very moist barbecue, and is especially helpful for meats that require a long cooking time, such as pork shoulder or whole hogs. You have to continue to add water to the pan during the cooking process, so you need to have access to water. Many Memphis in May World Championships have been won with water cookers.

CERAMIC COOKERS

These cookers are extremely versatile because they can cook at very high or very low temperatures, from 200°F to more than 700°F. They are very fuel efficient because of the insulative qualities of the ceramic material, and are fueled by either lump charcoal or charcoal briquettes, with chunks of wood added for additional smoke flavor. Ambient temperatures, whether hot or cold, don't seem to affect how they cook. Due to this versatility, ceramic cookers are used for cooking a broad range of foods such as pizza, seafood, barbecue, steaks, and chops. They can also handle larger cuts, such as brisket or pork shoulder.

There are many accessories made for ceramic grills, like heat diffusers, pizza stones, fire walls for creating 2-Zone cooking, rib racks, and more. The Primo Oval design is one I like because the oval shape allows hot coals to be set up on half of the bottom, with no coals on the other side. A cast-iron divider slides in the middle to ensure the coals stay put. I love to cook with two zones, where I can sear or brown directly over the fire, then move the meat to the cooler side and continue to cook without fear of burning the outside.

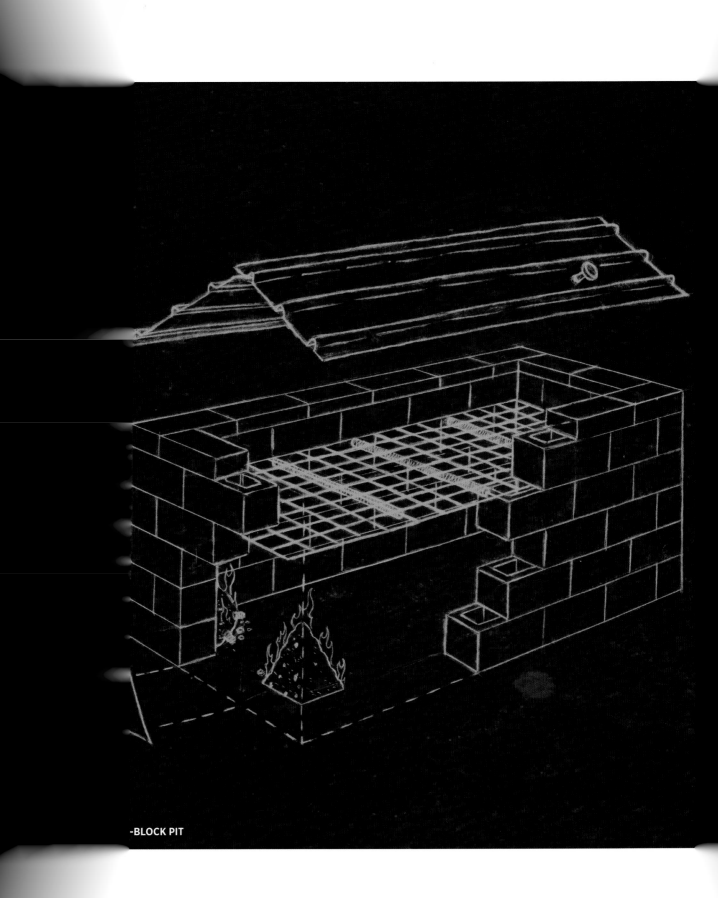

-BLOCK PIT

CINDER-BLOCK PITS

These have been around for a long time (see illustration, facing page). They can be built, inexpensively, with just a little space and time. The pit structure can be made permanent, or set up for occasional use and then taken apart when finished. They are direct cookers, with the meat positioned above the fire, and can cook large quantities and cuts of meat, including whole hogs. The fire is usually fueled by charcoal or coals created by cooking wood down to hot coals, which are then shoveled into the pit. The latter process makes for a sublime barbecue. The meat cooks very slowly at low heat, and the smoke is very mild.

MAINTENANCE: CLEANING AND SEASONING

I have heard many people say they don't believe a pit should be washed or cleaned—that you will wash away the flavor by doing so. I don't subscribe to that idea. I keep all my pits very clean, and power wash my offset pits on the inside with fresh water before every cook or competition. I clean the cookers thoroughly, paying close attention to the cooking grates, inside the top of the barrel, and inside the bottom where the cooking chamber meets the firebox. This ensures that nothing undesirable drips onto the meat from the top during the cooking and that no bitter flavors are imparted to the meat from a dirty cooking grate; and guards against any grease left over from previous use smoldering in the bottom of the cooking barrel beside the firebox (possibly causing the smoke to be bitter).

Regardless of the equipment you choose to cook with, I believe it is very important to keep a clean grill. I do like to season the metal of my cooking racks by heating the cooker and spraying any metal inside with cooking spray or spray oil, such as Pam.

TOOLS

See the Source Guide, page 279, for any item you can't find in a grocery or hardware store.

BURN BARRELS can be made from metal 55-gallon drums. Rebar rods are inserted into the middle of the barrel and crisscrossed to create a grate. An opening big enough for a flat shovel to fit inside is cut into the bottom, and the top is left open. A big fire is built on the top of the grate, and as the wood burns, hot coals drop to the bottom. These coals are then shoveled from the bottom and transferred to barbecue cookers like cinder-block pits to provide heat.

CHARCOAL CHIMNEYS are a great tool for lighting charcoal and will not impart any flavor to the grill or cooker that could cause the meat to taste bad.

ELECTRONIC TEMPERATURE CONTROL DEVICES are accessories that are attached to smokers at the air intakes. These devices blow air into the fire to maintain a set desired temperature. Some of these devices are so sophisticated that you can control them with a smartphone; there are also meat probes available, with alarms to alert you when the meat has reached the desired temperature.

FIRE TOOLS such as a **POKER** and **SHOVEL**, are important to have if cooking with an all-wood burning pit such as an offset or a cinder-block pit. Being able to manipulate or move logs around is necessary when tending a clean fire.

GRATES and **EXPANDED METAL** are used to hold meats on cookers, or to support fires so that the ash can fall below, allowing the fire to breathe properly.

GRILL BRUSHES are used to keep the cooking grates clean on all grills and barbecue smokers.

INJECTORS are large needles used to inject liquids into big cuts of meat for additional flavor.

INSULATED RUBBER GLOVES, COTTON GLOVES, and **DISPOSABLE GLOVES** are tools that I use every time I barbecue. You can buy bags of inexpensive cotton gloves at hardware stores that are great for insulating your hands from the heat. I put on a pair of the cotton gloves and then a pair of disposable gloves over them, which allows me to handle hot meat with ease.

A **MEAT TENDERIZER** (or a **JACCARD**), is a handheld professional tool that can be used to prepare meat by punching numerous little holes in the surface.

MEAT THERMOMETERS, or **DIGITAL COOKING THERMOMETERS**, are a necessary tool to have for cooking on a grill or cooker. It is important that they be accurate, and they should be tested periodically using the frozen water method. To check its precision by this method, fill a glass to the top with ice and add chilled water. Let sit for 5 minutes. Insert the thermometer into the glass, making sure the tip isn't touching the sides or the bottom, and stir the ice in this position for 30 seconds. The dial should read 32°F after this time. If it doesn't, the thermometer needs to be recalibrated.

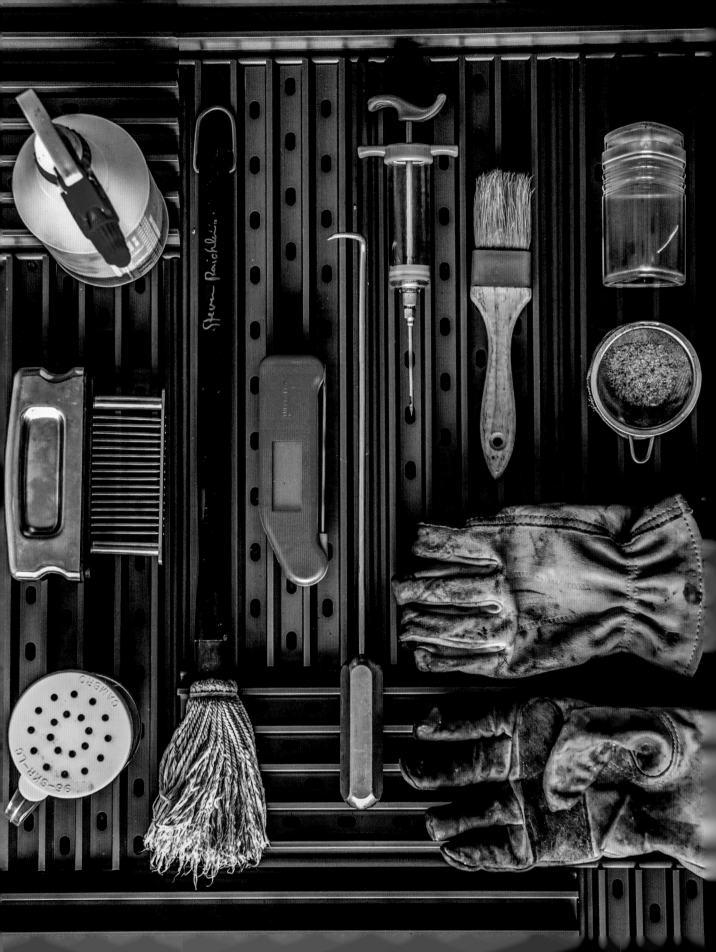

MOPS with small wooden handles and cotton mop heads are used for basting meat during cooking.

NEWSPAPER is what I use to light my charcoal chimney. Ball up three sheets of newspaper and place them in the bottom of the charcoal chimney. Pour the charcoal in the top, making sure to fill the chimney, and light the newspapers with a butane torch lighter.

PARAFFIN FIRE STARTERS are another simple way to light charcoal fires.

A **PIG TAIL TURNER** or **FLIPPER** is an important grill tool to have because it allows you to grab and flip your food on the grill when cooking.

SHAKERS are used to evenly apply seasonings and rubs to meat.

SPRAY BOTTLES can be found in hardware stores and are used to spritz the meat with water or juice.

TONGS and **SPATULAS** are familiar items to all home cooks, but for grilling you want to find long-handled versions for safely handling food over a fire or in a pit.

The humble **TOOTHPICK** is very useful for testing the doneness of ribs, and for pinning skin in place on chicken thighs.

A **TORCH LIGHTER** is a butane lighter on a long stick handle that extends your reach into a large pit, and is great for safely lighting fires.

BURN BARREL

FUEL

There are different sources of fuels to make a fire, and some are specific to the equipment you use to cook your barbecue. Regardless of which fuel you use, it's always important to use the best-quality fuel, because this will impact the taste and success of your barbecue whether grilling or smoking your food.

When I first started cooking barbecue, I planned to use applewood for my fire because it produces a mild, sweet smoke that is great with both meat and fish, but soon found I couldn't get a steady supply even though we have plenty of apple orchards two hours away from Richmond.

After some experimenting, I found that I liked and could easily acquire hickory wood, which produces a smoke that's not as mild as apple, but pairs well with pork and beef without overpowering the taste of the meat. This became the wood I learned to cook with. Historically, barbecue has always been cooked with wood that's local to the area, whether it's hickory, post oak, the stronger-flavored mesquite, or some other wood. Fruitwood tends to have a milder smoke and more delicate taste. Hardwoods can be a bit stronger, although many varieties of oak are in the mid-spectrum of smoky taste. Hickory and pecan are said to be stronger, but I believe most woods can be burned in a way to produce pleasing results. If you learn to manipulate the other elements of barbecue, you can produce good food using any of these woods as fuel. You just need to learn how best to cook with the wood you are using.

SEASONING OR CURING YOUR WOOD

When cooking barbecue on one of my large offset pits, I like to split the wood and let it cure or season for two to six months before I cook with it. I would recommend the same for wood used on a home grill. Wood can last much longer when it is still in whole logs or rounds and not split; however, wood that is split will cure more quickly than wood kept in rounds.

Wood should be appropriately seasoned before you cook. To check the dryness of wood, I measure the moisture in the wood using a moisture meter. The more moisture in the wood, the harder it is to burn. The wood that works best for me usually registers 10 to 25 percent moisture content on the meter. Make sure you store wood out of the rain and elements, and keep it dry.

WHEN TO USE A BURN BARREL: THE BEST USE OF GREEN WOOD

Green wood, or wood that is freshly cut, holds more moisture, making it harder to light. Green wood is often used in a burn barrel to produce coals that are great to cook with. This is an apparatus made from a metal drum (see illustration on facing page). Burning green wood in a burn barrel produces a hot fire, and the moisture in the wood will cause it to pop and produce small coals. These coals can then be shoveled into a pit or cooker and produce a nice heat with minimal smoke for cooking.

Green wood can be used in smaller cookers, but it must be split and cut into smaller pieces, which makes it easier to light and run a smaller fire. Cut your wood down to approximately 2 x 8-inch pieces to get a good fire. For larger cookers, use larger pieces.

LOGS OR STICKS?

The size of the wood you use is very important. The smaller the pit or firebox of your grill or smoker, the smaller the wood pieces should be. I first started cooking with 18-inch logs—like ones you would burn in a fireplace—placed over a bed of coals. As I watched the fire, I began to notice that the ends of these longer logs were not actually sitting in the coals, and would smolder and produce a heavy black smoke that I didn't want. I found that by cutting my logs much shorter—to a length of 9 inches—I was able to keep the entire length of the logs over the bed of coals. This produced a more pleasant-tasting smoke.

When I first started cooking barbecue, I was inspired greatly by a book written by John Willingham, who said we are "cooking, not smoking meat." He went on further to say that "smoke was dirt." This idea really stuck with me, and I became obsessed with learning how to manage a "clean" fire. This is a fire that produces very little smoke, because it is able to breathe and is not starved of oxygen. Fires are able to get the proper amount of oxygen by adjusting the opening of the air intake and by placing the logs in a way that allows good air circulation. A fire that is "choked" and cannot breathe well produces a heavy, bitter smoke that will convey to the taste of the food being cooked. The size and placement of the wood really impacts how clean or dirty a fire will be, especially on smaller grills or cookers. So if you are using a very small offset pit with a small firebox, smaller sticks of wood will allow you to build and run a clean fire that breathes and doesn't get too hot. This type of fire also helps the meat cook to the correct doneness without oversmoking.

WOOD CHIPS, WOOD CHUNKS, CHARCOAL, OR WOOD PELLETS

WOOD CHIPS are a great choice for providing smoke flavor when using small bullet and electric smokers and gas grills. The chips are placed in steel boxes—an accessory made for gas and electric grills—and the box is placed on a burner, allowing the wood to smoke while your food is cooking. Chips burn more quickly than wood chunks.

WOOD CHUNKS come in different sizes, but most are 2- to 3-inch pieces. These are great for providing smoke flavor when using bullet-style smokers, gravity-fed smokers, ceramic cookers, can or drum cookers, kettle grills, and very small offset barbecue pits. They burn more slowly than wood chips.

Although some people soak wood chunks or chips, I prefer not to. I just continue to add more chips or chunks during the cooking time. However, if you are using a smoke box or an electric smoker, sometimes soaking your wood chips for 30 minutes to an hour will slow the burning process of the wood and allow for a longer period of smoke production.

LOGS are best used for larger, all-wood-burning pits, or when using a burn barrel to produce hot coals. The size of the pit determines how big or small the logs need to be. For smaller pits, use split logs in about 2 x 8-inch lengths, and for larger wood-burning pits, split the logs into 3 x 16-inch lengths.

CHARCOAL BRIQUETTES AND LUMP CHAR-COAL are one of the most common fuels used by home cooks, and are very easy to find. Some brands are better than others, so look for a quality charcoal. Make sure to store them in a dry environment so they don't get wet.

I don't like to use charcoal treated with lighter fluid because of the chemical flavor it imparts. Hardwood lump charcoal burns hotter, and uses less oxygen without becoming sooty.

WOOD PELLETS can be found in most types of woods, from fruitwoods to hardwoods. These are used specifically in special electric barbecue pits or grills made to operate specifically with these wood pellets. They differ from chips in that they are made of pulverized and compressed wood and look like rabbit food.

FIRE

It is essential to know how to build and maintain a clean wood or charcoal fire. Being a Virginia boy, I define barbecue as pork. During my first experiments with cooking pork shoulders, the meat was bitter and not great to eat. Initially, I couldn't figure out what I had done that resulted in such a failure in flavor, but I eventually came to understand that flavor begins with building and keeping the right kind of fire.

For years, I watched and studied how a fire burns, paying close attention to the smoke that was produced. There are a lot of variables to consider when creating a good fire: how oxygen and airflow can be manipulated in different types of cookers; the burn properties of wood, including the different sizes of logs and the amount of curing time that produces different moisture contents; and how the wood is placed in the fire. All these things factor into what type of smoke is produced.

When building a fire, a general rule to keep in mind is that the logs must be placed in such a way that the fire breathes. Place the wood so there are gaps between the pieces to make sure the fire doesn't smolder and create a bitter smoke. Logs or wood sticks should be positioned "log cabin–style," two parallel logs laid to crisscross two parallel logs, back and forth, repeatedly, with big gaps between them allowing for airflow. If, when you light the fire, the smoke coming out of the exhaust is dark and heavy, this tells you there's a problem that can often be cleared up by repositioning the wood to allow more air into the fire.

STARTING A FIRE

There are different ways to start your fire, depending on the equipment you use and what you plan to cook. When using a large offset barbecue cooker, I start my fire with a charcoal chimney. I fill the chimney full of charcoal briquettes and light a few balled-up pieces of newspaper in the bottom section. When the coals are burning well, I pour the coals into the bottom of the firebox and start adding wood.

Charcoal chimneys are great for getting your grill going, too. If you're cooking on a ceramic cooker like a Primo Oval, it is very important not to use lighter fluid to start the fire. The ceramic material is very porous and will absorb the lighter fluid, and your barbecue will retain the chemical tastes and smell.

MINION METHOD If you have a bullet-style cooker, I suggest starting your fire using the Minion Method, created by Jim Minion. This process will help extend the cooking time on a load of charcoal, which can be helpful any time you're cooking large meats like butts and brisket that take a long time in the cooker. Fill a charcoal ring full of charcoal interspersed with chunks of wood, and leave a small open area to place the lighted briquettes. Fill a chimney with six to twelve charcoal briquettes and light. Once the briquettes are burning, empty the chimney into the empty space within the charcoal ring. The fire from the briquettes will slowly spread out to the other charcoal around the ring, and the chunks of wood will also burn during the cooking. Don't allow too much air at the intake, so that this fire burns slowly.

If you're cooking chicken or ribs, which have a shorter cooking time, use less charcoal in the charcoal ring; use even less when preparing fish.

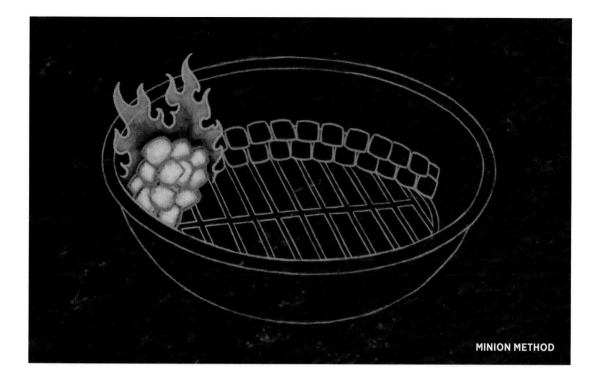

MINION METHOD

FIRE STARTER CUBES are a convenient way to light a fire. Add one or two of these starter cubes to your charcoal, and use a torch lighter to ignite them.

BISON AIRLIGHTERS and **LOOFTLIGHTERS** are portable air-driven fire lighters that are easy to use. They operate with butane and have an internal electric battery that needs charging or a power cord. They produce a small blue flame to ignite the charcoal. When your fire is started, an air-driven lighter can blast air to the wood to accelerate the burn and spread the fire.

WEED BURNERS are often used to assist in starting larger wood fires. On very cold days, weed burners can also be used to help heat the inside of big steel barbecue pits. These devices are a little tricky to operate, so be sure to follow the instructions carefully. They blow fire out like a small flamethrower or a big torch. Frankly, they scare me a little.

A **PROPANE TORCH**, which is like a plumber's torch, can also be used to start charcoal fires.

MAINTAINING AND CONTROLLING THE FIRE AND TEMPERATURE

You can control the temperature of a barbecue pit or grill by adjusting the intake and exhaust dampers, as well as by controlling the size of your fire. With smaller barbecue cookers, a small fire will reach the desired cooking temperature; similarly, larger pits may require larger fires. Insulated cookers will not need as big of a fire to heat to the desired cooking temperature. Once they come to temperature, they stay warm, because they hold and maintain the heat due to the insulation.

The barbecue recipes in this book indicate a specific temperature for optimal result. If your cooker doesn't come with a built-in temperature gauge, use an oven thermometer placed inside the cooking chamber to test the temperature often during cooking.

As a rule, I try to cook with the smallest fire necessary to reach the desired cooking temperature. By doing this, I am able to let the fire burn cleanly, using plenty of oxygen and producing good smoke. I like to start a fire that's a bit bigger than needed, then let it burn down some before putting my food

on. A smaller fire needs refueling more frequently. You need to have a good fire burning when you introduce the meat so it will cook longer before having to refuel.

Most grills or cookers have an intake damper and an exhaust damper. By adjusting these dampers, you can control the temperature and smoke while cooking. By opening the intake damper wide, you increase airflow to the fire and cause it to burn hotter. Closing down the intake damper reduces the airflow to the fire and causes the fire to burn cooler, lowering the cooking temperature.

The exhaust dampers can be adjusted to manipulate the temperature and smoke on a grill or cooker. Keeping the exhaust damper wide-open allows both the heat and the smoke to exit freely. This can ensure you don't oversmoke what you are cooking, but some grills will get too hot or too cool with the exhaust damper completely open. It takes some practice with your equipment to determine the best method to use for manipulating your fire temperature and smoke.

BISCUIT TEST

A trick to learning how heat travels in a new cooker is the biscuit test. Light a fire in your barbecue cooker and bring the cooking temperature up to approximately 275°F. Once the cooker is hot, open a couple of tubes of biscuits that you can buy in the grocery store. Place biscuits on the cooking grate in a grid pattern with 4 to 6–inch gaps, so that biscuits are resting on most areas of the cooking surface. Close the cooking doors and cook the biscuits for about 20 minutes. Open the

cooking doors and take a look at the biscuits. You will be able to learn how the heat travels in your pit, by seeing how the biscuits brown. The hotter areas of your pit will be where the biscuits are browner and the cooler areas will be where the biscuits are not as dark. This can be useful knowledge in helping you decide where to place meats on your cooker. I place bigger cuts of meat in the hotter spots and the smaller cuts of meat go in the cooler spots of my cooking chamber.

COOKING METHODS WITH FIRE

DIRECT COOKING OR GRILLING

This is when food is cooked directly over the fire. This method of cooking is best for foods such as steaks, chops, seafood, and vegetables, because they only need a short cook time in order to be done. Placing food on the grill directly over the fire is a more extreme heat, which shortens the cooking time. Direct-cooking temperatures can range from 300°F to more than 700°F. This hot radiant-cooking technique helps to sear, or char, the outside surfaces of the meat, adding a nice caramelized flavor.

This charring is called the Maillard reaction, or browning action. With the application of high heat, the amino acids and simple sugars change, causing foods not only to brown but to develop great flavor. The higher the heat is, the quicker the process. Direct cooking requires the cook to be more watchful during the process, paying careful attention to the color of the meat and flipping it when the food has browned nicely.

Using a grill brush to thoroughly clean the grates before you cook will help prevent sticking. You can cook direct using gas, charcoal, or wood for fuel. If you use charcoal or wood, it's important to let the fire burn down to hot coals before placing the food over the fire. With direct cooking or grilling, most foods will not take as long to cook, so the food will have a milder smoke flavor than a brisket that would cook for hours on an indirect cooker.

Direct cooking is the most common form of outdoor cooking. Old-school cinder-block pits are direct cookers, but the pit temperatures are usually kept low by not fueling them often and controlling the temperature. These types of pits are often fueled by charcoal or hot coals created from a burn barrel.

2-ZONE COOKING

This is a great method to use on a grill with meats that take longer to cook. You can do this with a gas or charcoal grill. Using a gas or charcoal grill, this method calls for a hot, or direct cooking side, and a cooler, or indirect cooking side. To set up 2-Zone cooking for a gas grill, the grill must have more than one burner. You must turn one burner on low to medium heat to create the hot side, and turn the other burner off completely to create the cooler side. You can sear or brown the meat using the hot side, then move the meat over to the cooler side and continue to let the meat cook until done. The same 2-Zone setup can be done with a charcoal grill by placing hot coals on only one half of the bottom. On the other half of the grill bottom, either leave the space empty or place a small aluminum drip pan.

INDIRECT COOKING

This happens when food is cooked not directly over the fire or source of heat, but is placed in a section of the grill or pit to the side of the fire. This allows the food to cook in a slower, gentler manner because the fire is not in direct contact with the product. Gravity-fed charcoal cookers

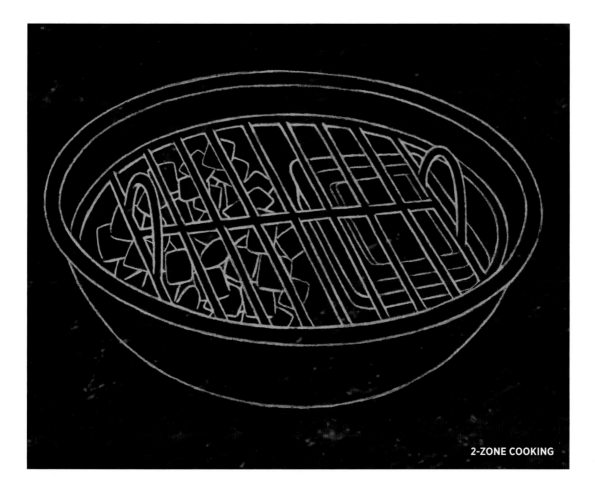

2-ZONE COOKING

and offset pits are two examples of barbecue cookers that are indirect cookers.

This type of cooking is great for larger cuts of meat that require a longer time to cook to tenderness. Pork shoulders or beef briskets can take as long as 7 to 16 hours to cook to tenderness, especially when cooking at lower cooking temperatures like 200°F to 250°F. By not having the fire directly under the meats, the cook doesn't have to tend the meat as often, making the process easier. This type of cooking also reduces the possibility of burning the meat. Quick-cook meats like chops, steaks, and seafood can be cooked with the indirect cooking method, but because the heat is lower, they will not brown as well as they would on a grill. Large cuts that require a long cooking time will eventually brown on the outside, achieving that extra dimension of flavor through the smoke and caramelization of the meat. Indirect cooking is usually fueled by charcoal, wood, or a combination of both.

TEXAS CRUTCH

SMOKE

Proper smoke management is key to making great-tasting food on a smoker or grill. Smoke is one of the most important factors in the success of my Cool Smoke cooking team on the competition circuit. I treat smoke like salt and pepper when cooking—as a flavor, not so much as the primary cooking process. Whatever I am cooking—poultry, meat, or seafood—I want the flavor of the meat to be the first thing you taste. I want the other tastes to play a supporting role: the taste of smoke should come after the other flavors of the food. For example, if I'm cooking chicken, I want to taste the meat first, then the seasoning, the sauce, and, finally, the smoke.

When you're cooking with an all-wood or charcoal fire, it's important to maintain quality smoke during cooking. Good smoke is thin and often said to be blue in color. In fact, it is very light and often difficult to see at all. This smoke is achieved by building a fire that has plenty of oxygen and "breathes" properly. When a wood or charcoal fire is allowed to breathe correctly, the smoke will be pleasant tasting. A poorly burning fire will produce a thick white smoke. Without enough oxygen, a fire will smolder, producing creosote, which imparts a bitter taste to the food. The flavor of smoke needs to be mild, not harsh or bitter.

Some foods can handle a lot of smoke, whereas others are more delicate and need less smoke. I suspect that back in the days when we only had wood-burning ovens, cooks knew these things better than anyone does now. A cook who had to bake a cake in a wood-burning oven must have been very proficient at running a clean fire. Imagine how a cake would taste if imbued with a heavy smoky flavor—I don't think it would be very good.

The bigger the cut of meat, the more smoke it can take. Meats such as pork butt and brisket require more smoke than small cuts do. Chicken will need even less smoke than ribs. Through experience, you learn how much smoke flavor you prefer for different foods, but in these recipes I have specified what I think is best. Often people ruin their first attempts at cooking with fire and wood by putting too much smoke on their meat.

TEXAS CRUTCH

You can control the amount of smoke you want on your barbecue using the "Texas Crutch" method. After meat has cooked, uncovered, for a period of time on the grill, it is removed and tightly wrapped in aluminum foil or butcher's paper, then returned to the cooker to finish cooking to the proper tenderness. This controls the level of smoke applied to the food and prevents oversmoking or drying out. The best time to remove the meat from the smoker or grill and wrap is when the meat has achieved a nice color—perhaps a bark—and has a good, smoky taste that doesn't overpower the taste of the meat itself, but is not yet tender. Once wrapped, the meat can then continue to be cooked until tender. (See photographs on opposite page.)

WEATHER

You can barbecue outside in most any type of weather, but it's important to factor the weather into your planning and timing of the cook. The size of your fire, or how much fuel you need to cook, is impacted by the ambient, or outdoor, temperature. Check the weather forecast: if it calls for rain, find a covered location where you can cook without being rained on. Keep in mind that your cooker may operate differently in hot and cold conditions. When it's very hot in the summer, a smaller fire is often better, and your cook times for food will be quicker. If your cooker isn't insulated, it will be harder to keep your cooking temperature low enough on a hot day, whereas in winter a bigger fire is often needed to keep your cooker at the desired temperature. It can take longer for a grill to get up to optimal temperature on a cold day, and the food may take longer to cook. Remember also that opening the door or lid to the cooker to check or spray meat will allow cool air in and slow the cooking process. By opening the intake damper, you can add more oxygen to the fire to increase the heat incrementally.

Wind is another thing to pay attention to as you cook. I try to strategically place my cooker or grill in a place that's protected from the wind. Wind rushing in the intake vents, or dragging across the exhaust stack, creates more draw and often makes it a challenge to maintain the desired cooking temperature. To prevent wind blowing into my intake vents, I sometimes create a makeshift windbreak using the backrest of a chair, or I move my grill or cooker behind a protective wall to help shield it.

PRODUCT

HOW TO SELECT MEAT

I like to start with a good product, so I recommend that you use the best meat you can afford. Outdoor grilling and smoking is fun and can be a rewarding way to coax flavor out of meat; but barbecue requires more time than cooking in an indoor kitchen. If you are going to invest time and effort into cooking barbecue, make sure you choose good meat. Pay attention to the age of the meat—fresh seafood and poultry will not keep as long as fresh pork does, and fresh pork doesn't keep as long as fresh beef.

To tell if meat and seafood are fresh, there should be no odor to the meat, and it should feel firm and not slimy to the touch. With pork and beef, I look for meat that is well marbled with internal fat, because this will produce a juicier bite when it is cooked to tender. The packing date of meat is typically the same day the animal has been processed and can be found on the shipping box or packaging (refer to the meat and poultry chapters for more information). There's nothing like old-school friendliness to solve this problem: develop a good relationship with your butcher or meat department manager to ensure you are buying the best meat.

DONENESS

TENDERNESS, OR THE ART OF DONENESS

Not enough can be said of the importance of tenderness, or doneness, in barbecue. If I had to pick two things that have been instrumental in the success Cool Smoke has had on the competition circuit, they would be (1) treating smoke like salt and pepper, and (2) achieving perfect tenderness in meat.

The best food not only tastes great, but is also cooked to perfection. Of course, perfect doneness is also a matter of taste. My mother, Charlotte, preferred her steaks, chops, and burgers cooked well-done, while I, on the other hand, prefer these cuts of meat cooked far less done. When it comes to "barbecue meats"—often referring to meats that are tough and require a long cooking time to break down the collagens and become tender—it is often said among competition cooks that "overs beat unders." This basically means that it's better to cook cuts of meat like ribs or brisket more tender, in other words, overcook rather than undercook these tough cuts of meat.

No one likes tough barbecue. It is said often with pride that a rib has been cooked until the meat is "falling off the bone"—a statement that reinforces the idea that people want their barbecue tender. That said, a perfectly cooked rib is one that is cooked long enough to render the meat tender; and when the rib cools down, it still has a nice gentle chew. In a perfect barbecue scenario, the meat would not fall off the bone, but come cleanly off the bone when you take a bite—but only where your teeth bites. The remaining (unbitten) meat would stay affixed to the bone.

Tough barbecue meats are cooked to internal temperatures as high as 190°F to 210°F. This can take hours and hours, and often,

inexperienced home cooks won't cook meat long enough. When barbecue isn't cooked long enough to completely break down the muscle fibers, it may seem done, but when the meat cools it will toughen up and the chew won't be as tender as you'd like. For that reason, and because we are particular about cook times, temperatures, and all aspects of creating a perfect dish, all the recipes in this cookbook give cooking times, pit/grill temperatures, and internal meat temperatures that have been tested many times.

I'm happy that these recipes will produce delicious results, but please remember that feel and touch are also important in getting a result that pleases you, the home cook. Through practice you can develop a better sense of feel in order to determine when meat is done to your liking. I call this "mastering the art of doneness or tenderness."

Doneness, or tenderness, is achieved with less time on the grill when cooking more delicate meats, whose optimal internal temperature can range from 120°F to 140°F. The longer these meats are cooked, the tougher they will become, so internal temperature is an important benchmark in the cooking process. Pork is a great example of a positive change in the public perception of when a meat is "done." The USDA at one time recommended cooking pork chops and tenderloin to 165°F because of the potential for trichinosis, caused by a parasite in the meat; however, because of changes in the feeding practices of the animals, this is no longer an issue. The USDA has lowered their recommended internal temperature of cooked pork to 145°F. This change vastly improves the taste and texture of pork loins and tenderloins that were, historically, overcooked. By cooking these pork cuts to a lower internal temperature, the meat will stay moist and be easier to chew.

Another necessary step to improve the taste and tenderness of grilled or barbecued meat is to allow the meat to cool for a few minutes before carving and serving. Letting meat "rest" when it comes off the grill allows the juices to be redistributed throughout the meat.

If you carve meat immediately off the grill or cooker, the juice will push out of the meat, and it will taste dry. Another benefit to allowing meat to rest after cooking is that the tendons and muscles in the meat relax as the juice is redistributed, and this enhances the quality of the chew. As a rule of thumb, steaks and chops—the smaller, more delicate cuts of meat—need a shorter resting time than larger cuts of meat like pork shoulders, beef brisket, and turkey breasts.

Think of a simple bell graph. As meat rests for a period of time, the product starts to improve, and at a certain time it tastes best—that's when it hits its peak. After that, the tenderness and mouthfeel start to decrease, the fats cool and the meat begins to dry out. However, understand that ambient temperature can greatly impact these rest times. If you are cooking and resting meat outside in cold weather, then the rest time will be shorter than if you are preparing and resting the meat in a very hot environment.

Another thing to know about meat is that when it comes off the grill or cooker, it will continue to cook—this is known as "carryover cooking." This is especially important to consider when cooking dishes such as steaks, chops, or fish, which take less time on the grill. The temperature range for perfection on these meats is much smaller. For example, if you grill a pork chop to an internal temperature of 140°F, then remove it from the heat, the meat will continue to cook off the grill, and the internal temperature will rise to 145°F, which is an optimal temperature. On the other hand, if you cooked the chop to 145°F and remove it from the grill, it will continue to cook to 150°F, and the meat will be drier and not as tender. So pay attention to the times and temperatures in these recipes. We have taken carryover cooking into account in the directions.

THE IMPORTANCE OF MOISTURE

From the very beginning of my barbecue career, I have liked to spray the meat as it cooks. While competing in 2006 at the Great American BBQ Contest in Kansas City, I had an experience that really impacted my thinking about moisture and its effect on cooking. It had rained very hard while I was cooking, and I noticed that my finished pork was really great that day—very moist and tender. That day at awards, we took first place in pork and received our first perfect score. It struck me that the finished barbecue was always better when I cooked in the rain. A lightbulb went off in my head, and I determined at that moment to learn how to "make it rain" whenever I cooked barbecue.

After that I became very focused on how important moisture is to making good barbecue. I looked at different ways I could bring more moisture into the process using water pans, sprayers, spritzes, and mops. Typically, meat such as beef brisket or pork shoulder takes a long time to cook. Depending on the type of equipment you are using, the cooking environment may be moist or dry. My big offset barbecue pits tend to have a lot of convection—or airflow—and the moisture level inside the cooking chamber tends to be low. I found that by placing a water pan on the cooking surface adjacent to the firebox and spraying big cuts of meats occasionally with water or apple juice, the quality of my finished meats improved greatly.

The water pan will produce moisture through steam. This steam helps produce a better exterior with a more enjoyable chew. Spritzes and mops are good ways to provide moisture while cooking, and also add subtle flavor to the meat.

THE TRAIN ANALOGY OF BIG CUTS, OR HOW IS COOKING BARBECUE LIKE A TRAIN?

When I began cooking barbecue back in 2004, I had never cooked beef brisket. Cooking my first 20-pound beef brisket over an all-wood-burning pit proved to be very challenging. Trying to figure out how the fire impacted both the cooking temperature in the pit and the smokiness of the meat was exciting but difficult.

A brisket needs to be cooked to a doneness that's not too hard to chew, not overcooked, but so perfectly tender that at times care must be taken when picking up the slices to avoid breaking them. In those first barbecue attempts, I knew that the cook times needed to be very long, and as I watched the internal temperature slowly creep higher, it seemed like those briskets would never get done. It dawned on me that cooking these big cuts of meat, like beef brisket, is akin to the speed of a train. When a train starts to move forward from a stopped position, it is slow to get moving. As the speed starts to pick up, momentum increases and the speed begins to increase more rapidly. Big cuts of meat are very much like that: When they are first put on the cooker, internal temperatures will be slow to rise. The internal temperature of beef brisket will take a long time to go from 40°F to 120°F, but the temperatures will start to rise more quickly the hotter it gets. Once a brisket reaches a temperature over 170°F, the time it takes for the meat to cook to a perfect doneness becomes faster. Remember this analogy when cooking and do not let the slowness alarm you, but also pay attention as the meat temperatures get higher, as you will need to check for doneness more frequently.

Of course, there are always going to be problem situations when cooking for long periods of time, and throughout the recipes in this cookbook we've provided tips to help guide you through these. One of the most common problems that occurs is "the stall." During the process of cooking large, tough cuts of meat, such as beef brisket and pork shoulder, the internal temperature of the meat will increase to around 165°F and moisture will naturally begin to push out from inside the meat. This causes the internal temperature to stall and remain at that same temperature for a period of time. For cooks who experience this for the first time, it can be a bit stressful. Two things can get you through the stall: time and heat. Just know that it will happen and it is okay to keep cooking until the internal temperature begins to rise again. If you need to get through the stall more quickly, simply increase the pit temperature.

MISE EN PLACE

Mise en place is a French term I learned in the beginning of my cooking apprenticeship under Chef Alain. It translates to "put in place," and refers to a chef needing to be organized and prepared. Having all your equipment and ingredients gathered, cleaned, and prepped before you start cooking will make for a smooth experience. This is especially important when cooking outdoors on a grill or cooker, because of the potential additional challenges that outside elements can cause.

"It's all in how you handle catastrophes" has been one of my sayings for a long time. This credo came from years of experiences at my catering company. Off-premise catering can be very challenging, and we have overcome many obstacles, including hurricanes, thunderstorms, snowstorms, and electrical outages, to get the job done. Working through these obstacles has helped make me both a better competition cook and a better all-around cook.

When people host their first barbecue gathering, inviting friends and family, it can be stressful. Barbecue sometimes involves cooking for long hours and feeding large groups of people—both daunting tasks. Make a good plan, listing on a timeline things that need to be bought and prepared, and noting when these duties need to be accomplished. Always allow yourself a cushion of time. An old friend always told me, "Plan your work and work your plan." This is definitely applicable to outdoor cooking.

Another great piece of advice I can impart to home cooks is how to respond to mishaps during cooking: be prepared. We've already discussed "the stall" and how to work through it. If you get behind in your schedule because your large cuts of meats are taking too long on the cooker, make adjustments in order to reach

your predetermined goal. In this case, raise the temperature of your cooker to help accelerate the cooking process.

On the other hand, if meat is cooking too fast and you fear the food will be done too soon, there are two adjustments you can make. The first is to lower the temperature of your cooker to slow down the cooking time. And another remedy for meat that cooks too quickly is to hold it properly until ready to serve. A cooler is an excellent place to hold hot meat until serving. Note: If you place large quantities of hot meat in a cooler, you may need to open the lid occasionally and allow some heat to be released so that your properly cooked meat doesn't continue to cook in the cooler and become mushy.

The point I am trying to make is that there are often steps you can take to correct a potentially bad situation.

COMPETITION
BARBECUE

I OFTEN SAY THAT COMPETITION BARBECUE IS "ONE-
bite food," because we have one chance—one bite—to get the judge's attention with our entries. To make sure that one bite is spectacular, I work to achieve big flavors that are bolder than what I cook at home. I tend to make competition barbecue so flavorful and rich through additional spice rubs, injections, brines, and butter that I wouldn't want to eat it as a full meal. The barbecue I cook at home and serve in our restaurants is more toned down in flavor, and makes for a better meal. Don't get me wrong—competition barbecue is very good, but it's much more assertive in its flavors.

As I began to compete on the circuit, traveling around the country and making friends with competition barbecue cooks, I really began to learn what it took to be successful as a competitive cook. I paid close attention to all the details in making barbecue, and I barbecued a lot. I watched the fire, smoke, and meat I was cooking with a focused eye, and I got better and better. I have competed in barbecue contests all over the United States and in many different sanctioned organizations, but most of the contests I have competed in were sanctioned by the Kansas City Barbecue Society (KCBS).

JUDGING BARBECUE

In KCBS contests, the rule is, you must cook chicken, pork ribs, pork shoulders or butts, and beef brisket. These meats must be placed in white Styrofoam boxes to be judged—there's no fancy plating to distract from the product. The cooks may elect to use garnish or not, but the only legal garnishes are parsley, cilantro, green-leaf lettuce, or kale. A typical entry will have greenery covering the bottom of the box, with the meat placed neatly on top of the greens. A cook must turn in a minimum of six portions of each meat to be judged. The meat entries are judged on appearance, taste, and tenderness, with taste being the most important factor. The judging is "blind"—the judges do not know whose food they are sampling. Numerical scores are given by each of the judges, and all the entries are ranked by the highest score to the lowest in each individual meat category and then overall finish, which is the accumulated score from all the meat categories. The team or cook who has the highest score is the winner, or Grand Champion.

There are numerous competition barbecue–sanctioning organizations, and the rules vary from organization to organization. At the Memphis in May World Championship Barbecue Cooking Contest, you can only enter one category to compete for the overall champion title. The choices are all pork: pork ribs, whole hog, or whole pork shoulders. At this contest, the meat to be judged must be turned in to the judges in a Styrofoam container with no garnish, but competitors are allowed to turn in barbecue sauce on the side, if they choose. Once the entry is submitted, you then serve your barbecue to three different judges, one at a time, and tell them about your cooking processes. Those judges evaluate your barbecue and give you a score. At Memphis in May, the judging is comparative, meaning the judges will compare your food against the other barbecue entries that they taste, giving the highest score to their favorite. All the scores are tallied up and the top three scores in ribs, pork shoulders, and whole hog (a total of nine teams) will make what is called the "finals." They will then serve their barbecue to four judges and tell their processes to them. These judges will again comparatively judge all nine finals teams, and the team with the highest score will be the Grand Champion. The Houston Livestock Show and Rodeo World's Championship Bar-B-Que Contest is another contest where cooks must make the "finals" before going on to another round of judging.

In competition barbecue, it is important to present barbecue that has a taste everyone will like. I try to make competition barbecue that has a little sweetness, tanginess, spiciness, and saltiness—with just the right amount of smoke. I try to balance these tastes so the meat will please pretty much everyone's palate. I also stay away from flavors that are polarizing or not as universally liked, so as not to displease any judge's taste preferences.

Barbecue is a food that most people are passionate about, and there are many regional styles. I find that by serving barbecue that has something for everyone's tastes, I score very well.

TENDERNESS

In addition to taste, which is the most heavily weighted score, I put great importance on the tenderness, or doneness, of the meat. In fact, in my Cool Smoke classes I teach that this is a tenderness contest. I believe that the meat with the best chew will always do better than the others. I always select the meat that has the best tenderness for my contest entries, and I can always tweak the taste with last-minute adjustments.

A great competition trick is to pulverize some of your rub using an electric coffee grinder and place it in a fine-mesh shaker. With this, you can lightly apply additional flavor to the cooked meat before turning it in to the judges. With the help of a light spray of apple juice on the meat, the finely ground rub will pretty much disappear on the meat and won't change the texture or mouthfeel like the application of a coarse rub would do.

Another way to make a last-minute flavor adjustment is to go heavier or lighter with an application of sauce, depending on how the meat tastes. You can sweeten up a finishing sauce by adding honey or sugar to it, if you think your barbecue has too much tang. The added sweetness can balance out something that's too acidic. On the other hand, if you feel the barbecue is too sweet, you could make a last-minute addition of vinegar to a sauce, and this will help make a flavor improvement. The important thing to understand here is that we can make flavor adjustments to barbecue after it has finished cooking and before we hand it in to be judged. This is why I always select the best-cooked meats in terms of tenderness for the judges to try. Tenderness is not easy to correct after we have cooked our competition meats, so it is very important to monitor closely when cooking.

It is also very important to evaluate your cooked barbecue properly and select the best samples to turn in to the judges. When I first started competing, I was told by another competition cook that if you cooked six racks of ribs, you sliced six racks of ribs. The lesson here is that sometimes we make a decision as to what ribs are the best based on how they look, but it is better to slice all the ribs to truly determine which have been cooked the best.

SAVING OVER- AND UNDERCOOKED MEAT

While it is harder to make adjustments to tenderness after a meat has been cooked, there are a few things we can do in addition to careful meat selection. If you overcook a meat, the best thing to do is cool it down quickly by getting air on it. I have a friend who once wrapped an overcooked pork butt in plastic wrap and submerged it into an ice bath to stop it from cooking. (Nice save, Donny!)

Another tenderness adjustment for brisket is to cut thicker slices if it is overly tender and thinner slices if it is a bit undercooked. Another thing I teach in my class is that your barbecue entries should chew and taste good when they are cool. We plate our meat presentations, carry them to the judging area, where they are then carried to the table of judges who will be judging them, then they get passed around to be looked at (but not tasted) for a presentation score before finally being tasted by the judges, and in that time, our meats will cool down considerably. Sometimes if the meat has not cooked long enough, it will be a bit chewy when it cools. Test your meats after they have cooled down to see if the texture is right. If the meat is a bit tough, you'll know to cook it longer to be more tender next time. The recipes in this book will give you a really nice bite, but through practice you will get better. Every piece of meat has its own nuances, and through experience you will develop a better feel for when the meat is properly cooked. A thermometer is always helpful, but in time you will start to rely on your touch.

SAUCES

I stated earlier that the meat should be the star, and the other flavors—the smoke, rub, and sauce—should be supporting flavors; but in competition barbecue, the sauce work is even more critical. I make sure I am not too heavy with my application of sauce on competition meats, and definitely not let the sauce get too hot after it is applied to the meat. Most sauces contain sugar, and when they get too hot, the sauce becomes tacky, or gummy. I do not want this to happen with my competition barbecue meats and I normally do not do as well in a contest if I overset my sauce. I am also careful to not apply sauce too heavily, to show the judges that my meats are great on their own and that the sauce is carefully applied to give a nice complementary pop of flavor. I make sure the sauce is applied evenly and does not pool in my presentation box. I like to use tongs to dip my chicken pieces in a pot of gently warmed sauce; then I hold the pieces over the pot and shake the excess sauce off so the chicken shines like jewels of meat.

PRESENTATION

Presentation, or appearance, is the lowest-weighted score in Kansas City Barbecue Society grading, but it's still very important. I have taken second place in contests, missing a grand championship by only one appearance point. I also think that beautifully presented meat can be a positive start to a judging experience, especially if it's followed up with great taste and a perfectly cooked piece of meat. Competition barbecue has grown a lot in popularity, and as it has grown, so has the availability of information. There are many classes now offered for competitive barbecuing, as well as books on the subject and information on the Internet. We also have more cooks competing and more

judges judging, and they seem to be more focused on doing a good job. So while presentation scores have a lower numerical impact on overall scores, every point is important and competition barbecue is more competitive than ever. I take great care in seeing that my best-cooked food looks beautiful in the turn-in box. That said, I also think my barbecue entries look like food and aren't overly styled. Some folks, such as my good friend Myron Mixon, like their chicken pieces to look like cupcakes—and they do well. My chicken looks like chicken and it does well also, so there are many ways to win. The main thing with presentation is to make your entry look tasty and great to the eye.

STAYING ORGANIZED

I am very organized when it comes to competition barbecue, and everything has a place. My cook site is always neat, and we keep things very clean. Training with Chef Alain and the Marine Corps instilled in me the importance of keeping a clean workplace. On competitions, I have a timeline that lays out what to do when for every cook on our team, so I don't have to think about what comes next. I think it is important to have a cooking timeline written out—an idea that Lee McWright of Music City Pig Pals gave me at a barbecue contest in Florida years ago. The good thing about having a cooking timeline written out is that not only do you not have to think about what to do next, but you can plan future adjustments if you find something is not working. So, for example, if your ribs are not done on time, you can modify your cooking timeline for your next contest, and either put them on sooner or raise your cooking temperature. I try to give myself a little wiggle room with my timeline so that I have plenty of time for all my meats to be cooked and presented properly. I don't know who I heard say this first, but "it's better to be looking at it than looking for it!"

The voice I hear in my mind when I think about it is Chris Capell's, who is the head cook and owner of Dizzy Pig. So make sure you give yourself enough time to do what you need to get done. It is also helpful to put comments or notes on your cooking timeline to keep records of your cooking, which can be very useful later. We kept journals in the beginning years of Cool Smoke. My first cooking partner, Kendall Lamp, was the one who put our cooking outline into spreadsheets and color-coded them, making them so easy to follow.

PRACTICE BARBECUES

Another thing that's very important to becoming a competition cook is to do practice barbecues, because they really help develop your timing. What works in practice will work at a contest. Times and temperatures are important when cooking barbecue, and these things are repeatable for the most part. So when we do a practice cook, the timing can be close to the same when we go to the contest, and if we write our timeline down, then we have a written guide to help us in competitions. I like to review our cooking on the way home from a contest; I find that's the best time to make notes of our observations because the experience is still fresh in our minds. Even when we do well, we are always looking for things we can do better.

SLEEP

Rest is also very important when cooking at a barbecue contest. Cooking big cuts of meat like beef brisket or pork shoulder take hours, and with the additional time it takes to prep everything, it all makes for a lot of work. Tending a fire all night long and getting a face full of smoke can take its toll on a competition cook, and the fatigue can cause us to lose our edge—and our focus—when putting our entries together. I was able to add valuable rest time to our schedule by raising my cooking temperatures. In the beginning I was cooking at 250°F; now we cook between 275°F and 300°F, which allows us to be fresh when it is most important.

Most of the time these days the Cool Smoke team is just my father, George, and me. Dad gets up at two a.m. to light the fire and tend to the meat. I wake up at five a.m. and start to work on ribs. At seven a.m. my father goes back to sleep for two to three hours. By scheduling our team efforts like this, we are better rested and cook better as a result.

NEVER LEAVE YOUR BEST MEAT ON THE TABLE

In my early years of competition barbecue, Steve Farin, a great barbecue cook, shared an important lesson with me: "Don't leave your best meat on the table." The idea here is that we cook a multitude of meats for a contest so that we can choose the best barbecue to present to the judges. The rest of the meat is literally "left on the table."

We were in Florida competing at a contest, and Steve watched me put my brisket entry together. When I was done, he asked why I wasn't going to turn any of the point end of the brisket in for judging. I told him that I didn't know how to separate the point meat from the flat meat. I turned my brisket entry in to the judges without the point end, and when I returned to my cook site, Steve showed me how to separate the two muscles. We ended up placing ninth in brisket that day—I had definitely left my best meat on the worktable, but I learned a good lesson.

MIND-SET

The mental part of competition barbecue is very important to me. I am so busy with my work that I don't have time to compete as often as I once did. So when I get in my RV to drive to a contest, I use that time to visualize my cook. An old friend, Paxton Campbell, used to say, "Plan your work and work your plan!" This is what I try to do when I am at a contest: I think of all the teams as being tied for first place until the first meat is turned in. If I turn in an entry that I felt was not as good as I wanted, I try to make up for it in the next entry, and I keep that attitude through to the last category. If I miss my marks on one of my meats, I keep my head and try to make the best of it. I always say, "It's all in how you handle catastrophes." I believe this kind of thinking helps me do a better job competing. One of my favorite sayings is, "The harder I work, the luckier I get," so I work really hard when I am competing. All the details are important to me, and I come to a contest with a clean pit, good wood, sharp knives, fresh rubs, and good cuts of meat. Having these things helps me be a more confident cook.

Competition barbecue has taken me on a journey that I never could have imagined. The friends I have made and the people I have met are amazing, such as John Markus, who gave me the nickname "The Professor," put me on the television show *BBQ Pitmasters*, and gave me the opportunity to cook for the troops in Kuwait. Cooking with my father has also been very special for us both, and winning our fifth World Championship at the 2016 Jack

Daniels Invitational Barbecue event together last year was unreal. As I type this, I still cannot believe it. I tell people all the time that if we never win again, we have still won more than our fair share. I think my mom, Charlotte, who has passed, helped me put things into a great perspective on a phone call one day in our beginning years of competing. We had competed one week and had done very well, then at the next contest we did not win any awards. A couple of days later my mom called and said she heard that we had not done so well that weekend. I said, no, ma'am, we hadn't. She said to me, "Last week it was your turn and this week it was someone else's." That has always stuck with me, and now seeing different teams win keeps it fun for everyone.

"IF YOU'RE LOOKING, YOU'RE NOT COOKING!" . . . OR ARE YOU?

This statement is often made about cooking barbecue, but it's not one I adhere to completely. Let me share an anecdote from my first barbecue competition by way of explanation.

As a cook, I use all my senses—hearing, taste, smell, touch, and sight. I am a very visual cook and I watch things very closely while cooking. Initially, a cook must keep a close eye on the food in order to tell when something is perfectly cooked. If you cook a dish enough over time, however, you get to know by touch or smell when the meat is done.

I was cooking at my first barbecue contest in September 2004 in Lynchburg, Virginia, which just happened to be the town where I grew up. This was a contest sanctioned by the Kansas City Barbecue Society. That weekend, my main goal was to turn in all the meats on time and not be late. We were cooking brisket, pork butts, pork ribs, and chicken.

We set up our equipment next to a cook named Tater Bug who had built his own pit. He spent most of the contest sitting in a chair letting the cooker do its job. He rarely opened the doors of his cooker, but sat with confidence, knowing his cooker and that the meat was fine. I, on the other hand, was constantly tending to the meat, spritzing and spraying away. I opened the door often to check the color of my meat, making sure that everything was cooking to my satisfaction. Almost every time I opened that door, Tater Bug would shake his head at me and let me know that I was doing it wrong and "if you're looking, you're not cooking!"

There are two reasons barbecue people believe this. One is experience. If you cook barbecue long enough and get to know your cooker well, it's not necessary to constantly watch the meat; you will learn when it is time to tend it. The second reason has to do with the need for the pit temperature to rise back to the desired temperature after the pit has been opened. The recovery time on some pits can be very long, so the less you open them, the shorter time it takes to cook the meat. I like to look at the food while it's cooking to make sure it isn't drying out or overcooking, so I prefer to cook on a cooker that has a fast temperature-recovery time.

After Tater Bug's disapproval of my style of cooking, I had little hope we would win anything that day, but we ended up getting second place in Pork and seventh place in Brisket. A legend in barbecue, Johnny Trigg, won the contest. Little did I know that we would become friends and have many life experiences together on and off the competition circuit.

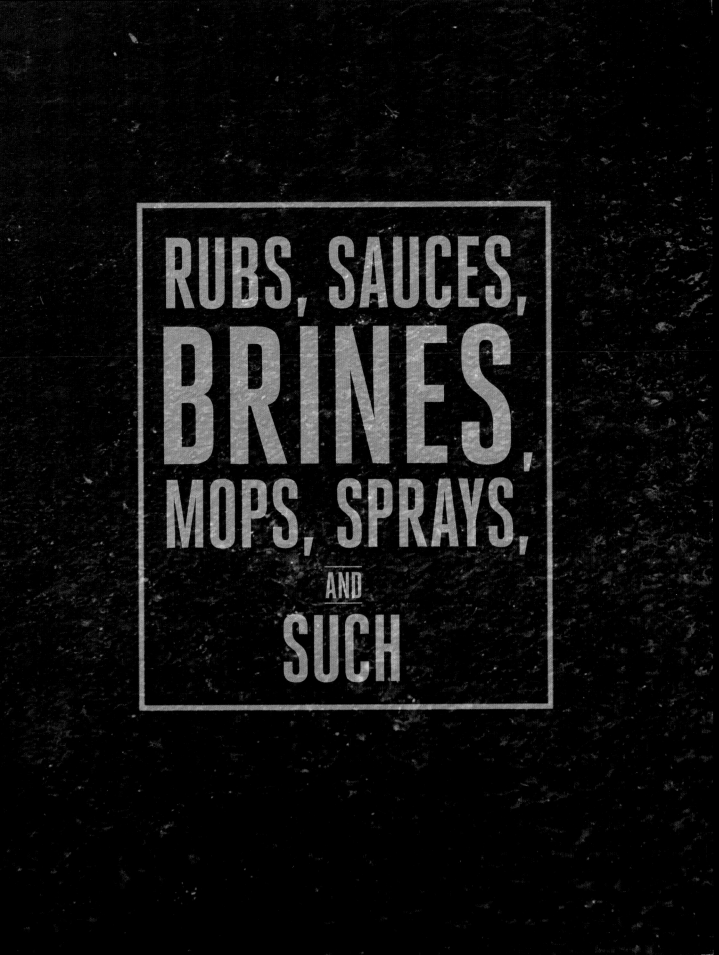

RUBS, SAUCES, BRINES, MOPS, SPRAYS, AND SUCH

HAVING SPENT YEARS AS A CHEF IN A FRENCH KITCHEN, I had many interesting ideas when I began cooking barbecue. I thought demi-glace and white truffle salt would taste great on sliced brisket. They both do, but I learned firsthand that they don't do well in a barbecue contest.

As I really began to dig into the preparation of barbecue—and especially competition barbecue—I began to learn what I call the "expected flavors of barbecue." While there are regional tastes that exist in barbecue, there are also tastes that seem to be universal. First of all is the flavor of the meat itself. Whether I'm cooking chicken, pork, or beef, I want the protein to be the star, and the other tastes (smoke, seasonings, and sauce) to be more of a background or supporting flavor. Other expected flavors of barbecue are smoke, salt, pepper, sugar, and vinegar. These ingredients, when used properly in sauces, mops, and rubs, will always fit into the expectations of someone hungry for barbecue. The varying amounts of each added flavor are what make for different regional styles of cooking. If vinegar is used as a dominant flavor in a sauce, you would achieve a Carolina- or Virginia-style barbecue; but when vinegar is used only moderately it still works well with smoked or grilled meats. Sugar is another ingredient used heavily in some regions, but when its use is subtle, most people will still like the flavor it adds to the barbecue.

RUBS

I think most of us are guilty of having spices in our cupboard that have been there too long and have diminished in flavor. A number of years ago, I went through my spice cabinet and threw out all the old ones and replaced them with fresh new spices. I can attest to this: the difference in the taste of fresh spices and stale spices is huge. When I am competing on the barbecue circuit, I make sure that my spices and rubs are of the best quality. If we are going to take the time to cook a big piece of meat like a pork shoulder or brisket, or an expensive cut of meat like a nice steak, we should make sure the seasoning blends and rubs applied to those meats are the best in terms of flavor.

The spices and seasoning ingredients for the rub recipes in this chapter must be fresh. Black, white, and pink peppercorns should be ground fresh, as well as coriander seeds, freshly toasted cumin seeds, whole allspice, whole juniper berries, and any other spice that can be bought in whole form to make these seasoning blends. Listed in our Source Guide (page 279), you can find our favorite spice grinders, glass storage jars, and shakers used to apply rubs as well as the contact info for some of our favorite spice purveyors.

Freshly made rubs and spice blends can be kept for months in an airtight container in a cool, dark environment. Rubs actually seem to improve if made a few days before using. When the spices commingle for 2 to 3 days before the rub is used, the color improves with rubs containing paprika, and some rubs actually have better flavor development. It is also best to make sure you shake or mix the spices well just prior to using, as heavier ingredients will often settle to the bottom if they have been sitting.

When applying seasonings to foods, you should be careful to season your food evenly. A good shaker is a useful tool to apply rubs to meat. Small fine-mesh shakers and sieves are great for evenly applying spices that tend to clump, such as cayenne pepper. It's important to follow the application time directions in these recipes, because the timing of rub application is based on three things: developing flavor, allowing the rubs to dissolve, and making sure the meats do not cure. Most rubs contain salt, so if they are left on meat for an extended period of time, they will pull out internal moisture and, in essence, cook the meat, giving it an undesirable "hammy" texture.

In developing these recipes, we determined the ideal amount of time the rub should be applied to the food before cooking. Some general guidelines to follow are that larger cuts of meat should have the rub on them longer, and smaller or more delicate meats do not have to be seasoned as far in advance. Another thing to consider when cooking foods that have been rubbed, or in the creation of your own rub, is sugar. Rubs that contain sugar cannot take high heat for a long period of time. Sugars can burn easily and the resulting taste can be very bitter. When using rubs that contain sugar, it's best to cook the meat using indirect heat, or at a lower cooking temperature. A barbecue competition trick is to put some of your barbecue rub in a coffee grinder and grind it into a fine dust, and place it in a fine-mesh shaker like one used for confectioners' sugar or cocoa powder. Once your barbecue is cooked, you can add zip to your food by dusting it lightly with the powdered rub. This addition of flavor cannot be seen or felt in your mouth, because the seasoning is so fine.

Another thing that is very important with rubs or seasoning blends is how much to apply. I want the food to be full flavored, but I never want the rub to overpower the taste of the meat or the food being cooked. In the recipes for competition-style barbecue, we push the flavor a bit more, because competition barbecue is what I call "one-bite food." We get one chance to get the judges' attention.

Bark is the slightly crispy, caramelized exterior of the meat that contains concentrated flavor from the rub and smoke. This can be really delicious and is often the best part of the meat, when done properly.

SAUCES

Good sauces used the right way can make a grilled or smoked dish much better by adding complementary flavors. There are some key things to remember when working with sauces for barbecued or grilled foods. Don't apply too much sauce on the cooked meat—let the grilled or smoked meat be the star and serve your sauce on the side, or pass it around the table. When I am serving competition barbecue, I apply sauce to my meats, but I'm not too heavy-handed with it. My goal is to cook my barbecue perfectly in terms of taste and tenderness, so that the sauce becomes that final little complementary pop of flavor. Be sure the meat is cooked to the desired doneness before applying the sauce. When you apply sauce to cooked meat and return it to the grill to set, be careful not to burn it. Many barbecue sauces contain sugar and it is easy to burn or overset, which causes the mouthfeel of the sauce to be too tacky or sticky. The sauce should be just barely set, and this doesn't take much time. Make saucing a finishing step of your dish,

watch it carefully on the grill, and you will be fine. Some of the sauce recipes in this chapter were created specifically for a dish, and others may be used more generally, so feel free to try these sauces with other recipes. For example, tamarind sauce goes well with ribs and pork shoulder. Barbecue sauces traditionally go well with most grilled and smoked meats.

BRINES

The multiple brine recipes in this chapter are a great way to bring a variety of flavors into cooked meats. Think of brines as a liquid seasoning soak. Bigger cuts of meats will need a longer soaking time, which helps infuse flavors deep inside the meat. Recipes that include brining will specify exactly how long to soak the meat. These times have been tested extensively to give the best results. The goal in determining the best soak time for a brine is imparting the best flavor without curing the meat. I've cooked with other brine recipes that call for rinsing the brine-soaked meat with cold water to avoid an overly salty taste. You won't have to do that for these brines: all these recipes give the exact soaking times, resulting in salt levels that do not require rinsing.

These brine recipes are not cooked, but made in advance and refrigerated for at least twenty-four hours, allowing the flavors to develop and for the brine to cool to 40°F or lower. All these brine recipes contain solid aromatics that are strained out while the brine is poured over the meat. Another step for our brines is that brined meats are removed from the liquid and dried with a clean towel or paper towels before cooking.

MARINADES

Marinades are another great way to bring flavor to grilled or smoked meats, and these are usually used on thinner cuts of meats, but they can be delicious on big cuts as well. Marinades often contain some type of oil or acid, or both. The acid can actually cook a meat—this is what happens when making a dish like ceviche with lime juice. Our recipes give times for how long to marinate to achieve the best results. Note: Marinades that contain soy sauce are delicious, but be careful when grilling them over high heat. Soy sauce will burn much like sugar if it gets too hot.

MOPS AND SPRAYS

Mops and sprays are great ways to apply more flavor to meats while grilling or barbecuing, and they also add moisture to the exterior of the meat during cooking. This is essential when cooking meats like ribs, pork shoulders, or beef brisket for a long time. When I began learning how to cook barbecue, I observed that my barbecue seemed to turn out better when I cooked in the rain. The increased moisture in the air due to the rain resulted in a more succulent finished product. With that observation, I decided that I would figure out how to "make it rain" all the time.

In our recipes that include a spritz or a mop, we give specific directions on times to spray or mop, but in general you should watch your meat closely. After meat starts to develop a nice bark or sear is the time to give it a quick spray or mop. I then allow the meat to cook, spraying occasionally. Don't be afraid to get creative by making your own mops and spritzes. Apple juice is one of my simple, go-to sprays, and I use it on many of my competition meats. Spray bottles, barbecue mops, basting brushes, and basters are simple tools needed for applying spritzes or mops, and most are available at grocery and specialty stores.

INJECTIONS

Injections are another way to get extra flavor deep inside larger cuts of meat. I mostly use them for competition barbecue, but they are still an excellent method for creating great-tasting barbecue that isn't intended for competition. There are many products on the market that are injection bases mixed with a liquid. Some of these products contain phosphates, and although phosphates don't really add much in terms of flavor, they help maintain moisture and texture.

RUBS

While some of these rubs were originally created for a specific dish, I found, through experimentation, that they actually are very versatile. Also, we are fans of salt and love what it does for taste, but feel free to reduce the amount if you prefer.

COOL SMOKE RUB

MAKES A GENEROUS 1½ CUPS

½ cup turbinado sugar

¼ cup plus 2 tablespoons kosher salt

¼ cup Smoked Chili Powder (page 50)

2 tablespoons plus 2 teaspoons ground cumin

1 teaspoon cayenne pepper

1 tablespoon plus 1 teaspoon cracked black pepper

1 tablespoon plus 1 teaspoon granulated garlic

1 tablespoon plus 1 teaspoon granulated onion

In a medium bowl, mix all the ingredients together thoroughly. Store in an airtight container in a cool, dark place until ready to use.

FENNEL POLLEN RUB

MAKES 2¼ CUPS

1 cup kosher salt

½ cup freshly ground white pepper

¼ cup rubbed sage

2 tablespoons plus 2 teaspoons fennel pollen

5 tablespoons plus 1 teaspoon turbinado sugar

2 tablespoons plus 2 teaspoons ground aji amarillo (found at most specialty groceries)

In a medium bowl, mix all the ingredients together thoroughly. Store in an airtight container in a cool, dark place until ready to use.

POULTRY RUB

MAKES A GENEROUS 1½ CUPS

1 cup kosher salt

2 tablespoons freshly ground black pepper

1 tablespoon plus 1 teaspoon granulated garlic

2 teaspoons ground cumin

2 teaspoons cayenne pepper

2 tablespoons smoked paprika

2 tablespoons ground sumac

1 tablespoon plus 1 teaspoon dried Greek oregano (available at most groceries)

In a medium bowl, mix all the ingredients together thoroughly. Store in an airtight container in a cool, dark place until ready to use. Also great with pork.

QUAIL RUB

MAKES ¾ CUP

½ cup kosher salt

¼ cup cracked black pepper

1 tablespoon plus 1 teaspoon granulated garlic

2 teaspoons fennel pollen

In a small bowl, mix all the ingredients together thoroughly. Store in an airtight container in a cool, dark place until ready to use.

CARAWAY RUB

MAKES A GENEROUS ⅓ CUP

3 tablespoons kosher salt

1 tablespoon freshly ground black pepper

1 teaspoon crushed red pepper

1 tablespoon freshly ground caraway seeds

1 teaspoon granulated garlic

½ teaspoon granulated onion

In a medium bowl, mix all the ingredients together thoroughly. Store in an airtight container in a cool, dark place until ready to use.

DUCK RUB

MAKES ¾ CUP PLUS 2 TABLESPOONS

½ cup kosher salt

2 tablespoons cracked black pepper

1 tablespoon freshly ground coriander seeds

1 teaspoon freshly ground fennel seeds

3 tablespoons turbinado sugar

2 teaspoons granulated garlic

In a small bowl, mix all the ingredients together thoroughly. Store in an airtight container in a cool, dark place until ready to use.

TARRAGON AND ALEPPO RUB

MAKES 2¾ CUPS

2 cups kosher salt

½ cup Aleppo pepper

2 tablespoons plus 2 teaspoons dried tarragon

2 teaspoons ground dried lemon peel

2 teaspoons granulated garlic

1 teaspoon ground chile de árbol (see Source Guide, page 279)

In a medium bowl, mix all the ingredients together thoroughly. Store in an airtight container in a cool, dark place until ready to use.

SMOKED CHILI POWDER

MAKES A GENEROUS 2 CUPS

1 cup smoked paprika

5 tablespoons plus 1 teaspoon dried Greek oregano (available at most groceries)

3 tablespoons plus 1 teaspoon ground cumin

3 tablespoons plus 1 teaspoon granulated garlic

3 tablespoons plus 1 teaspoon cayenne pepper

2 tablespoons granulated onion

In a medium bowl, mix all the ingredients together thoroughly. Store in an airtight container in a cool, dark place until ready to use.

FENNEL GARLIC RUB

MAKES A GENEROUS ¾ CUP

½ cup kosher salt

¼ cup cracked black pepper

1 teaspoon crushed red pepper

1½ teaspoons granulated garlic

2 teaspoons freshly cracked fennel seeds

In a small bowl, mix all the ingredients together thoroughly. Store in an airtight container in a cool, dark place until ready to use.

DILL RUB

MAKES A GENEROUS ½ CUP

¼ cup kosher salt

¼ cup freshly ground pink peppercorns

1 tablespoon plus 1 teaspoon dried dill

½ teaspoon ground dried lemon peel

½ teaspoon freshly ground juniper berries

In a small bowl, mix all the ingredients together thoroughly. Store in an airtight container in a cool, dark place until ready to use.

GOOSE RUB

MAKES A GENEROUS 1 CUP

6 tablespoons kosher salt

2 tablespoons cracked black pepper

2 tablespoons freshly ground pink peppercorns

1 tablespoon plus 1 teaspoon freshly ground coriander seeds

1 tablespoon plus 1 teaspoon freshly ground juniper berries

2 teaspoons granulated garlic

1 teaspoon granulated onion

1 tablespoon plus 1 teaspoon celery seeds

1 tablespoon plus 1 teaspoon freshly ground caraway seeds

In a small bowl, mix all the ingredients together thoroughly. Store in an airtight container in a cool, dark place until ready to use.

LEMON PEPPER RUB

MAKES A GENEROUS ½ CUP

2 tablespoons whole black peppercorns

2 tablespoons dried lemon peel

¼ cup kosher salt

2 teaspoons granulated garlic

2 teaspoons granulated onion

Grind the peppercorns and dried lemon peel in a spice grinder until medium coarse. In a small bowl, combine the ground pepper and lemon peel with the salt, granulated garlic, and granulated onion and mix thoroughly. Store in an airtight container in a cool, dark place until ready to use.

VENISON RUB

MAKES A GENEROUS ⅓ CUP

3 tablespoons kosher salt

1 tablespoon freshly ground black pepper

1 tablespoon freshly ground pink peppercorns

2 teaspoons freshly ground coriander seeds

2 teaspoons freshly ground juniper berries

1 teaspoon granulated garlic

½ teaspoon granulated onion

In a small bowl, mix all the ingredients together thoroughly. Store in an airtight container in a cool, dark place until ready to use.

COFFEE RUB

MAKES A GENEROUS ½ CUP

¼ cup kosher salt

2 tablespoons cracked black pepper

2 tablespoons medium-roast ground coffee

1 tablespoon light brown sugar

½ teaspoon freshly ground cumin seeds

½ teaspoon unsweetened cocoa powder

¼ teaspoon chipotle chile powder

In a small bowl, mix all the ingredients together thoroughly. Store in an airtight container in a cool, dark place until ready to use.

STEAK RUB

MAKES 1¼ CUPS

½ cup cracked black pepper

¼ cup coarsely ground brown mustard seeds

3 tablespoons coarsely ground dill seeds

1 tablespoon plus 1 teaspoon coarsely ground coriander seeds

5 tablespoons plus 1 teaspoon kosher salt

5 tablespoons plus 1 teaspoon granulated garlic

1 tablespoon plus 1 teaspoon crushed red pepper

In a small bowl, mix all the ingredients together thoroughly. Store in an airtight container in a cool, dark place until ready to use.

CELERY SEED RUB

MAKES A GENEROUS ¾ CUP

½ cup kosher salt

¼ cup plus 1 tablespoon cracked black pepper

2 teaspoons celery seeds

1 teaspoon granulated garlic

2 teaspoons ancho chile powder (see Source Guide, page 279)

In a small bowl, mix all the ingredients together thoroughly. Store in an airtight container in a cool, dark place until ready to use.

SAUCES

COOL SMOKE BARBECUE SAUCE

MAKES 1 QUART

3 cups ketchup

1 cup packed dark brown sugar

¾ cup distilled white vinegar

¼ cup molasses

3 tablespoons Worcestershire sauce

1 tablespoon Smoked Chili Powder
   (page 50)

½ teaspoon kosher salt

2 teaspoons ground cumin

1 tablespoon smoked paprika

1 tablespoon sweet paprika

2 teaspoons granulated onion

2 teaspoons granulated garlic

2 teaspoons cayenne pepper

1½ teaspoons freshly ground black pepper

¼ cup apple cider vinegar

In a 4-quart saucepan, whisk together all
the ingredients with ¾ cup water. Bring to a
simmer over medium heat and cook, stirring
continuously, for 20 minutes, until the sauce
thickens. Set aside to cool completely. Transfer
to an airtight container and refrigerate until
ready to use, up to 2 weeks.

TIPS

• For a sweeter version of this sauce, increase
  brown sugar or reduce amount of vinegar.

• Best if it sits overnight.

COOL SMOKE VINEGAR SAUCE

MAKES 1¼ CUPS

1 cup apple cider vinegar

¼ cup Cool Smoke Rub (page 49)

In a small bowl, thoroughly mix the vinegar
and rub. Transfer to an airtight container and
refrigerate until ready to use, up to 6 months.

CHIMICHURRI

MAKES 2 CUPS

½ cup chopped fresh flat-leaf parsley

½ cup chopped fresh cilantro

1 tablespoon minced garlic

¼ cup minced shallot

¼ cup plus 2 tablespoons canola oil

¼ cup plus 2 tablespoons olive oil

1 tablespoon chopped lemon zest (remove the
   zest with a vegetable peeler, then chop)

½ teaspoon crushed red pepper

½ teaspoon dried Greek oregano
   (available at most groceries)

½ teaspoon freshly ground cumin seeds

2 tablespoons red wine vinegar

½ teaspoon kosher salt

In a small bowl, toss all the ingredients
together until well combined. Use immediately.

COOL SMOKE SALSA

MAKES 3 CUPS

1 (7-ounce) can chipotles in adobo sauce, sauce reserved

1 (14.5-ounce) can diced tomatoes

5 garlic cloves

¼ cup fresh lime juice (from about 2 medium limes)

1 cup packed fresh cilantro leaves

½ cup chopped red onion

1 teaspoon kosher salt

½ jalapeño, seeded

In a blender, combine 1 chipotle pepper and 1 teaspoon adobo sauce from the can. Add the remaining ingredients and puree for 1 minute until smooth. Refrigerate in an airtight container until ready to use, up to 5 days.

CUMBERLAND SAUCE

MAKES 1½ CUPS

1 cup port wine

¼ cup finely diced shallots

½ cup demi-glace (see Source Guide, page 279)

1 tablespoon lemon zest

1 tablespoon orange zest

½ teaspoon dry mustard

½ teaspoon Caraway Rub (page 50)

½ cup red currant jelly (available at most groceries)

½ teaspoon freshly ground black pepper

In a small saucepan, combine the port wine and shallots over medium heat. Cook, stirring occasionally, for 10 minutes, until the sauce has reduced by half.

Reduce the heat to medium-low, add the demi-glace, lemon zest, orange zest, dry mustard, and Caraway Rub, and simmer 3 minutes. Remove the pot from the heat and stir in the jelly and pepper. Cover and keep the sauce warm until ready to use.

PEPPER RELISH

YIELDS 2 CUPS

1½ pounds tomatoes, minced

1 large green bell pepper, minced

1 large red bell pepper, minced

1 large shallot, minced

2 tablespoons sugar

1 teaspoon cinnamon

¼ teaspoon ground clove

¼ cup white vinegar

⅛ teaspoon hot mustard powder

⅜ teaspoon crushed red pepper

⅜ teaspoon ground espelette (see Source Guide, page 279)

1 teaspoon kosher salt

⅛ teaspoon granulated garlic

In a heavy-bottomed saucepan over medium heat, bring all the ingredients to a simmer, then lower the heat and continue to cook covered, for 1 hour, stirring occasionally. Taste to adjust for your desired seasoning.

Allow to cool to room temperature. Then transfer to an airtight container and refrigerate until ready to use.

TARRAGON AND ALEPPO WHITE SAUCE

MAKES A GENEROUS 2½ CUPS

1½ cups Duke's Mayonnaise, or your favorite brand

¼ cup plus 2 tablespoons distilled white vinegar

¼ cup plus 2 tablespoons fresh lemon juice

¾ teaspoon granulated garlic

¼ cup plus 2 tablespoons buttermilk

1½ teaspoons Aleppo pepper (see Source Guide, page 279)

1½ teaspoons Simple Syrup (page 74)

1 tablespoon kosher salt

3 tablespoons finely chopped tarragon

3 tablespoons finely chopped Italian flat leaf parsley

In a medium bowl, combine all the ingredients except the tarragon and parsley, and whisk thoroughly. Use a rubber spatula to fold in the tarragon and parsley. Refrigerate in an airtight container until ready to use, up to 3 days.

TAMARIND BARBECUE SAUCE

MAKES 2½ CUPS

1 cup packed dark brown sugar

½ cup corn syrup

¼ cup plus 2 tablespoons ketchup

½ cup plus 2 tablespoons apple cider vinegar

1 tablespoon Worcestershire sauce

1½ tablespoons tamarind paste (available at most Asian markets)

1 tablespoon granulated garlic

1 teaspoon freshly ground black pepper

1 teaspoon granulated onion

1 teaspoon Smoked Chili Powder (page 50)

1 teaspoon ground ginger

1 teaspoon smoked paprika

1 teaspoon hot sauce, your favorite brand

½ teaspoon mustard seeds

½ teaspoon dried thyme

½ teaspoon dried basil

1 teaspoon kosher salt

½ teaspoon pure vanilla extract

½ teaspoon ground cumin

1½ tablespoons unsalted butter, at room temperature

¼ cup apple juice

¼ teaspoon ground cinnamon

½ teaspoon chipotle chile powder (available at most major groceries)

½ teaspoon smoked salt (see Source Guide, page 279)

Whisk together all the ingredients in a 4-quart saucepan. Bring to a simmer over medium heat. Cook, stirring continuously, for 15 minutes, until the sauce thickens. Set aside to cool completely. Transfer to an airtight container and refrigerate until ready to use.

SAUSAGE GRAVY

MAKES 1½ QUARTS

2 cups whole milk

2 cups half-and-half

10 sprigs thyme

2 medium bay leaves

7 large fresh sage leaves

2 cups chicken stock

6 tablespoons (¾ stick) unsalted butter

1 pound hot Italian sausage

¾ cup finely diced onion

¾ cup finely diced celery

¾ cup finely diced fennel

1 tablespoon plus 2 teaspoons Quail Rub (page 49)

¼ teaspoon freshly ground coriander seeds

2 large garlic cloves, minced

½ cup all-purpose flour

1 tablespoon Worcestershire sauce

2 teaspoons hot sauce, your favorite brand

In a heavy-bottomed 2-quart pot, combine the whole milk, half-and-half, thyme, bay leaves, and sage. Bring just to a simmer over medium-low heat, then remove from the heat and let it steep for 30 minutes to 1 hour. Strain the mixture into a bowl; discard the solids. Set aside.

In a small saucepan, warm the stock over low heat, then set aside until ready to use.

In a heavy-bottomed 3-quart saucepan, melt 1 tablespoon of the butter over medium-high heat. Add the sausage and cook, stirring often and breaking it up into small pieces with a wooden spoon as it cooks, for 3 to 5 minutes, until the meat is evenly browned. Reduce the heat to low and use a slotted spoon to transfer the sausage to paper towels to drain.

In the same saucepan, add the onion, celery, and fennel and increase the heat to medium. Add the Quail Rub and ground coriander and stir to combine. Cook, stirring often, for 5 minutes, until the onion is translucent, then add the garlic and cook, stirring continuously, for 1 minute more.

Add the remaining 5 tablespoons butter and stir until the butter melts and the foam subsides, then whisk in the flour and reduce the heat to low. Cook, whisking continuously, for 5 minutes. Gradually whisk in the warm stock. When the mixture is smooth and the flour is completely incorporated, whisk in the milk mixture. Decrease the heat to medium-low and add the Worcestershire and the hot sauce. Cook, stirring often, for 15 minutes more, until the gravy is thick and bubbling.

Remove the pot from the heat and stir in the sausage. Keep warm until ready to use, or refrigerate the gravy, covered, and rewarm in a saucepan over low heat before serving. It will keep for a few days.

CHIPOTLE WHITE SAUCE

MAKES 2½ CUPS

1½ cups Duke's Mayonnaise, or your favorite brand

¼ cup plus 2 tablespoons fresh lemon juice

¼ cup plus 2 tablespoons apple cider vinegar

¾ teaspoon granulated garlic

2 tablespoons chipotle puree (see Source Guide, page 279; available in most groceries)

1½ teaspoons Simple Syrup (page 74)

2¼ teaspoons dried Greek oregano (available in most groceries)

1 tablespoon kosher salt

In a medium bowl, whisk together all the ingredients thoroughly. Refrigerate in an airtight container until ready to use, up to 3 days.

MUSTARD SAUCE

MAKES 1½ CUPS

¾ cup yellow mustard

¼ cup whole-grain mustard

¼ cup apple cider vinegar

3 tablespoons honey

1 teaspoon kosher salt

1 teaspoon freshly ground black pepper

¼ teaspoon cayenne pepper

In a small bowl, stir together all the ingredients until thoroughly combined. Refrigerate in an airtight container until ready to use, up to 2 weeks.

CHERRY BARBECUE SAUCE

MAKES 1 QUART

3 cups ketchup

1 cup packed light brown sugar

¾ cup distilled white vinegar

2 tablespoons molasses

1 tablespoon Worcestershire sauce

1 teaspoon chipotle chile powder (available at most major groceries)

1 tablespoon chili powder

1 tablespoon sweet paprika

1 teaspoon granulated onion

1 teaspoon granulated garlic

1½ teaspoons kosher salt

½ teaspoon freshly ground black pepper

½ cup cherry preserves

½ cup sun-dried cherries (available in most specialty groceries)

In a 4-quart saucepan, combine all the ingredients with ½ cup water over medium heat. Bring to a simmer and cook, stirring continuously, for 20 minutes, until the sauce thickens. Set aside to cool slightly.

Puree the cooled sauce in a blender until smooth, and set aside until ready to use, or transfer the sauce to an airtight container and refrigerate until ready to use, up to 2 weeks.

ROASTED TOMATO, HONEY, AND CHIPOTLE SAUCE

MAKES 4 CUPS

2 tablespoons olive oil

1 cup diced onion

1 tablespoon diced garlic

¼ cup tomato paste

1 (14.5-ounce) can roasted tomatoes

1 teaspoon smoked paprika

2 teaspoons Smoked Chili Powder (page 50)

½ cup honey

¼ cup apple cider vinegar

3 tablespoons chipotle puree (available at most specialty groceries)

1½ teaspoons kosher salt

In a large saucepan, heat the olive oil over medium-low heat. Add the onion and garlic and cook, stirring often, for 3 minutes. Add the tomato paste and cook, stirring continuously, for 2 minutes. Stir in the remaining ingredients and cook, stirring occasionally, for 15 minutes.

Remove from the heat and set the sauce aside to cool slightly. Transfer to a blender and puree for 1 minute, or until smooth. Set the sauce aside at room temperature to cool completely, then transfer to an airtight container and refrigerate until ready to use, up to 2 weeks.

HERB GRAVY

MAKES 1½ QUARTS

1 cup half-and-half

1 small fennel bulb, coarsely chopped

3 celery stalks, coarsely chopped

½ medium yellow onion, coarsely chopped

10 sprigs thyme

2 medium bay leaves

1 teaspoon whole black peppercorns

1 garlic clove, smashed

4 cups chicken stock

3 tablespoons unsalted butter

¼ cup all-purpose flour

1 tablespoon Fennel Pollen Rub (page 49)

2 tablespoons finely chopped fresh flat-leaf parsley

In a heavy-bottomed 2-quart pot, combine the half-and-half, fennel, celery, onion, thyme, bay leaves, peppercorns, and garlic. Bring just to a simmer over medium-low heat, then remove the pot from the heat and let the mixture steep for 30 minutes to 1 hour. Strain the mixture into a bowl; discard the solids.

In a small saucepan, warm the stock over low heat. Set aside until ready to use.

In a large, heavy-bottomed pot, melt the butter over medium-low heat. When the foam subsides, stir in the flour and reduce the heat to low. Cook, whisking continuously, for 2 minutes. Gradually add the warm stock and whisk continuously until the mixture is smooth and thoroughly combined. Add the steeped half-and-half and the Fennel Pollen Rub, and whisk continuously for 10 minutes, until the gravy is thick and bubbling. Remove from the heat and stir in the parsley. Keep the gravy warm until ready to serve.

CHILI CATSUP

MAKES 1½ CUPS

1 cup ketchup

¼ teaspoon granulated garlic

½ teaspoon kosher salt

6 tablespoons distilled white vinegar

½ teaspoon Smoked Chili Powder (page 50)

½ teaspoon chipotle chile powder (available in most major groceries)

½ teaspoon pasilla chile powder (see Source Guide, page 279)

¼ teaspoon granulated onion

In a medium bowl, mix together all the ingredients thoroughly. Transfer to an airtight container and refrigerate until ready to use, up to 2 weeks.

SPICY MAYONNAISE

MAKES A GENEROUS ½ CUP

½ cup Duke's Mayonnaise, or your favorite brand

1 tablespoon hot sauce, your favorite brand

½ teaspoon kosher salt

In a small bowl, whisk together all the ingredients until thoroughly combined. Refrigerate in an airtight container until ready to use, up to 2 weeks.

STEAK SAUCE

MAKES 3¼ CUPS

2 tablespoons canola oil

1 cup diced yellow onion

5 garlic cloves, thinly sliced

2 tablespoons serrano pepper, seeded and minced

2 tablespoons tomato paste

½ cup raisins

2 tablespoons Dijon mustard

½ cup red wine vinegar

½ cup Worcestershire sauce

2 tablespoons light brown sugar

1 teaspoon kosher salt

1 teaspoon chipotle puree (see Source Guide, page 279), available in most grocery stores

½ teaspoon cracked black pepper

In a small, heavy-bottomed saucepan, heat the canola oil over medium heat. Add the onions and cook, stirring frequently for 5 minutes, until translucent. Add the garlic and serrano pepper and cook, stirring often, for 4 minutes. Add the tomato paste and cook, stirring continuously, for 3 minutes. Add the raisins, mustard, vinegar, Worcestershire, sugar, salt, chipotle puree black pepper, and ¼ cup water and stir to combine. Bring the sauce to a simmer and cook for 5 minutes, then set aside to cool slightly.

Transfer the cooled sauce to a blender and puree until it is smooth and uniform in color. Transfer to an airtight container and let cool completely at room temperature, then cover and refrigerate until ready to use, up to 1 month.

BLOOD ORANGE AND CRANBERRY CHUTNEY

MAKES 1 QUART

2 tablespoons canola oil

1 cup minced shallot

¼ cup minced jalapeño

6 blood oranges, suprêmed, juice reserved

2 cups fresh cranberries

½ cup julienned orange zest
(remove the zest—avoiding the white
pith—with a vegetable peeler and
cut into thin strips)

2 star anise pods

¼ cup sugar

2 teaspoons mustard seeds

¼ teaspoon ground cinnamon

½ teaspoon finely chopped fresh ginger

2 tablespoons red wine vinegar

½ teaspoon kosher salt

2 tablespoons chopped fresh mint

In a small, heavy-bottomed saucepan, heat the canola oil over medium-low heat. Add the shallots and jalapeño and cook, stirring, for 2 minutes. Add the blood orange suprêmes and juice, the fresh cranberries, and the orange zest. Stir to combine and cook for 1 minute. Add the star anise, sugar, mustard seeds, cinnamon, ginger, vinegar, and salt and cook, stirring often, for 10 minutes.

Remove from the heat and fold in the mint. Let the chutney cool to room temperature, then transfer to an airtight container and refrigerate until ready to use, up to 2 weeks.

SMOKED CHILI POWDER SOUR CREAM

MAKES ¾ CUP

¾ cup sour cream

½ teaspoon kosher salt

½ teaspoon Smoked Chili Powder
(see page 50)

In a small bowl, combine all the ingredients and stir well. Transfer to an airtight container and refrigerate until ready to use. It will keep for about 3 days.

CELERY SEED WHITE SAUCE

YIELDS 2½ CUPS

1½ cups mayonnaise

½ cup plus 1 tablespoon cider vinegar

3 tablespoons fresh lemon juice

¾ teaspoon granulated garlic

1½ teaspoons celery seed

¾ teaspoon cayenne pepper

2¼ teaspoons kosher salt

3 teaspoons Simple Syrup (see page 74)

In a medium mixing bowl, whisk all ingredients together thoroughly. Refrigerate in an airtight container until ready to use. This sauce will keep, refrigerated, for 3 days.

BRINES,
MOPS, AND SPRAYS

WORCESTERSHIRE MOP

MAKES A GENEROUS 5 CUPS

1 quart apple cider vinegar

¼ cup kosher salt

⅛ cup freshly ground white pepper

¼ cup Worcestershire sauce

¼ cup hot sauce, your favorite brand

8 tablespoons (1 stick) unsalted butter,
    room temperature

In a 2-quart saucepan, combine the vinegar, salt, white pepper, Worcestershire, hot sauce, and butter and whisk over medium heat until the butter has melted. Bring to a simmer, whisking continuously, then immediately remove from the heat and pour the mop into a lidded heatproof container. Keep warm until ready to use, or cool the sauce completely at room temperature, and refrigerate, covered, until ready to use. It will keep in the refrigerator for up to 5 days. (Thanks to Pat Burke for letting me use this recipe!)

LEMON SPRAY

MAKES A GENEROUS 2½ CUPS

¼ cup Simple Syrup (page 74)

¼ cup plus 2 tablespoons fresh lemon juice

In a medium bowl, combine all the ingredients with 2 cups water and pour into a spray bottle. The lemon spray will keep in the refrigerator for 4 to 5 days.

APPLE SPRAY

MAKES 2¾ CUPS

½ cup Caramel Simple Syrup (page 74)

2 cups apple juice

¼ cup fresh lemon juice

In a medium bowl, combine all the ingredients and pour into a spray bottle. Apple spray will keep in the refrigerator for 4 to 5 days. It will be used on the grill to moisten the meat.

APPLE BRINE

MAKES ABOUT 3 QUARTS

2½ quarts apple juice

½ cup kosher salt

⅓ cup packed light brown sugar

⅓ cup coriander seeds

8 small bay leaves

2 tablespoons plus 1 teaspoon whole
    black peppercorns

2 tablespoons plus 1 teaspoon fennel seeds

1 teaspoon crushed red pepper

In a 3-quart container with a lid, combine all the ingredients and stir until the salt and sugar have dissolved. Cover and refrigerate for 24 to 48 hours before using. Strain before using.

FENNEL SAGE BRINE

MAKES A GENEROUS 6 QUARTS

½ cup plus 2 tablespoons kosher salt

1 cup sugar

2 large carrots, coarsely chopped

2 celery stalks, leaves included,
    coarsely chopped

½ medium yellow onion, coarsely chopped

1 bunch fresh flat-leaf parsley, torn in half

1 bunch fresh thyme

3 or 4 bay leaves

2 tablespoons whole black peppercorns

½ fennel bulb, fronds included,
    coarsely chopped

½ bunch sage

In a large bowl or 8-quart plastic container, combine 6 quarts water with the salt and sugar. Stir until most of the salt and sugar have dissolved. Add the vegetables, parsley, thyme, bay leaves, peppercorns, fennel, and sage and refrigerate for 24 to 48 hours before using. Strain before using.

CHICKEN BRINE

MAKES 3¼ QUARTS

½ cup plus 1 tablespoon kosher salt

½ cup sugar

1 large carrot, coarsely chopped

1 celery stalk, leaves included, coarsely
    chopped

¼ medium yellow onion, coarsely chopped

½ bunch fresh flat-leaf parsley, torn in half

½ bunch fresh thyme

1 or 2 bay leaves

1 tablespoon whole black peppercorns

In a large bowl or 4-quart plastic container, combine 3 quarts water with the salt and sugar. Stir until most of the salt and sugar have dissolved. Add the vegetables, parsley, thyme, bay leaves, and peppercorns and refrigerate for 24 to 48 hours before using. Strain before using.

SPICED PECANS

MAKES 2 CUPS

1 teaspoon canola oil

1 egg white

¼ cup sugar

2 teaspoons ground chile de árbol
(see Source Guide, page 279)

1½ teaspoons smoked salt (see Source Guide,
page 279)

2 cups pecan halves

Preheat the oven to 350°F. Line a baking sheet
with parchment paper or a silicone baking mat
and grease the parchment or mat with the
canola oil.

In a medium bowl, whip the egg whites until
they hold soft peaks. Fold in the sugar, chile
de árbol, and smoked salt. Fold in the pecan
halves just until they are well coated with the
egg white mixture.

Arrange the pecans in a single layer on the
prepared baking sheet. Bake for 45 minutes,
stirring the pecans every 10 minutes with
a wooden spoon. Watch to make sure the
pecans do not burn. Remove from the oven
and set aside to cool to room temperature. The
spiced pecans will keep in an airtight container
at room temperature for up to 3 weeks.

SPICY WALNUTS

MAKES 2 CUPS

1 teaspoon canola oil

2 tablespoons unsalted butter, melted

1 tablespoon Caramel Simple Syrup
(page 74)

1 teaspoon smoked salt (see Source Guide,
page 279)

1 teaspoon ground chile de árbol (see Source
Guide, page 279)

2 cups walnuts

Preheat the oven to 350°F. Line a baking sheet
with parchment paper or a silicone baking mat
and grease the parchment or mat with the
canola oil.

In a medium bowl, combine the butter,
Caramel Simple Syrup, salt, and chile de árbol.
Add the walnuts and toss to evenly coat.

Arrange the walnuts in a single layer on the
prepared baking sheet. Bake for 45 minutes,
stirring the pecans every 10 minutes with
a wooden spoon. Watch to make sure the
walnuts do not burn. Remove from the oven
and set aside to cool to room temperature. The
spicy walnuts will keep in an airtight container
at room temperature for up to 3 weeks.

BREAD-AND-BUTTER PICKLES

MAKES 6 (12-OUNCE) JARS

PICKLING LIQUID

½ cup kosher salt

1 quart apple cider vinegar

1 quart sugar

1 teaspoon celery seeds

2 tablespoons mustard seeds

1 tablespoon ground ginger

1 teaspoon ground turmeric

1 teaspoon whole white peppercorns

3 pounds pickling cucumbers, cut into ¼-inch-thick rounds

1 large white onion, halved and thinly sliced

Make the pickling liquid: In a 3-quart saucepan, combine the salt, vinegar, sugar, celery seeds, mustard seeds, ginger, turmeric, and white peppercorns and stir over medium heat until the salt and sugar have dissolved. Increase the heat to medium-high and bring just to a boil, then remove the pot from the heat and set aside to cool slightly.

Place the cucumber rounds and onion slices in a large stockpot. Pour the warm pickling liquid over the cucumbers, then set aside, uncovered, to cool to room temperature. You may need to weigh the cucumber slices down with a plate to keep them submerged during the cooling process.

Distribute the cucumbers, onions, and pickling liquid among six 12-ounce jars (or put them all in a large 3-quart lidded container), cover tightly, and refrigerate until chilled. The pickles will keep in the refrigerator for up to 3 months.

CARAMEL SIMPLE SYRUP

MAKES 1 CUP

¾ cup sugar

Combine the sugar and 2 tablespoons water in a small, heavy-bottomed saucepan over medium-low heat. Do not stir the mixture, as this will cause crystallization. Cook for 5 to 7 minutes. As the water evaporates, the sugar will begin to caramelize. Once the sugar turns a medium caramel color, reduce the heat to low, add ¼ cup water, and stir to fully incorporate. Remove from the heat and let the syrup cool before pouring into a lidded heatproof container.

The caramel simple syrup will keep in the refrigerator for up to 3 months.

SIMPLE SYRUP

MAKES 2 CUPS

1 cup sugar

Combine the sugar with 1 cup water in a small, heavy-bottomed saucepan. Bring to a boil over medium-high heat, stirring occasionally, then reduce the heat to low and simmer for 3 minutes, or until the sugar has dissolved. Remove from the heat and set aside to cool before using, or let cool completely, then transfer to an airtight container and refrigerate until ready to use, up to 6 months.

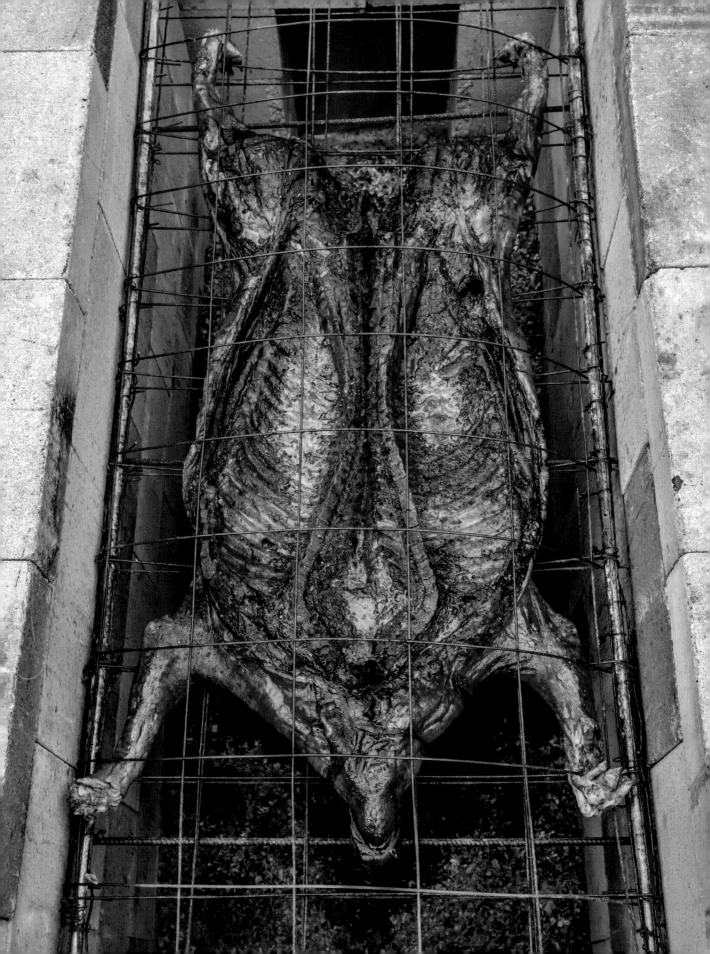

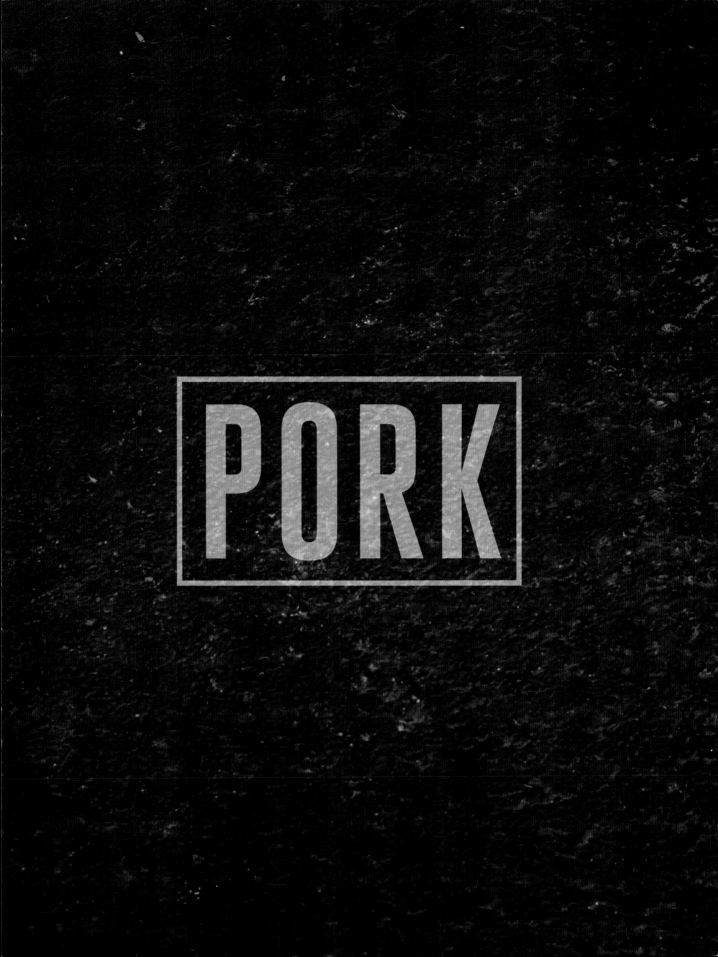

WHEN I WAS GROWING UP IN VIRGINIA, BARBECUE SANDWICHES

were made with meat that was chopped or pulled from the pork shoulder. Today, if someone orders a barbecue sandwich at one of my restaurants and doesn't specify chicken, pork, or beef, we will know you mean pork and not beef or chicken. The Pork Butt Sandwich (page 119) with Dill Coleslaw (page 220) is a perfect example of the barbecue sandwiches I grew up eating.

Bacon and salty pork hams were also important staples in our home, and pork chops are one of my go-to meats to grill for dinner. The USDA's decision in the last decade to lower the recommended internal temperature of cooked pork from 165°F to 145°F (with the exception of ground pork) is especially beneficial to the taste and tenderness of pork loins and tenderloins. By cooking these meats to a lower internal temperature, the quality of the finished dish is greatly improved. These tender and leaner cuts become dry and do not chew as well when overcooked. Apple-Brined Pork Loin with Applesauce and Spicy Peanut–Brown Butter Vinaigrette (page 82), Kale and Bacon–Stuffed Pork Loin (page 86), and Thick-Cut Pork Chops with Mustard Sauce (page 79) all benefit from being cooked to 145°F.

The three things I look for when selecting pork are marbleization, age, and quality of butchering. Pork, unlike beef, is not graded by fat content. Pork that is well marbled will show striations of fat within the meat, giving the pork a lighter red color. Pork that is well marbled with fat will yield moist and juicy meat once it is cooked. Most pork producers state that the pork is fresh for twenty-one days for bone-in, and twenty-eight days for boneless cuts. I prefer fresh pork that is seven to fourteen days old from its harvest date. I look for ribs that don't have any "shiners" (when the bones are exposed because too much meat was cut from the ribs). I look for single-pack, vacuum-sealed ribs because they are easier to inspect than double or triple packs.

Pulled pork is often specified for use in some of these recipes. There's no hard-and-fast rule about how to pull the meat from the cooked pork—just use your hands to pull bite-size chunks of meat.

THICK-CUT PORK CHOPS
WITH MUSTARD SAUCE

MAKES 4 SERVINGS

Some people like skinny chops, some people like thick ones. (I happen to like all chops.) These thick chops take on more smoke during the longer cooking time, so you get more of that great smoky flavor.

2½ cups Pork Chop Brine (recipe follows)

1½ cups Mustard Sauce (page 63)

4 thick-cut pork chops (¾ to 1 inch thick)

1 tablespoon salted butter

2½ teaspoons kosher salt

2½ teaspoons freshly ground black pepper

Prepare the Pork Chop Brine 24 hours in advance.

Prepare the Mustard Sauce and warm gently in a saucepan over low heat or, if made in advance, rewarm gently over low heat.

Arrange the pork chops in a casserole dish in one layer. Strain the chilled brine and pour it over the pork chops. Refrigerate, uncovered, for 3 hours before cooking.

Remove the pork chops from the brine and pat the meat dry using paper towels.

In a small bowl or cup, combine the butter, ½ teaspoon of the salt, and ½ teaspoon of the pepper and microwave on high for 30 seconds to melt the butter. Brush the pork chops evenly on both sides with the seasoned butter, then dust the chops uniformly on both sides with ½ teaspoon of the salt and ½ teaspoon of the pepper each.

When you are ready to cook, heat the grill to 400°F, using the direct grilling method (see Direct Cooking or Grilling, page 22).

Place the pork chops on the hot side of the grill and cook for 4 minutes, then rotate each chop 90 degrees and cook for an additional 4 minutes. Flip the chops and cook for 4 minutes, and once again rotate each chop 90 degrees. Cook for 4 additional minutes, or until a meat thermometer placed in the thickest part of the meat reads an internal temperature of 140°F. Transfer the chops to a platter and let them rest for 5 minutes before serving.

Serve with the Mustard Sauce.

PORK CHOP BRINE

MAKES A GENEROUS 2¾ CUPS

2½ cups apple juice

3 tablespoons honey

¼ cup kosher salt

2 small bay leaves

2 teaspoons caraway seeds

1 teaspoon mustard seeds

2 teaspoons whole black peppercorns

¼ teaspoon granulated garlic

In a large pot or lidded container, whisk together the apple juice, salt, and honey until the salt and honey have dissolved. Add the bay leaves, caraway, mustard seeds, peppercorns, and garlic, cover, and refrigerate for 24 hours.

SKINNY PORK CHOP
WITH CHILI CATSUP AND SOFT SCRAMBLED EGGS

MAKES 4 SERVINGS

The idea behind this dish is that sometimes it's nice to have breakfast for dinner, especially on those nights when you don't feel like cooking for hours. Prepare the soft scrambled egg ingredients before cooking the chops so that the eggs can be cooked quickly while the meat is resting.

2 tablespoons plus 2 teaspoons Poultry Rub
(page 49)

1 tablespoon salted butter

6 (3- to 4-ounce) pork chops

1½ cups Chili Catsup (page 65)

9 large eggs

6 tablespoons half-and-half

1½ teaspoons kosher salt

½ cup chopped scallions

2 tablespoons chopped fresh chives

3 tablespoons unsalted butter

Prepare the Poultry Rub.

In a small bowl or cup, combine the salted butter with 1 teaspoon of the Poultry Rub, and microwave on high for 30 seconds to melt the butter.

Brush the pork chops evenly on both sides with the seasoned butter, then dust the chops evenly on both sides with 1 teaspoon of the Poultry Rub each. Let the chops sit, uncovered, for 30 minutes at room temperature.

Prepare the Chili Catsup and warm it gently in a saucepan over low heat or, if made in advance, rewarm gently over low heat.

In a medium bowl, whisk together the eggs, half-and-half, and salt for 30 seconds, until

well combined and pale yellow in color. Fold in the scallions and chives.

When you are ready to cook, heat the grill to 400°F, using the direct grilling method (see Direct Cooking or Grilling, page 22).

Place the seasoned pork chops on the hot side of the grill and cook for 4 minutes. Flip the chops over and cook for an additional 4 minutes, or until a meat thermometer placed in the thickest part of the chop reads an internal temperature of 140°F. Remove from the heat and let the chops rest for 5 minutes.

While the pork chops are resting, in a medium nonstick skillet, melt the unsalted butter over medium-low heat. Add the egg mixture and cook for 30 seconds, until the eggs begin to set on the outside edges of the pan. With a rubber spatula, release the edges of the egg and push them toward the center of the skillet. Cook, continuously fluffing and moving the eggs around the skillet, for 1 to 2 minutes more, until they are set. The eggs should look slightly runny. Immediately transfer to a serving platter and sprinkle with the remaining 1 teaspoon Poultry Rub.

Top each chop with 2 tablespoons of the Chile Catsup, and serve with the soft scrambled eggs. Pass any remaining sauce around the table.

APPLE-BRINED PORK LOIN
WITH APPLESAUCE AND
SPICY PEANUT–BROWN BUTTER VINAIGRETTE

Having apprenticed under a French chef, one of my favorite things to do is brown butter in a pan. The French call it *beurre noisette,* and it adds a nice nutty flavor to both savory and sweet dishes.

1½ quarts Pork Loin Brine (recipe follows)

1 (2- to 2½-pound) pork loin

3 cups Caramelized Applesauce (page 233)

3 tablespoons plus 1 teaspoon Poultry Rub (page 49)

1 tablespoon unsalted butter, at room temperature

2 cups Spicy Peanut Brown Butter Vinaigrette (recipe follows)

The day before you plan to grill, prepare the Pork Loin Brine.

The next day, strain the brine. Place the pork loin in a lidded container and pour enough strained brine over the loin to cover. Refrigerate for 4 hours.

Prepare the Applesauce and refrigerate until ready to serve.

After 4 hours, remove the loin from the brine and pat it dry with paper towels. Discard the brine.

Prepare the Poultry Rub.

Combine the butter and 1 teaspoon of the Poultry Rub in a small bowl. Microwave the butter mixture for 30 seconds to melt the butter, and brush it on all sides of the pork loin. Dust the loin on all sides with the remaining 3 tablespoons Poultry Rub. Let the loin sit for 30 minutes at room temperature before cooking.

When you are ready to cook, heat the grill to 400°F using the 2-Zone setup (see 2-Zone Cooking, page 22).

Place the seasoned pork loin on the hot side of the grill and cook for 10 minutes, turning the loin frequently to evenly brown all sides. Move the loin to the cool side of the grill and cook for 10 minutes, or until a meat thermometer placed in the thickest part of the loin reads an internal temperature of 140°F. Remove the loin from the heat and let it rest 10 minutes before slicing.

Prepare the Spicy Peanut Brown Butter Vinaigrette.

Using a sharp knife, slice the pork loin ¼ to ½ inch thick. Place the slices on a platter, spoon 1 cup of the Spicy Peanut Brown Butter Vinaigrette over the loin, and serve with the applesauce. Pass the remaining vinaigrette around the table.

PORK LOIN BRINE

MAKES 1½ QUARTS

1 quart plus 1 cup apple juice

½ cup kosher salt

¼ cup plus 2 tablespoons packed
 light brown sugar

2 tablespoons coriander seeds

4 small bay leaves

1 tablespoon plus 1 teaspoon whole black
 peppercorns

2 teaspoons black mustard seeds

½ teaspoon crushed red pepper

In a large pot or lidded container, whisk
together the apple juice, salt, and sugar until
dissolved. Stir in the coriander, bay leaves,
peppercorns, mustard seeds, and red pepper
and refrigerate for 24 hours before using.

SPICY PEANUT–BROWN BUTTER VINAIGRETTE

MAKES 2 CUPS

⅓ cup apple cider vinegar

2 teaspoons honey

2 teaspoons kosher salt

¾ teaspoon chipotle chile powder
 (available at most major groceries)

⅛ teaspoon cayenne pepper

½ teaspoon granulated garlic

16 tablespoons (2 sticks) unsalted butter

½ cup chopped roasted peanuts

In a medium bowl, whisk together the vinegar,
honey, salt, chipotle powder, cayenne, and
granulated garlic until well combined.

In a small sauté pan, melt the butter over
medium-low heat. Cook, stirring often, for 4 to
6 minutes, until the milk solids are nutty and
brown.

While whisking, add the brown butter in a slow
stream to the vinegar mixture, whisking continuously to incorporate thoroughly. Fold in the
chopped peanuts. Keep the vinaigrette warm
until ready to use.

STUFFING AND ROLLING A PORK LOIN

1 Using a sharp knife, make a slice lengthwise through the middle of the pork loin. Slice three-quarters of the way through the entire length of the pork loin. Avoid cutting all the way through. **2** Spread open and press flat, fat-side down. Season butterflied pork loin with Caraway Rub. Press rub into the pork loin. **3** Place kale mixture down the center of the butterflied pork loin. Press down the kale mixture evenly and compact. **4** Rolling away from you, roll the pork loin up lengthwise, jelly-roll style. **5** Take a piece of butcher's twine about 4 to 5 times the length of the pork loin and tie one end of it around one end of the pork loin firmly to keep it from unrolling. Run the butcher's twine underneath the entire length of the pork loin. Loop the butcher's twine around the pork loin and through the twine running lengthwise and pull snug to shape the pork loin. Make another loop with the twine 2 inches down from the first loop and pull tight. Make the pork a uniform shape as you go. **6** Continue to place loops of butcher's twine every 2 inches until the entire pork loin is pulled tight and the same diameter from one end to the other. Tie off at the end, so that the butcher's twine cannot unravel. **7** Season the outside of the trussed and stuffed pork loin with the Caraway Rub.

KALE AND BACON-STUFFED PORK LOIN

MAKES 4 TO 6 SERVINGS

Having grown up in the South, I'm a big fan of cooked greens—collards, mustard, and kale are some of my favorites. The heartiness of the kale and the salty bacon make a nice accompaniment to the pork here. Don't be intimidated by the stuffing technique for this dish—it's as easy as tying your shoes!

2 tablespoons olive oil

1 cup finely diced smoked bacon (about 14 slices)

1 cup julienned yellow onion

1 tablespoon minced garlic

4 cups packed sliced kale

1 tablespoon plus 2 teaspoons Caraway Rub (page 50)

1 tablespoon plus 1 teaspoon kosher salt

¼ cup apple cider vinegar

1 (2- to 2½-pound) pork loin, butterflied

1 tablespoon unsalted butter, melted

3 cups Roasted Tomato, Honey, and Chipotle Sauce (page 64)

½ cup apple juice, in a spray bottle, for the grill

Prepare the Caraway Rub.

In a large, heavy-bottomed pot, heat the olive oil over medium-low heat. Add the bacon and cook for 3 to 5 minutes, until the fat is rendered and the bacon is golden brown. Reduce the heat to low and add the onion and garlic to the pot. Cook, stirring with a wooden spoon, for 3 to 5 minutes, until the garlic is a light golden and the onion is transparent. Add the kale and 2 teaspoons of the Caraway Rub and

cook, stirring often, for 5 minutes. Add the vinegar and cook for another 2 to 3 minutes, or until the vinegar has evaporated and the kale is tender. Remove from the heat and transfer the stuffing to a plate or platter to cool until ready to use.

Prepare the Roasted Tomato, Honey, and Chipotle Sauce and keep warm until ready to use, or, if made in advance, rewarm the sauce gently over low heat.

Cut a 24-inch length of butcher's twine and soak it in water.

On a clean cutting board, brush both sides of the butterflied pork loin with the melted butter, and use a shaker to dust with ½ tablespoon of the Caraway Rub. Place the loin fat-side down and spoon the kale mixture horizontally down the center of the loin. Rolling away from you, roll the pork up lengthwise, jelly-roll style. With the fat side up, use the soaked butcher twine to tie the loin. Evenly dust the outside of the stuffed loin with the remaining ½ tablespoon Caraway Rub. (See photographs on pages 84–85.)

When ready to cook, heat the grill to 400°F, using the direct grilling method (see Direct Cooking or Grilling, page 22).

Place the stuffed pork loin directly on the grill and cook for 10 minutes, then spray with apple juice to moisten. Cook for 35 to 40 minutes more, rolling the meat a quarter turn and spraying with apple juice every 5 minutes. The pork is done when a meat thermometer placed in the thickest part of the loin reads an internal temperature of 140°F. Let the loin rest for 15 minutes before removing the twine and slicing.

With a sharp knife, cut the loin crosswise into 1-inch-thick slices. Spoon 1½ cups of the warm Roasted Tomato, Honey, and Chipotle Sauce over a platter and top with the sliced pork. Pass the remaining sauce around the table.

FENNEL GARLIC PORK SHOULDER

WITH WORCESTERSHIRE MOP

MAKES 10 TO 20 SERVINGS

This mop recipe is a gift from my good friend Pat Burke, who is a legend in barbecue. The mop not only keeps the meat moist while cooking, it adds tanginess to the finished dish. Thank you, Pat!

½ cup Fennel Garlic Rub (page 53)

1 (8- to 10-pound) bone-in pork shoulder, trimmed (ask your butcher to do this)

1 quart Worcestershire Mop (page 69)

Prepare the Fennel Garlic Rub. Dust the pork shoulder evenly all over with the rub. Refrigerate, uncovered, overnight.

Prepare the Worcestershire Mop. Keep warm until ready to use.

When you are ready to cook, heat the smoker to 300°F pit temperature (see Smoke, page 25). Alternatively, heat the grill to 300°F using the 2-Zone setup (see 2-Zone Cooking, page 22), using five or six chunks of your favorite wood in addition to the charcoal or gas.

Place the pork shoulder in the smoker, or on the cool side of the 2-Zone grill, close the grill lid, and cook for 1 hour, then baste with the mop. Cook with the lid closed for 3 hours more, basting the shoulder with the mop every 30 minutes.

Wrap the shoulder tightly in heavy-duty aluminum foil and return it to the smoker or to the cool side of the grill. Cook at 300°F for 2½ to 3½ hours more, checking the temperature after 2½ hours with a meat thermometer. The meat will be done when a thermometer placed in the thickest part of the shoulder reads an internal temperature of 195°F. Allow to rest for a minimum of 30 minutes.

Serve the pork sliced, chopped, or pulled.

SMOKED LOIN BACK RIBS
WITH CHERRY BARBECUE SAUCE

MAKES 4 SERVINGS

While this is a tomato-based sauce, the addition of dried cherries and cherry preserves add just the right sweetness to the pork.

1 cup Cool Smoke Rub (page 49)

2 racks loin back pork ribs (about 1½ pounds each), trimmed with membrane removed (ask your butcher to do this or follow photographs pages 94–95)

½ cup apple juice, in a spray bottle, for the grill

3 cups Cherry Barbecue Sauce (page 63)

Prepare the Cool Smoke Rub.

An hour before you plan to cook the ribs, season each rack with ½ cup of the Cool Smoke Rub (use ¼ cup per side), using a shaker to dust evenly on both sides.

When you are ready to cook, heat the smoker to 275°F pit temperature (see Smoke, page 25). Alternatively, heat a grill to 275°F, using the 2-Zone setup (2-Zone Cooking, page 22), using three or four chunks of your favorite wood in addition to the charcoal or gas.

Place the ribs meat-side up in the smoker, or on the cool side of the grill, close the grill lid, and cook for 1 hour, then spray the ribs with apple juice to moisten. Cook the ribs for 1 hour more, spraying them with juice again after 30 minutes and a final time at the 2-hour mark.

Prepare the Cherry Barbecue Sauce.

Cut two 18 x 24-inch lengths of foil to wrap each rib rack in a tight package.

When the ribs have a reddish-brown mahogany color, transfer them from the grill and place each rack meat-side down on a sheet of foil and wrap tightly, being careful not to puncture the foil. Place the rib packages meat-side down in the smoker, or on the cool side of the grill, and cook for 1½ to 2 hours more, until tender. Open the foil packages and use a skewer or a toothpick to check for tenderness.

Remove the ribs from the foil, brush each rack with ½ cup of the Cherry Barbecue Sauce (use ¼ cup per side), and return them meat-side up to the smoker, or to the cool side of the grill, for 5 to 10 minutes to set the sauce. Watch them carefully so you do not burn or overset the sauce.

Transfer to a platter and serve with any remaining sauce on the side.

SMOKED LOIN BACK RIBS
WITH ROASTED TOMATO, HONEY, AND CHIPOTLE SAUCE

MAKES 4 TO 6 SERVINGS

Barbecue sauces tend to be the norm with smoked pork loin back ribs (often called baby back ribs); this dish is unique because of the savory flavors that come from the Roasted Tomato, Honey, and Chipotle Sauce.

1 cup Cool Smoke Rub (page 49)

2 racks loin back pork ribs (about 1½ pounds each), trimmed with membrane removed (ask your butcher to do this or follow photographs pages 94–95)

½ cup apple juice, in a spray bottle, for the grill

3 cups Roasted Tomato, Honey, and Chipotle Sauce (page 64)

Prepare the Cool Smoke Rub.

An hour before you plan to cook the ribs, use a shaker to dust each rack evenly on both sides with ½ cup of the Cool Smoke Rub (use ¼ cup per side).

When you are ready to cook, heat the smoker to 275°F pit temperature (see Smoke, page 25). Alternatively, heat the grill to 275°F, using the 2-Zone setup (see 2-Zone Cooking, page 22), using three or four chunks of your favorite wood in addition to the charcoal or gas.

Place the ribs meat-side up in the smoker, or on the cool side of a grill, close the grill lid, and cook for 1 hour. Spray the ribs with apple juice to moisten and cook for 1 hour more, spraying again after 30 minutes, and a final time at the 2-hour mark.

Cut two 18 x 24-inch lengths of foil to wrap each rib rack in a tight package.

When the ribs turn a reddish-brown mahogany color, transfer them from the grill and place each rack meat-side down on a sheet of foil; wrap tightly, being careful not to puncture the foil. Place the rib packages meat-side down in the smoker, or on the cool side of the grill, and cook for 1½ to 2 hours more, until tender. Open the foil packages and use a skewer or a toothpick to check for tenderness.

Meanwhile, prepare the Roasted Tomato, Honey, and Chipotle Sauce and keep it warm in a covered saucepan over low heat until ready to use; if made in advance, rewarm the sauce gently over low heat.

When they are done, remove the ribs from the foil packets, brush each rack with ½ cup of the Roasted Tomato, Honey, and Chipotle Sauce (use ¼ cup per side), and return them meat-side up to the smoker, or to the cool side of the grill, for 5 to 10 minutes to set the sauce. Watch them carefully so you do not burn or overset the sauce.

Remove from the heat and serve immediately with any remaining sauce on the side.

SPARERIBS
WITH MUSTARD SAUCE

MAKES 4 TO 6 SERVINGS

The mustard sauce is a big departure from the typical way spareribs are served in many places. This sauce gives a big nod to South Carolina–style barbecue, and the addition of whole-grain mustard makes it even more unique.

1 cup Fennel Garlic Rub (page 53)

2 (4½-pound) racks pork spareribs, trimmed and membrane removed (ask your butcher to do this or follow photographs pages 94–95)

½ cup apple juice, in a spray bottle, for the grill

1½ cups Mustard Sauce (page 63)

Prepare the Fennel Garlic Rub.

An hour before you plan to cook the spareribs, dust each rack with ½ cup of the Fennel Garlic Rub (use ¼ cup per side).

When you are ready to cook, heat the smoker to 275°F pit temperature (see Smoke, page 25). Alternatively, heat the grill to 275°F, using the 2-Zone setup (see 2-Zone Cooking, page 22), using three or four chunks of your favorite wood in addition to the charcoal or gas.

Place the spareribs meat-side up in the smoker, or on the cool side of the grill. Cook for 1 hour, then spray the ribs with apple juice to moisten. Cook for 1 hour more, spraying again after 30 minutes and a final time at the 2-hour mark.

Meanwhile, prepare the Mustard Sauce and keep it warm until ready to use, or, if made in advance, rewarm it gently in a saucepan over low heat.

Cut two 18 x 24-inch sheets of aluminum foil to wrap each rib rack in a tight package.

When the ribs have a nice reddish-brown mahogany color, remove them from the grill and place each rack meat-side down on a sheet of foil and wrap tightly, being careful to not puncture the foil. Place the foil packages meat-side down in the smoker, or on the cool side of the grill, and cook for 2 to 2½ hours more, until tender. Open the foil packages and use a skewer or a toothpick to check for tenderness.

Remove from the heat, carefully unwrap the ribs, and discard the foil. Brush each rack with ½ cup of the Mustard Sauce (use ¼ cup per side). Return the ribs meat-side up to the smoker, or to the cool side of the grill, and cook for 5 to 10 minutes to set the sauce. Watch them carefully so you do not burn or overset the sauce.

Serve the ribs immediately with any remaining sauce on the side.

1 2

TRIMMING COMPETITION RIBS

1 Using the longest rib bone, make a cut to create a perfect rectangle. **2** Cut off the last bone on each end of the rack of ribs. **3** Completed trimmed rack of competition ribs. (See recipe page 96–97.)

COMPETITION RIBS
COOL SMOKE STYLE

MAKES 2 TO 4 SERVINGS

As I've often said, competition barbecue is "one-bite food"—we have one opportunity to get the judges' attention. These ribs have just the right amount of smoke to complement the natural flavor of the pork, and enough pop to take to a barbecue contest.

1 cup Cool Smoke Rub (page 49)

2 (3-pound) racks St. Louis–cut pork spareribs, trimmed with membrane removed (ask your butcher to do this or follow photographs pages 94–95)

½ cup apple juice, in a spray bottle, for the grill

1 cup Cool Smoke Barbecue Sauce (page 57)

½ cup honey

2 teaspoons apple cider vinegar

8 tablespoons (1 stick) unsalted butter, melted

¼ cup packed light brown sugar

Use a shaker to dust both sides of the rib racks generously with the Cool Smoke Rub (use ¼ cup per side), and let them sit at room temperature, uncovered, for 1 hour before cooking.

When you are ready to cook, heat the smoker to 275°F pit temperature (see Smoke, page 25). Alternatively, heat a grill to 275°F, using a 2-Zone setup (see 2-Zone Cooking, page 22), using three or four chunks of your favorite wood in addition to the charcoal or gas.

Place the ribs meat-side up in the smoker, or on the grill over indirect heat, and cook for 2 hours, spraying the spareribs with apple juice every 30 minutes to moisten.

Prepare the Cool Smoke Barbecue Sauce.

In a small bowl, stir together the Cool Smoke

Barbecue Sauce, ¼ cup of the honey, and the vinegar and set aside.

Cut two 18 x 24-inch lengths of foil to wrap each rib rack in a tight package.

When the ribs have cooked for 2 hours, transfer them from the grill and place each rack meat-side down on a sheet of foil. Drizzle the ribs evenly on both sides with the melted butter and remaining ¼ cup honey, and sprinkle evenly with the brown sugar. Wrap each rack tightly in the foil, being careful not to puncture.

Return the rib packages meat-side down to the smoker, or to the cool side of a grill, close the lid, and cook for 2 to 2½ hours more, or until the meat is tender. The ribs are done when a meat thermometer placed in the thickest part of the meat reads an internal temperature of 203°F to 211°F or use a skewer or a toothpick to check for tenderness.

Remove from the heat, carefully unwrap the ribs, and discard the foil. Brush the Cool Smoke Barbecue Sauce-honey mixture on both sides of the ribs to coat and return them meat-side up to the smoker or grill over indirect heat. Cook for 15 minutes to set the sauce. Watch them carefully so you do not burn or overset the sauce.

Serve immediately, with any remaining sauce on the side.

SMOKED PORK CHILI
WITH WHITE BEANS

MAKES 6 TO 8 SERVINGS

Texans often frown on having beans in their chili. Not being a Texan, however, I'm a sucker for the creamy white beans in this recipe—they add a great contrast in texture. Two hours of smoke on the pork brings a depth and complexity to this chili.

1 tablespoon plus 2 teaspoons Smoked Chili Powder (page 50)

3 pounds pork shoulder, cut into 1-inch cubes

1 tablespoon plus ½ teaspoon kosher salt

½ cup apple juice, in a spray bottle, for the grill

1 tablespoon canola oil

1½ cups diced yellow onion

1 cup diced green bell pepper

½ cup diced poblano pepper

¼ cup diced jalapeño

1 cup diced turnip

1 tablespoon thinly sliced garlic

1 teaspoon freshly ground black pepper

1 teaspoon dried Greek oregano (available at most groceries)

½ teaspoon freshly ground cumin seeds

½ teaspoon freshly ground coriander seeds

½ teaspoon chipotle chile powder

½ teaspoon Espelette pepper (see Source Guide, page 279)

½ cup beer, your favorite brand

2 quarts chicken stock

3 cups canned white beans, drained and rinsed

¾ cup Smoked Chili Powder Sour Cream (page 66)

1 bunch scallions, thinly sliced

2 limes, quartered

Prepare the Smoked Chili Powder.

Cover a rimmed baking sheet with parchment or aluminum foil and arrange the pork cubes in one layer, so that all the pieces are touching. Dust the top of the pork evenly with ½ tablespoon of the Smoked Chili Powder and ¾ teaspoon of the salt. Use your hands to flip the pork cubes over and repeat the dusting process with another ½ tablespoon of the Smoked Chili Powder and ¾ teaspoon of the salt. Transfer the pork to a wire rack.

When you are ready to cook, heat the smoker to 300°F pit temperature (see Smoke, page 25). Alternatively, heat the grill to 300°F, using the 2-Zone setup (see 2-Zone Cooking, page 22),

Place the wire rack of pork in the smoker, or on the cool side of the grill, close the lid, and cook for 2 hours, spraying every 30 minutes with apple juice to moisten. Remove the pork from the smoker or grill and set aside until ready to use.

In a heavy-bottomed 4-quart pot, heat the canola oil over medium-low heat. Add the onion, bell pepper, poblano pepper, jalapeño, and turnip and cook, stirring frequently, for 5 minutes. Add the garlic and cook, stirring continuously to avoid burning it. Season with the remaining 2 teaspoons salt, the black

(continued)

pepper, remaining 2 teaspoons Smoked Chili Powder, the oregano, cumin, coriander, chipotle powder, and Espelette, and cook for 3 minutes.

Deglaze the pot with the beer, using a wooden spoon to scrape up and incorporate all the browned bits on the bottom of the pot. (Feel free to drink the remaining beer in the can.) Add the stock and the smoked pork, cover, and cook for 60 to 75 minutes, or until the pork is fork-tender.

Meanwhile, prepare the Smoked Chili Powder Sour Cream.

When the pork is done, add the white beans to the pot and warm though. Check the seasoning and adjust as necessary. Serve in bowls. Top each serving with 1½ to 2 tablespoons of the Smoked Chili Powder Sour Cream, sprinkle with the scallions, and garnish with lime wedges.

BARBECUE, THE FRIENDLIEST FOOD

I like to tell people that barbecue is the friendliest food. Barbecue is historically made from large, modest cuts of tougher meats that take hours to cook until tender. There's a lot of time for talking and just having fun while you wait for the meat to cook, so it's often served at family reunions, picnics, and other celebrations with large groups of people. Barbecue is a food that doesn't discriminate— it's popular with everyone, and the aromas of cooking meat are like a dinner bell inviting everyone to come and enjoy. Having started my career in a French kitchen cooking fancy dishes, I like how barbecue doesn't seem to intimidate anyone. It's very casual and puts people at ease.

MUSTARD AND ROSEMARY-CRUSTED PORK SHOULDER

MAKES 10 TO 20 SERVINGS

Mustard and rosemary are a classic combo in many cuisines. Here they combine with the smoke to make for a savory dish. This recipe's temperature guide is for pulled pork. If you want sliced pork, cook it to an internal temperature of 180°F.

½ cup Mustard Sauce (page 63)

2 tablespoons minced garlic

2 tablespoons minced fresh rosemary

1 (8- to 10-pound) bone-in pork shoulder, trimmed (ask your butcher to do this)

1 tablespoon kosher salt

1 tablespoon cracked black pepper

2 cups apple juice, in a spray bottle, for the grill

Prepare the Mustard Sauce.

In a small bowl, combine the Mustard Sauce, garlic, and rosemary, stir well, and set aside.

Check the surface of the pork shoulder for any bone slivers and use a sharp knife to remove them. Season the pork shoulder evenly with the salt and pepper, and rub the Mustard Sauce mixture on all sides. Refrigerate, uncovered, overnight.

When you are ready to cook, heat the smoker to 300°F pit temperature (see Smoke, page 25). Alternatively, heat the grill to 300°F, using the 2-Zone setup (see 2-Zone Cooking, page 22), using five or six chunks of your favorite wood in addition to the charcoal or gas.

Place the pork shoulder in the smoker, or on the cool side of the grill, close the grill lid, and cook for 1 hour, then spray the meat with apple juice to moisten. Cook for 3 hours more, spraying the pork shoulder every 30 minutes.

At the end of 4 hours, wrap the shoulder tightly in heavy-duty aluminum foil and return it to the smoker, or to the cool side of the grill. Cook for 2½ to 3½ hours, checking the temperature after 2½ hours with a meat thermometer. The meat will be done when a thermometer placed in the thickest part of the shoulder reads an internal temperature of 195°F.

Serve the pork sliced, chopped, or pulled.

COMPETITION PORK BUTT
COOL SMOKE STYLE

MAKES 10 TO 20 SERVINGS

While this dish is reminiscent of Kansas City–style barbecue, we've added a little bit of sweetness, a little spice, and some tang, with the goal of having something to please everyone's tastes.

For competition cooks, the prize portion of the pork butt is what's known as the "money muscle," also called the coppa, a muscle at the top of the shoulder. It gets its name because of the many awards it tends to win for cooks. If prepared correctly, it has a tender, silky chew.

---

1 cup Cool Smoke Rub (page 49)

2 cups Pork Injection (recipe follows)

1 (8- to 10-pound) bone-in pork shoulder, trimmed (ask your butcher to do this)

2 cups apple juice, in a spray bottle, for the grill

3 cups Cool Smoke Barbecue Sauce (page 57)

Prepare the Cool Smoke Rub and the Pork Injection.

On a clean work surface, use a shaker to dust the pork shoulder evenly all over with the Cool Smoke Rub. Place the pork fat-cap down and fill a meat injector (see Source Guide, page 279) with the Pork Injection. Using 1 ounce of the liquid per injection, repeatedly inject the meat 1 inch apart over the surface of the pork. Refill the injector as needed. Refrigerate, uncovered, overnight.

When you are ready to cook, heat the smoker to 300°F pit temperature (see Smoke, page 25). Alternatively, heat the grill to 300°F, using the 2-Zone setup (see 2-Zone Cooking, page 22), using five or six chunks of your favorite wood in addition to the charcoal or gas.

Place the pork shoulder in the smoker, or on the cool side of the grill, close the lid, and cook for 1 hour, then spray with apple juice to moisten. Cook for 3 hours more with the lid closed, spraying the shoulder every 30 minutes.

Cut two 18 x 24-inch pieces of heavy-duty aluminum foil and join them lengthwise by crimping the edges. Lay the resulting piece out flat on a clean work surface.

Remove the shoulder from the smoker or grill and wrap it tightly in the length of foil. Return it to the smoker or to the cool side of the grill. Cook for 2½ to 3½ hours more, checking the temperature after 2½ hours with a meat thermometer. The meat will be done when a thermometer placed in the thickest part of the shoulder reads an internal temperature of 195°F. Rest 30 minutes to 1 hour.

Prepare the Cool Smoke Barbecue Sauce.

Remove the pork shoulder from the foil and brush with ½ cup of the Cool Smoke Barbecue Sauce. Return the pork, uncovered, to the smoker, or to the cool side of the grill, and cook for another 10 minutes to set the sauce.

Remove from the heat and let the shoulder rest for 45 minutes. (See photographs on pages 104–105.)

Serve the pork sliced, chopped, or pulled, with the remaining Cool Smoke Barbecue Sauce on the side.

PORK INJECTION

MAKES 2 CUPS

1½ cups apple juice

3 tablespoons brown sugar

⅓ cup Butcher's BBQ pork injection powder (see Source Guide, page 279)

¼ teaspoon xanthan gum (see Source Guide, page 279)

Thoroughly whisk all the ingredients together in a medium bowl. Will keep in refrigerator for up to 5 days.

SERVING COMPETITION PORK BUTT

1 Using a very sharp slicing knife, cut the "money muscle" at the top of the shoulder off at the seam. This is a small muscle that looks somewhat like a small tenderloin and is prized for both its texture and flavor. **2** Once the money muscle has been sliced off the pork butt, place it on a cutting board cut-side down, and make a slice on the bias about 1 inch from one end of the "money muscle." Continue to make a series of slices every inch or so, on the bias, until the "money muscle" has been cut into five to seven 1-inch slices. **3** Search the remaining larger portion of the cooked pork butt for the best pieces to serve the judges. **4** Be careful to avoid crushing the meat when pulling the cooked pork shoulder to find the samples for the judges.

PORK T-BONE STEAKS
WITH TAMARIND SAUCE

This is a quick and easy grilled dish, but you'll need to prepare the brine the day before you cook. If you like Asian flavors, you'll love the ginger in the rub and the sweet-and-sour tamarind fruit in the sauce.

½ recipe Apple Brine (page 69)

4 (6- to 8-ounce) T-bone pork steaks

2½ cups Tamarind Barbecue Sauce (page 60)

2 tablespoons unsalted butter

2 teaspoons T-Bone Rub (recipe follows)

½ cup apple juice, in a spray bottle

The day before you cook the steaks, prepare the Apple Brine.

The day you plan to cook, place the steaks in a casserole dish or a container with high sides. Strain the cold brine, discarding the solids, and pour enough brine over the steaks to cover. Refrigerate for 3 hours, uncovered.

Prepare the Tamarind Barbecue Sauce, cover, and keep warm until ready to use or, if made in advance, rewarm it gently in a saucepan over low heat. Prepare the T-Bone Rub.

Remove the steaks from the brine and pat them dry with paper towels.

In a microwavable dish, combine the butter and 2 teaspoons of the T-Bone Rub. Microwave for 30 seconds to melt the butter, stir, then brush the seasoned butter on both sides of the steaks. Let them sit at room temperature for 30 minutes before cooking.

When you are ready to cook, heat the grill to 400°F.

Place the steaks directly on the grill and cook for 4 minutes, then rotate them 90 degrees and cook for another 4 minutes. Flip the steaks, spray them with apple juice to moisten, and cook for another 4 minutes. Spray again with apple juice, rotate 90 degrees, and cook for a final 4 minutes, or until a meat thermometer placed in the thickest part of the steak reads an internal temperature of 140°F.

Transfer the steaks to a platter and let them rest for 5 minutes before serving.

Top each steak with 3 to 4 tablespoons of the warm Tamarind Barbecue Sauce. Pass the remaining sauce around the table.

T-BONE RUB

MAKES A GENEROUS ¾ CUP

½ cup kosher salt

2 teaspoons granulated garlic

1 tablespoon freshly ground coriander seeds

2 teaspoons cracked black pepper

1 tablespoon dried basil

2 teaspoons ground ginger

2 tablespoons turbinado sugar

Combine all the ingredients thoroughly in a small bowl. Store in an airtight container until ready to use. Will keep for a few months.

SMOKED AND BRAISED PORK SHANK
WITH WHITE BEANS

Braised meat is a comfort food, with a depth of flavors that comes from a longer cooking time. The addition of smoke lends another layer of taste that contributes to the complex flavor of these pork shanks.

3 quarts Apple Brine (page 69)

2 cups dry white beans

3 (¾- to 1-pound) pork shanks

2 tablespoons plus 2 teaspoons Fennel Garlic Rub (page 53)

3 tablespoons olive oil, divided

1 tablespoon chopped fresh thyme

1 tablespoon chopped fresh rosemary

½ cup apple juice, in a spray bottle, for the grill

1 cup medium-dice celery

1 cup medium-dice carrots

1 cup medium-dice yellow onion

5 garlic cloves, thinly sliced

½ cup chopped canned tomatoes

1 large bay leaf

1 sprig thyme

4 sprigs rosemary

6½ cups chicken stock

¼ cup chopped fresh flat-leaf parsley

Prepare the Apple Brine 1 day before you plan to cook.

Put the white beans and 2 quarts water in a large bowl or 3-quart pot, and soak them overnight, uncovered, at room temperature.

The day you plan to cook, place the pork shanks in a large container with high sides. Strain the cold Apple Brine, discarding the solids, and pour enough over the pork shanks to cover. Refrigerate for 4 hours, then remove the shanks from the brine and pat them dry with paper towels.

Prepare the Fennel Garlic Rub.

Brush the shanks with 1 tablespoon of the olive oil and sprinkle with the chopped thyme, chopped rosemary, and 1 tablespoon of the Fennel Garlic Rub. Refrigerate, uncovered, for 2 hours.

When you are ready to cook, heat the smoker to 300°F pit temperature (see Smoke, page 25). Alternatively, heat the grill to 300°F, using the 2-Zone setup (see 2-Zone Cooking, page 22).

Place the shanks on the smoker, or on the cool side of the grill. Close the lid and cook for 1 hour, then spray the shanks with apple juice to moisten and cook for 1 hour more.

Meanwhile, drain the white beans and discard any broken beans or stones.

In a large Dutch oven, heat the remaining 2 tablespoons olive oil over medium-high heat. When the oil is hot, add the celery, carrots, and onion and cook, stirring, for 5 to 7 minutes, or until the vegetables are a light golden brown. Reduce the heat to medium-low, add the garlic, and cook, stirring continuously, for 5 minutes. Add the tomatoes and remaining 1 tablespoon plus 2 teaspoons Fennel Garlic Rub, and cook for 5 minutes more. Stir in the white beans, bay leaf, and the thyme and rosemary sprigs. Add the pork shanks to the Dutch oven and pour in enough stock to cover. Cover and cook over low heat for 1 to 1½ hours, or until the white beans and pork shanks are tender.

Transfer the tender shanks to a platter and loosely cover them with aluminum foil to keep warm.

Continue cooking the white beans over medium-low heat, uncovered, for 10 minutes, until the liquid thickens and is creamy. Return the pork shanks to the Dutch oven to warm, and serve the shanks garnished with the parsley.

SMOKED PORK BELLY
WITH PEANUT-GINGER SAUCE

MAKES 6 TO 8 SERVINGS

This pork belly recipe wanders a bit from traditional barbecue, going in an Asian direction. The acidity and heat of the Peanut-Ginger Sauce cuts through the fattiness of the pork belly. We recommend serving it with crunchy Sesame Cucumber Salad (page 247).

2½ to 3 quarts Apple Brine (page 69)

1 (4-pound) pork belly, skin removed (ask your butcher to do this)

¾ cup plus 1 tablespoon Duck Rub (page 50)

2 cups apple juice, in a spray bottle, for the grill

4 tablespoons packed light brown sugar

4 tablespoons (½ stick) unsalted butter, at room temperature

2 tablespoons honey

2 cups Peanut-Ginger Sauce (recipe follows)

Two or three days before you plan to cook, prepare the Apple Brine.

The day before you plan to cook, place the pork belly in a large roasting pan. Holding a strainer over the pan, pour enough Apple Brine over the pork belly to completely cover. Cover the pan with a lid or plastic wrap and refrigerate overnight.

The next day, transfer the pork belly to a clean work surface and pat completely dry with paper towels. Discard the brine and clean and dry the roasting pan.

Prepare the Duck Rub.

Return the pork belly to the roasting pan. Fill a shaker with the Duck Rub and dust the meat evenly on all sides. Cover the pan with a lid or plastic wrap and refrigerate for 3 hours. Remove the pork belly from the refrigerator 1 hour before cooking and let it sit, uncovered, at room temperature.

When you are ready to cook, heat the smoker to 285°F pit temperature (see Smoke, page 25). Alternatively, heat the grill to 285°F, using the 2-Zone setup (see 2-Zone Cooking, page 22),

Place the pork belly fat-side up on the smoker, or on the cool side of the grill. Close the lid and cook for 1 hour, then spray the pork with apple juice to moisten. Cook for 1 hour more, then turn the belly and cook for another 2 hours, spraying the meat with apple juice every 30 minutes.

Cut two 18 x 24-inch pieces of heavy-duty aluminum foil and join them lengthwise by crimping the edges. Lay the resulting piece out flat on a clean work surface.

Remove the pork belly from the smoker or grill and place it fat-side up on the length of foil. Season it on one side with 2 tablespoons of the brown sugar, 2 tablespoons of the butter, and 1 tablespoon of the honey. Turn, and season the other side with the remaining brown sugar, butter, and honey. Wrap the pork belly tightly in the foil, as you would a package, being careful not to puncture the foil.

Place the foil package in the smoker or on the grill, close the lid, and cook for 2½ to 3½ hours, or until the meat is tender and a meat thermometer placed in the thickest part of the pork reads an internal temperature of 195°F. Let the foil-wrapped pork belly set, venting the package by unsealing it, at room temperature for 1 hour before serving.

When you are ready to serve, transfer to a cutting board and remove the foil. At this point, you may choose to pull, slice, or cube the meat. Serve each 4- to 5-ounce portion with 3 to 4 tablespoons of the Peanut-Ginger Sauce. Prepare this sauce the same day you plan to cook or up to a day in advance and refrigerate until ready to use. Pass any remaining sauce around the table.

PEANUT-GINGER SAUCE

MAKES 2 CUPS

5 ounces roasted peanuts

1 tablespoon plus 1½ teaspoons minced fresh ginger

1 garlic clove, crushed

2 teaspoons sugar

½ teaspoon crushed red pepper

2 tablespoons soy sauce

2 tablespoons rice vinegar

2 tablespoons fresh lime juice

½ teaspoon kosher salt

Combine all the ingredients in a blender and blend on high speed until well combined. With the blender running on medium speed, slowly add 1 cup lukewarm water and blend until the sauce is smooth and creamy. Transfer to an airtight container and refrigerate until ready to use. It will keep 2 to 3 days in the refrigerator.

PORK SAUSAGE

While this dish is a bit labor-intensive, you can freeze any unused sausage for future dinners.

---

2 or 3 pork casings, if using

2 pounds pork shoulder, cut into 1-inch cubes

½ pound pork fatback, cut into 1-inch cubes

1½ tablespoons kosher salt

½ teaspoon pink curing salt

1 tablespoon fennel seeds

½ teaspoon fennel pollen

1 teaspoon crushed red pepper

1½ teaspoons dried oregano

1 teaspoon granulated garlic

If you plan on casing the sausage, soak two or three pork casings in cold water and set aside until ready to use.

In a large bowl, combine all the ingredients and toss to thoroughly combine, ensuring that the pork is evenly seasoned. Place the seasoned pork in a shallow rimmed pan and freeze, uncovered, for 30 to 45 minutes, or until the pork is firm but not frozen. Put your grinder parts and a large metal bowl in the freezer at the same time.

First remove the grinder parts and bowl from the freezer and set up the grinder. Remove the pork from the freezer and grind the mixture into the cold bowl.

Transfer the ground pork to the bowl of a stand mixer fitted with the paddle attachment. Add ¼ cup ice water and mix on medium speed for 15 seconds, or until just incorporated. Be careful not to overmix, or the fat will melt.

If you are using the sausage uncased, transfer the sausage meat to large resealable plastic bags, removing as much air as possible to prevent the sausage from oxidizing. The sausage will keep in the refrigerator for up to 5 days or in the freezer for up to 3 months.

If you choose to case the sausage, rinse the insides of the casings by placing the open end under a running faucet. Return the casings to a small bowl of cold water.

Fill the sausage stuffer with ground sausage, making sure there are no gaps or air pockets. Thread the casing onto the tube of the sausage stuffer, leaving about 3 inches of casing hanging off the end of the tube. Tie a knot in the hanging casing and position it so the knot is up against the tube.

Begin feeding the sausage into the casings. Do not overstuff the casings, or you will not be able to twist it into links. Leave an additional 3 inches of casing at the top end of the sausage, remove it from the stuffer, and use a toothpick or cake tester to prick tiny holes in any existing air pockets. Repeat the process until all the ground sausage has been cased. Twist the sausage three turns to divide the sausage into 6-inch links, and tie off the last sausage link. Transfer the links to a paper towel–lined pan and refrigerate overnight. (See photographs on pages 114–115.)

The next day, use scissors to cut the links apart at the twist points. Sausage links will keep

in the refrigerator for up to 5 days or in the freezer for up to 3 months.

Note: This sausage should be ground using a small die. Everything is put in the freezer so the fat stays solid despite the heat of the grinder. If you are making sausage links, you will need pork casings. The sausage does not need to be cased if used for Fennel Sausage Stuffing (page 248) or Sausage Gravy (page 61). I recommend serving the sausage links with Mustard Sauce (page 63).

MAKING SAUSAGE

1 Soak 2 to 3 pork casings in cold water and set aside until ready to use. **2** Bowl of seasonings. **3** In a large bowl, combine all the ingredients and toss to thoroughly combine, ensuring that the pork is evenly seasoned. **4** Next, remove the pork from the freezer, and grind the mixture into the cold bowl. **5** Transfer the ground pork to the bowl of a standing mixer fitted with a paddle attachment. Add ¼ cup ice water and mix on medium speed for 15 seconds, or until just incorporated. Be careful not to overmix because the fat will melt. If you choose to case the sausage, rinse the insides of the casings by placing the open end under a running faucet. Return the casing to a small bowl of cold water. **6** Thread the casing onto the tube of the sausage stuffer, leaving about 3 inches of casing hanging off the end of the tube. Tie a knot in the hanging casing, and position it so that the knot is up against the tube. Begin feeding the sausage into the casings. Do not overstuff the casings, or you will not be able to twist it into links. Leave an additional 3 inches of casing at the top end of the sausage, remove it from the stuffer, and use a toothpick or cake tester to prick tiny holes in any existing air pockets. Repeat the process until all the ground sausage has been cased. **7** Twist the sausage three turns to divide the sausage into 6-inch links, and tie off the last sausage link. Transfer the links to a paper towel–lined pan and refrigerate overnight.

FRIED PORK TENDERLOIN SANDWICH
WITH SPICY MAYONNAISE

MAKES 6 SANDWICHES

Fried pork tenderloin sandwiches are popular in the Midwest, where many restaurants offer them as a specialty. This sandwich was first served to me by a barbecue friend Darren Warth while we were competing at the American Royal. The trick to this sandwich is getting the meat crispy on the exterior, but still have it be tender—all without overcooking the meat.

¼ cup Spicy Mayonnaise (page 65)

½ to ¾ cup Bread-and-Butter Pickles (page 74), or your favorite pickles

1 cup all-purpose flour

1 tablespoon plus 1½ teaspoons kosher salt

1 tablespoon cracked black pepper

½ teaspoon MSG

1 teaspoon granulated garlic

1 teaspoon granulated onion

1 teaspoon cayenne pepper

1 (1-pound) pork tenderloin, cut in 6 (1-inch-thick) medallions

4 large eggs

¼ cup buttermilk

½ cup canola oil

6 Hawaiian rolls, halved and toasted

1½ cups shredded iceberg lettuce

Prepare the Spicy Mayonnaise and the Bread-and-Butter Pickles.

In a small bowl, combine the flour, 1 tablespoon of the salt, ½ tablespoon of the black pepper, MSG, garlic, onion, and cayenne and mix thoroughly. Transfer to a shallow casserole dish and set aside until ready to use.

Sandwich the pork medallions between two large sheets of plastic wrap and use a meat mallet to pound the meat to ½-inch-thick slices. Season each side of the pork with ⅛ teaspoon of the salt and ⅛ teaspoon of the black pepper.

In a medium bowl, whisk together the eggs and buttermilk until thoroughly combined.

Dredge the pork on each side in the seasoned flour, shake off any excess flour, and dip the pork into the egg mixture. Shake off the excess egg and return the pork to the seasoned flour, dredging again to coat both sides completely.

In a 12-inch cast-iron skillet, heat the canola oil over medium heat. When it is hot, carefully place 3 pork slices in the oil and cook for 2 minutes, until golden brown, then use tongs to turn and cook the other side for 2 minutes, or until golden brown. Carefully transfer the pork medallions to a paper towel–lined platter to drain. Repeat the process for the remaining medallions.

Spread 1 teaspoon of the Spicy Mayonnaise on the cut sides of each roll (2 teaspoons total per roll). Place ¼ cup of the shredded lettuce on the bottom half of each roll and layer with a piece of pork and some pickles (you may include onions from the Bread-and-Butter Pickles for extra flavor). Sandwich with the roll top and serve immediately.

PORK BUTT SANDWICH
WITH DILL COLESLAW

This is a great use for leftover Competition Pork Butt. The crunchiness of the dill slaw adds a nice bite and tang to the pork. If you like a sweet barbecue sauce, use Cool Smoke Barbecue Sauce, and if you like tangy, use Cool Smoke Vinegar Sauce.

½ cup Cool Smoke Barbecue Sauce (page 57) or Cool Smoke Vinegar Sauce (page 57)

½ recipe Dill Coleslaw (page 220)

2¼ pounds chopped or pulled Competition Pork Butt, Cool Smoke Style (page 102), warmed through

1 tablespoon apple cider vinegar

Kosher salt and freshly ground black pepper

6 to 8 potato rolls, halved and toasted

Prepare the Cool Smoke Barbecue Sauce or the Cool Smoke Vinegar Sauce, or use leftover sauce.

Prepare the Dill Coleslaw.

Toss the warm pork with the vinegar and season with salt and pepper.

To assemble, place 4½ to 6 ounces of the pork (depending on the number served) on the bottom half of each roll. Top the pork with 1 tablespoon of the Cool Smoke Barbecue Sauce or Cool Smoke Vinegar Sauce, about ¼ cup of the Dill Coleslaw, and then sandwich with the top half of each roll. Serve immediately.

PORK BURGER
WITH APPLE-ONION JAM AND APPLE COLESLAW

MAKES 6 BURGERS

In a burger-crazed world, this burger is a standout. The ground pork makes it unique, and although slaw is usually found on hot dogs, it's a welcome addition here.

1 tablespoon plus 1 teaspoon Caraway Rub (page 50)

1½ cups Apple Coleslaw (page 245), Spicy Walnuts omitted

2¼ pounds ground pork

6 slices white cheddar cheese

¾ cup Apple-Onion Jam (recipe follows)

9 bacon slices, cooked

6 potato rolls, halved and toasted

Prepare the Caraway Rub and the Apple Coleslaw (omitting the Spicy Walnuts). The Apple-Onion Jam can be prepared up to 5 days in advance, or sooner allowing enough time to cool before using.

In a medium bowl, combine the ground pork and Caraway Rub and use your hands to gently mix. Divide the pork mixture into 6 portions and shape them into patties.

When you are ready to cook, heat the grill to 450°F, using the direct grilling method (see Direct Cooking or Grilling, page 22).

Place the pork patties directly on the grill and cook for 5 minutes, then flip them and cook for an additional 5 minutes, or until a meat thermometer placed in the thickest part of the meat reads an internal temperature of 160°F.

A minute before you remove the burgers from the grill, top each with a slice of cheese and heat just long enough to melt the cheese.

To assemble, spread 1 tablespoon Apple-Onion Jam on the cut sides of each roll (2 tablespoons total per roll). On the bottom half of each roll place a cheeseburger patty and 3 pieces of bacon. Top with about ¼ cup of the Apple Coleslaw and sandwich with the roll top. Serve immediately.

APPLE-ONION JAM

MAKES ABOUT 1 QUART

1 tablespoon canola oil

2½ cups finely diced yellow onions

3 cups finely diced peeled tart apples

3 tablespoons sugar

1 tablespoon kosher salt

2 tablespoons apple cider vinegar

5 sprigs thyme

2 teaspoons mustard seeds

In a heavy-bottomed 2-quart saucepan, heat the canola oil over medium heat. Add the onions and cook, stirring, for 5 to 7 minutes, or until the onions begin to caramelize. Add the apples, sugar, salt, vinegar, thyme, and mustard seeds, cover, and reduce the heat to low. Cook for 15 minutes, or until the apples are tender and mash easily with a fork. Remove from the heat, uncover, and let the jam cool completely. Refrigerate in an airtight container until ready to use, up to 5 days.

WHOLE HOG

My first experience with a whole hog was one summer when my friend's father cooked one down the street from where I lived. We were two young boys, curious about what the men were doing. At the time, it seemed like a secret ritual only grown men knew how to do. Now I think it was just an excuse for the men to stay up all night and drink!

This is an old-school recipe because of the cinder-block pit and burn barrel used to burn wood down to coals (see page 15). While the process is a long endeavor, it is the essence of what I like about barbecue—taking a wood-burning fire and trying to coax something great out of a large cut of meat. The key challenge is to cook the shoulders and hams to doneness while not overcooking the loin.

You'll need a hog rack for this project, and you'll find illustrations for how to prepare a cinder-block pit and burn barrel on pages 11–14.

1½ cups kosher salt

¾ cup cracked black pepper

1 tablespoon crushed red pepper

1½ tablespoons granulated garlic

2 tablespoons cracked white pepper

1 (140- to 160-pound) whole hog, dressed and butterflied

3 cups distilled white vinegar, in a spray bottle, for the grill

4 quarts Worcestershire Mop (page 69)

In a small bowl, combine the salt, black pepper, crushed red pepper, garlic, and white pepper. Transfer to a shaker.

Position half a hog rack on a large, clean worktable. Place the whole hog skin-side down atop the hog rack and spray the hog with the vinegar until the surface area is completely wet. Use a shaker to dust all the exposed meat with a liberal amount of the garlic-pepper mixture, and let the hog sit at room temperature for 1 to 2 hours.

Meanwhile, prepare a cinder-block pit and burn barrel. Heat the pit to 200°F to 225°F,

and maintain that temperature throughout the duration of the cooking. Prepare the Worcestershire Mop.

Top the whole hog with the second half of the hog rack and secure it on both sides. Position the rack with the hog skin-side up in the cinder-block pit. Shovel the coals into the four corners of the pit, maintaining the temperature at 200°F to 225°F. This helps to not overcook the loins and tenderloins. Cook for 4 hours, then flip the hog rack over and baste the meat side with 1 cup of the Worcestershire Mop.

Cook the hog for 8 to 12 hours more, basting every hour with 1 cup of the Worcestershire Mop, until the meat is tender and a meat thermometer placed in the thickest part of the hams and shoulders reaches an internal temperature of 190°F to 195°F, or until the probe on the thermometer slides into the meat with ease.

When the hog is done, stop fueling the pit. As the pit cools, let the hog rest in the pit for 2 to 3 hours before carving. Serve with your favorite sauces. (See page 56–67.)

WHEN SELECTING BEEF, I LOOK FOR MEAT THAT IS WELL MARBLED with fat. Meat should be red in color with white fat. The Whole Beef Tenderloin with Cumberland Sauce (page 149) demonstrates the importance of marbling in beef. Because fat is flavor, it is very important to choose a tenderloin that is well marbled. Otherwise, your end product will be anemic and lackluster in flavor. Prime rib or rib-eye cuts have naturally high fat content. On the other hand, tenderloin is a leaner cut with a less robust beef flavor.

USDA grades of beef—Select, Choice, and Prime—are determined by marbling. Select is the leanest grade with the least marbling; Choice shows some marbling; and Prime is the most marbled beef. American Wagyu beef—the result of crossbreeding a Japanese breed of cattle with an American breed—is prized for its flavor and rich marbling. Kobe beef comes from the region of Kobe in Japan, and is also prized for it's great flavor and marbling.

Dry aging typically occurs in refrigeration outfitted with additional fans to create air circulation. The fans facilitate the evaporation of moisture from within the meat, thereby intensifying the beef flavor. The longer the meat ages, the more complex the flavors will become. Additionally, the aging process allows for the muscle fibers to break down, resulting in a more tender chew.

Wet aging is great for briskets and really impacts the flavor and texture. Raw briskets are packaged in vacuum-sealed bags and refrigerated for twenty-one to fifty-plus days in cold refrigeration. It is important that the temperature of the refrigerator stays very cold, preferably 39°F or lower, but does not freeze. Because the meat is not exposed to air, there is minimal shrinkage (as opposed to dry aging). During the wet-aging process, muscle fibers break down, giving the end product a more tender texture and an intense, complex flavor. Briskets will soften during this process, enhancing the texture of the beef and creating earthy and more complex flavors. It's good to note that properly refrigerated beef will keep fresh much longer than pork or poultry.

SPICE-RUBBED BRISKET

While I'm a big fan of salt and pepper on brisket and steaks, I prefer using the Steak Rub here because it adds a more robust, dynamic flavor to the meat.

1 (12- to 14-pound) beef brisket

1½ cups Steak Rub (page 54)

2 teaspoons olive oil

2 cups apple juice, in a spray bottle, for the grill

Steak Sauce (page 65) or Cool Smoke Barbecue Sauce (page 57)

The day before you plan to cook, clean and prepare the brisket. Alternatively, have your butcher do this. (See photographs on pages 130–131.)

Prepare the Steak Rub and Steak Sauce or Cool Smoke Barbecue Sauce.

Rub the brisket on all sides with the olive oil and dust evenly with the Steak Rub, patting the rub evenly over all sides of the meat. Transfer to a pan and refrigerate, uncovered, overnight.

When you are ready to cook, heat the smoker to 300°F pit temperature (see Smoke, page 25). Alternatively, heat the grill to 300°F, using the 2-Zone setup (see 2-Zone Cooking, page 22), using five or six chunks of your favorite wood in addition to the charcoal or gas.

Place the brisket fat-side down in the smoker or on the cool side of the grill. Close the lid and cook for 1 hour, then spray with apple juice to moisten. Cook for 3 hours more, spraying the brisket every 30 minutes. Do not turn the meat.

Cut two 18 x 24-inch pieces of heavy-duty aluminum foil and join them lengthwise by crimping the edges. Lay the resulting piece out flat on a clean work surface. Transfer the brisket from the grill or smoker and place it fat-side down on the length of foil. Spray lightly with apple juice overall, applying a heavier concentration of juice on the crispier areas to rehydrate them. Wrap the brisket tightly as you would a package, being careful not to puncture the foil (see illustration, page 24).

Set the brisket package in the smoker or on the cool side of the grill, close the lid, and cook for 2½ to 3½ hours, or until the meat is fork-tender. Check the internal temperature after 2½ hours. The brisket is done when a meat thermometer inserted into the thickest part of the brisket reads an internal temperature of 205°F to 207°F.

Remove the brisket from the heat again and let it rest, vented in the foil, for 1–2 hours.

Transfer the meat to a cutting board or a clean surface and cut it across the grain into ¼-inch-thick slices. Serve with your choice of Steak Sauce or Cool Smoke Barbecue Sauce on the side.

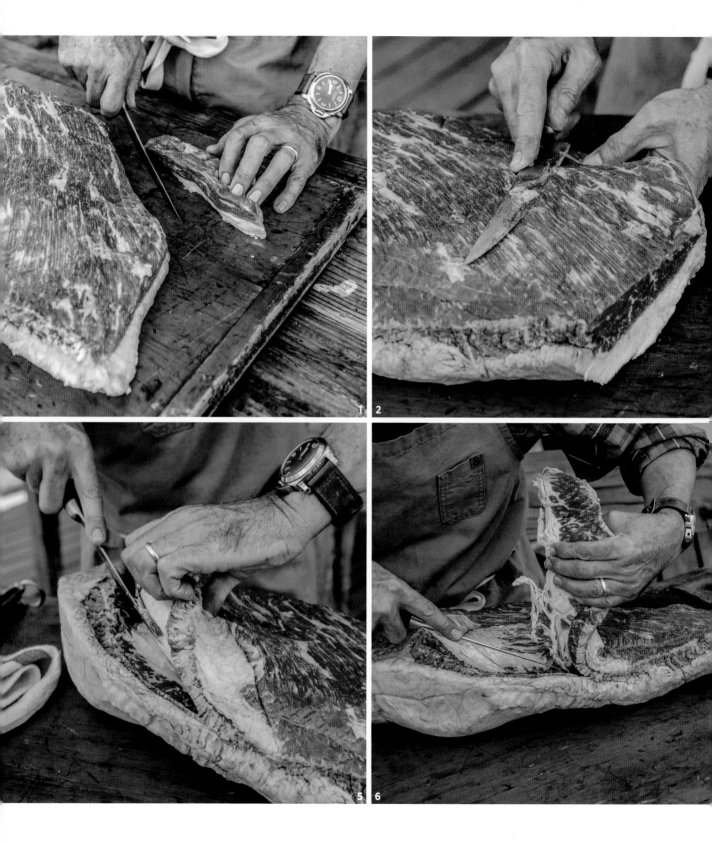

CLEANING AND PREPARING A BRISKET

1 Trim both edges of the brisket flat by making two parallel slices going with the grain to cut about 1 inch of each brisket flat edges off. The brisket flat should still be 7 to 10 inches wide after trimming. I like to cut off a piece of the flat at the "toe" of the flat (the end opposite of the "point"). Make sure that the cut is against the grain of the meat. This makes it easier to know how to slice after the meat has been rubbed and cooked. Brisket flats are best carved against the grain for the best chew. **2** On the meat side of the flat, I remove any membrane or exterior flat. **3** There is a seam of fat that separates the "point" and the "flat." Using a sharp boning knife, make a cut running parallel with the grain of the "flat" that follows the edge of the seam of the fat about 2 inches deep. **4** Make a second cut from the "point" side into the fat seam on the bias, cutting into the bottom of the first cut made into the fat seam to notch out the fat seam. **5** Continue to cut and excavate the fat seam that separates the point and the flat. **6** You will be able to see what is fat and what is meat. Take your time and be careful. Through experience, this will become easier. Remove all exterior meat from the "point" muscle of the brisket. **7** By removing all of the exterior fat from the "point," you can apply seasoning all over the exterior and make "Burnt Ends." I leave all of the fat on the bottom of the "flat," but I will cut it down so that the brisket sits level to help it cook evenly. Make a final inspection to insure that all fat is removed from the "point," membrane and from the meat side of the "flat," and that the brisket is sitting level.

COMPETITION BRISKET
COOL SMOKE STYLE

MAKES 12 TO 14 SERVINGS

Brisket is often treated much like a pot roast, which is cooked until it falls apart. When competition brisket is perfectly cooked, you're able to slice the flat to about the thickness of a number 2 pencil, and can pick up the slice and pull it apart with a gentle tug.

1 (12- to 14-pound) beef brisket

1½ cups plus 2 tablespoons Cool Smoke Rub (page 49)

2 teaspoons olive oil

2 cups apple juice, in a spray bottle, for the grill

2 teaspoons minced dehydrated onions

2 cups Cool Smoke Barbecue Sauce (page 57)

The day before you plan to cook, clean and prepare the brisket. Alternatively, have your butcher do this. (See photographs on pages 130–131.)

Prepare the Cool Smoke Rub.

Rub the brisket on all sides with the olive oil and dust with 1½ cups of the Cool Smoke Rub, patting the rub evenly over all sides of the meat. Transfer to a pan and refrigerate, uncovered, overnight.

When you are ready to cook, heat the smoker to 300°F pit temperature (see Smoke, page 25). Alternatively, heat the grill to 300°F, using the 2-Zone setup (see 2-Zone Cooking, page 22), using five or six chunks of your favorite wood in addition to the charcoal or gas.

Place the brisket fat-side down in the smoker, or on the cool side of the grill. Close the lid and cook for 1 hour, then spray with apple juice

to moisten. Cook for 3 hours more, spraying the brisket every 30 minutes. Do not turn the meat.

Cut two 18 x 24-inch pieces of heavy-duty aluminum foil and join them lengthwise by crimping the edges. Lay the resulting piece out flat on a clean work surface. Transfer the brisket from the grill or smoker and place it fat-side down on the length of foil. Sprinkle the dehydrated onions evenly over all sides of the meat. Spray with apple juice overall, applying a heavier concentration of juice on the crispier areas to rehydrate them. Wrap the brisket tightly as you would a package, being careful not to puncture the foil.

Set the brisket package in the smoker or on the cool side of the grill, close the lid, and cook for 2½ to 3½ hours, or until the meat is fork-tender. Check the internal temperature after 2½ hours. The brisket is done when the thickest part of the brisket reaches an internal temperature of 205°F to 207°F, or until the probe of a thermometer slides into the meat with ease.

Remove the brisket from the heat again and let it rest, vented in the foil, for 1–2 hours.

Meanwhile, grind the remaining 2 tablespoons Cool Smoke Rub in a coffee grinder until

(continued)

super-fine, and transfer to a fine-mesh shaker. Prepare the Cool Smoke Barbecue Sauce as well.

Fifteen to 20 minutes before you are ready to serve, unwrap the brisket. Pour the liquid in the bottom of the foil into a fat separator. Pour the fat off from the fat separator and discard, reserving the remaining juices.

Using a sharp knife, separate the point from the flat. Reserve the point for Burnt Ends (page 137). If you are cooking at home and want to save the point for serving at a later date, seal the point in foil or plastic wrap and refrigerate for up to 5 days.

Brush a light coating of Cool Smoke Barbecue Sauce over the meat side of the flat and return it to the smoker or to the cool side of the grill, fat-side down. Cook for 10 minutes to set the sauce. Transfer the meat to a cutting board or a clean surface and cut it across the grain into ¼-inch-thick slices.

Brush each slice of brisket lightly with the juices in the fat separator. Dust each slice lightly with the finely ground Cool Smoke Rub and brush with a light coating of Cool Smoke Barbecue Sauce.

If preparing the brisket for competition, serve with Burnt Ends.

For home presentation, serve the sliced brisket with the remaining Cool Smoke Barbecue Sauce on the side.

BURNT ENDS

Burnt ends are a specialty of Kansas City. They come from the point of a brisket. Because the point has more marbleization than the flat of the brisket, the cubes of meat in this recipe burst with flavor. Note that you need to make the Competition Brisket, Cool Smoke Style first, and use the reserved point for this recipe.

1 (4-pound) brisket point, reserved from Competition Brisket, Cool Smoke Style (page 133)

¾ cup Cool Smoke Barbecue Sauce (page 57)

½ cup apple juice, in a spray bottle, for the grill

Prepare the Competition Brisket and separate the brisket point from the flat.

Prepare the Cool Smoke Barbecue Sauce.

When you are ready to cook, heat the smoker to 300°F pit temperature (see Smoke, page 25). Alternatively, heat the grill to 300°F, using the 2-Zone setup (see 2-Zone Cooking, page 22), using five or six chunks of your favorite wood in addition to the charcoal or gas.

If the reserved point is hot, cut it into ¾- to 1-inch cubes. In a medium bowl, toss the meat with ½ cup of the Cool Smoke Barbecue Sauce to coat. Place the meat in a shallow pan and return it to the smoker or to the cool side of the grill, close the lid, and cook for 5 to 10 minutes to set the sauce. Transfer the cubes to a plate or platter and serve with the remaining Cool Smoke Barbecue Sauce on the side.

Alternatively, if the reserved point has been refrigerated to this point, spray it with apple juice to moisten, wrap it in aluminum foil, and place it in the smoker or on the cool side of the grill for 1 hour, until the meat is hot. Remove from the heat and set aside to cool slightly.

When it is cool enough to handle, cut the meat into ¾- to 1-inch cubes. In a medium bowl, toss the meat with ½ cup of the Cool Smoke Barbecue Sauce to coat. Place the meat in a shallow pan and return it to the smoker or the cool side of the grill, and cook for 5 to 10 minutes to set the sauce. Transfer the cubes to a plate or platter and serve with the remaining Cool Smoke Barbecue Sauce on the side.

SMOKED BRISKET CHILI
WITH SMOKED CHILI POWDER SOUR CREAM

MAKES 4 TO 6 SERVINGS

Because briskets weigh 12 to 20 pounds, there's usually leftover meat. This recipe elevates leftover Competition Brisket, Cool Smoke Style, or Spice-Rubbed Brisket. The addition of chipotle and adobo sauce, cilantro, lime, and chili powder sour cream brings a Latin freshness to this chili.

4 cups large-dice cooked Brisket (see recipes pages 129 and 133)

2 tablespoons Smoked Chili Powder (page 50)

1 teaspoon canola oil

1 cup chopped bacon

1½ cups medium-dice yellow onion

1½ cups medium-dice green bell pepper

1½ cups medium-dice red bell pepper

2 tablespoons thinly sliced garlic

1 (7-ounce) can chipotles in adobo sauce, available in the Hispanic section of most grocery stores, plus 1 tablespoon adobo sauce from the can

¼ cup tomato paste

1 tablespoon kosher salt

½ teaspoon freshly ground black pepper

2 tablespoons light brown sugar

1 (12-ounce) can or bottle of dark beer

1 (14½-ounce) can diced tomatoes

2 bay leaves

2 cups beef stock

¾ cup Smoked Chili Powder Sour Cream (page 66)

1 bunch scallions, thinly sliced

1 cup fresh cilantro leaves

2 limes, quartered

Prepare the Brisket and the Smoked Chili Powder.

In a heavy-bottomed 4-quart pot, heat the canola oil over medium-low heat. When the oil is hot, add the bacon and cook for 3 to 5 minutes, until golden brown and most of the fat has rendered out. Add the onion, green and red bell peppers, and garlic to the pot and cook, stirring frequently, for 5 minutes. Add 2 chopped chipotles, the adobo sauce, the tomato paste, Smoked Chili Powder, salt, black pepper, and brown sugar and cook, stirring continuously, for 3 minutes. Be careful not to burn the sugar. Add the beer and cook for 7 to 10 minutes, or until the liquid has reduced by half. Add the tomatoes, bay leaves, brisket, and stock and cook, uncovered, for 30 minutes.

Meanwhile, prepare the Smoked Chili Powder Sour Cream. Refrigerate in an airtight container until ready to use.

When you are ready to serve, taste the chili and adjust the seasoning as needed. Serve in bowls and top with 1½ to 2 tablespoons of the Smoked Chili Powder Sour Cream. Sprinkle each serving with scallions and cilantro and serve with a wedge of lime.

SALISBURY STEAK

WITH SHIITAKE MUSHROOM GRAVY

MAKES 6 SERVINGS

Typically, Salisbury steaks are cooked in a pan on the stove, but these are cooked on the grill, adding a tasty, smoky char to the meat. The Steak Rub in the patties and shiitake mushrooms in the gravy elevate this homey dish.

2 tablespoons Steak Rub (page 54)

1 tablespoon canola oil

1 cup finely diced yellow onion

2 large eggs

2 pounds 80% lean ground beef

¼ cup Worcestershire sauce

½ cup ketchup

1 tablespoon plus 1 teaspoon kosher salt

1 teaspoon mustard powder

¼ cup fine bread crumbs

Shiitake Mushroom Gravy (recipe follows)

Prepare the Steak Rub.

In a small sauté pan, heat the canola oil over medium-low heat. Add the onion and cook, stirring, for 3 to 5 minutes, until soft. Set aside to cool slightly.

In a small bowl, whisk the eggs until combined.

In a large bowl, combine the ground beef, sautéed onion, eggs, Worcestershire, ketchup, Steak Rub, salt, mustard powder, and bread crumbs. Use your hands to gently mix until all the ingredients are well incorporated. Divide the mixture into 6 equal portions and form each into an oblong patty.

Prepare the Shiitake Mushroom Gravy.

When you are ready to cook, heat the grill to 400°F, using the direct grilling method (see Direct Cooking or Grilling, page 22).

Place the patties over direct heat and cook for 4 minutes, then rotate the patties 90 degrees and cook for another 4 minutes. Flip the patties over and cook for 5 minutes more, or until a meat thermometer placed in the thickest part of the patty reads an internal temperature of 145°F.

Pour ¼ to ⅓ cup of the Shiitake Mushroom Gravy over each steak and pass any additional sauce around the table.

(continued)

SHIITAKE MUSHROOM GRAVY

MAKES ABOUT 6 CUPS

2 teaspoons Smoked Chili Powder (page 50)

2 tablespoons canola oil

4 cups thinly sliced shiitake mushrooms

¼ cup finely diced shallots

1 tablespoon minced garlic

2½ teaspoons kosher salt

1 teaspoon freshly ground black pepper

5 tablespoons unsalted butter

¼ cup all-purpose flour

2½ cups warm beef stock

1 tablespoon Worcestershire sauce

2 tablespoons ketchup

2 tablespoons chopped fresh flat-leaf parsley

Prepare the Smoked Chili Powder.

In a large, heavy-bottomed saucepan, heat the canola oil over medium-high heat. When the oil is hot, add the mushrooms and cook, stirring, for 7 minutes, until golden brown.

Reduce the heat to medium-low and add the shallots. Cook, stirring often, for 5 minutes, until translucent. Add the garlic and cook, stirring continuously, for 1 minute. Stir in the salt, pepper, and Smoked Chili Powder. Add the butter, and when butter has melted and the foam subsides, stir in the flour and reduce the heat to low. Cook, stirring continuously, for 5 minutes. Gradually add 2 cups of the warm stock, continuing to stir. When the mixture is smooth and well combined, stir in the Worcestershire and ketchup.

Increase the heat to medium-low and cook, stirring often, for 10 minutes, until the mixture is thick and bubbling. Remove the pot from the heat and stir in the parsley. Cover and keep the gravy warm until ready to use. Check the consistency of the gravy before serving. If it has thickened too much, thin it by adding the remaining stock, 1 tablespoon at a time, as needed.

REVERSE-SEARED PRIME RIB
WITH HORSERADISH AND RED WINE SAUCES

Prime rib is best cooked rare or medium-rare. By reverse searing—cooking the meat at a lower temperature first, then increasing the temperature to finish the cooking—you're able to infuse the meat with a deep, smoky flavor without overcooking it. Note that most of the prime rib roasts you buy in a grocery store are already trimmed.

Prime Rib Seasoning Blend (recipe follows)

1 (4-pound) prime rib roast, trimmed (ask your butcher to do this)

Horseradish Sauce (recipe follows)

Red Wine Sauce (recipe follows)

2 cups apple juice, in a spray bottle, for the grill

Prepare the Prime Rib Seasoning Blend and set aside ½ teaspoon for the Red Wine Sauce. Pat the remaining seasoning evenly onto all sides of the prime rib to coat, and refrigerate, uncovered, for 6 hours.

Remove the prime rib from the refrigerator 1 hour before cooking and let it sit at room temperature.

Make the Horseradish Sauce and the Red Wine Sauce.

When you are ready to cook, heat the grill to 225°F, using the 2-Zone setup (see 2-Zone Cooking, page 22).

Place the prime rib fat-cap down on the cool side of the grill, close the lid, and cook for 1 hour. Spray the roast with apple juice to moisten and transfer the meat to the hot side of grill. Increase the grill temperature to 400°F, close the lid, and cook for 1 hour more, spraying it with apple juice every 15 minutes. The meat is done when a meat thermometer placed in the thickest part of the roast reads an internal temperature of 120°F. Allow the roast to rest 20 minutes before serving.

Serve with the Horseradish Sauce and Red Wine Sauce on the side.

PRIME RIB SEASONING BLEND

¼ cup kosher salt

2 tablespoons cracked black pepper

1 tablespoon coarsely ground coriander seeds

1 teaspoon granulated onion

1 teaspoon granulated garlic

1 tablespoon dried thyme

2 teaspoons hot mustard powder

Stir together all the ingredients in a small bowl. Set aside ½ teaspoon for the Red Wine Sauce (recipe follows) and use the rest for the prime rib.

(continued)

HORSERADISH SAUCE

MAKES ABOUT ¾ CUP

½ cup sour cream

2 tablespoons prepared horseradish

¼ teaspoon kosher salt

¼ teaspoon freshly ground black pepper

½ teaspoon lemon zest

½ teaspoon fresh lemon juice

¼ teaspoon Worcestershire sauce

1 tablespoon chopped fresh chives

Stir together all the ingredients in a small bowl until well combined. Transfer to an airtight container and refrigerate until ready to use, up to 3 days.

RED WINE SAUCE

MAKES ABOUT 1½ CUPS

1½ cups red wine of your choice

5 sprigs fresh thyme

2 bay leaves

1 garlic clove, smashed

½ cup demi-glace (see Source Guide, page 279)

½ teaspoon Prime Rib Seasoning Blend (page 143)

2 tablespoons unsalted butter

¼ cup finely chopped fresh chives

In a small saucepan, combine the red wine, thyme, bay leaves, and garlic and cook over medium heat for 10 minutes, or until the sauce has reduced by half. Add the demi-glace and the Prime Rib Seasoning Blend and simmer for 3 minutes. Remove the pot from the heat and gently stir in the butter and chives until the butter has melted. Cover the pot and keep the sauce warm until ready to use. Check the consistency of the sauce before serving. If it is too thick, stir in hot water, 1 teaspoon at a time, as needed to reach the desired consistency.

CHARRED TRI-TIP
WITH CELERY SEED RUB

MAKES 4 TO 6 SERVINGS

Beef tri-tip is a local specialty of Santa Maria, California. I had always thought tri-tips should be cooked medium-rare, but a good friend from California, Sterling Ball, shared that they are best cooked to 140°F (medium). I now agree!

¼ cup Celery Seed Rub (page 54)

2 pounds beef tri-tip

½ cup apple juice, in a spray bottle, for the grill

Prepare the Celery Seed Rub.

Use a sharp knife and carefully remove and discard enough of the fat cap from the beef tri-tip to expose the meat. (It's okay if some fat remains on the meat.) Dust evenly on all sides with the Celery Seed Rub and let the meat sit at room temperature for 1 hour.

When you are ready to cook, heat the grill to 400°F, using the direct grilling method (see Direct Cooking or Grilling, page 22).

Place the tri-tip directly over the heat and cook for 5 minutes, then rotate the meat 90 degrees and spray it with apple juice to moisten. Cook for another 5 minutes, then flip the tri-tip over, spray again with apple juice, and cook for 5 minutes more. Rotate the meat 90 degrees and cook for an additional 5 minutes, or until a meat thermometer placed in the thickest part of the beef reads an internal temperature of 140°F. Remove the tri-tip from the heat and let it rest for 5 minutes before carving.

Carve the tri-tip across the grain into ¼- to ½-inch-thick slices, and serve immediately.

COFFEE-RUBBED COWBOY STEAKS
WITH PINTO BEANS

MAKES 4 SERVINGS

As much as I like cooking barbecue, I love to eat a steak. Cowboy steak is a big, bone-in rib-eye. While you wouldn't normally associate umami with cowboys, that's exactly the savory taste that the coffee rub provides. I like steaks prepared medium-rare, and that's what you will get if you follow these directions.

1 cup dried pinto beans

1 cup apple juice, in a spray bottle, for the grill

¼ cup finely diced bacon

½ cup finely diced yellow onion

4 garlic cloves, thinly sliced

¼ to ½ jalapeño, sliced, with seeds

1 teaspoon kosher salt

½ teaspoon freshly ground black pepper

1 small bay leaf

4 cups chicken stock

6 tablespoons Coffee Rub (page 54)

2 (2-pound) bone-in rib-eye steaks, 2 to 2½ inches thick, frenched (ask your butcher to do this)

Coffee Sauce (recipe follows)

Put the pinto beans in a medium bowl or pot and add cool water to cover. Set aside to soak overnight, uncovered. In the morning, discard any partial beans that have floated to the top, along with any stones, then drain and rinse the beans.

The day you plan to cook, in a heavy-bottomed 2- to 3-quart saucepan, cook the bacon over medium-low heat, stirring frequently, for 3 to 5 minutes, until the fat has rendered and the bacon is browned. Add the onion and cook, stirring often, for 3 to 5 minutes, until translucent. Add the garlic and jalapeño and cook, stirring often, for 2 to 3 minutes, until the garlic turns a light golden brown. Stir in the salt, pepper, bay leaf, pinto beans, and stock. Cook, uncovered, stirring occasionally, for 1 hour, or until the beans are tender. Add additional water, if needed, during the cooking to keep the beans submerged. Remove the saucepan from the heat and let it sit, covered, for 30 minutes to 1 hour.

Prepare the Coffee Rub.

Dust the steaks evenly with the Coffee Rub. Let them sit at room temperature for 30 minutes to 1 hour.

Meanwhile, prepare the Coffee Sauce.

When you are ready to cook, heat the grill to 400°F, using the direct grilling method (see Direct Cooking or Grilling, page 22).

Place the steaks directly over the heat and cook for 4 minutes, then rotate them 90 degrees and spray with the apple juice to moisten. Cook for another 4 minutes. Flip the steaks, spray them with apple juice, and cook for 4 minutes more, then rotate 90 degrees, and cook for another 4 minutes, or until a meat thermometer placed in the thickest part

(continued)

of the steak reads an internal temperature of 125°F. Transfer the steaks to a platter or cutting board and let them rest 5 minutes before slicing.

Slice the steaks across the grain and serve them with the Coffee Sauce on the side.

COFFEE SAUCE

2 teaspoons Coffee Rub (page 18)

1½ cups brewed medium-roast coffee

½ cup port wine

¼ cup minced shallot

1 tablespoon minced garlic

¼ cup demi-glace (see Source Guide, page 279)

1 tablespoon Dijon mustard

1 teaspoon balsamic vinegar

2 tablespoons unsalted butter

Prepare the Coffee Rub.

In a small saucepan, combine the coffee, port, shallot, and garlic. Stir and cook over medium heat for 5 to 7 minutes, or until the sauce has reduced to ½ cup.

Stir in the demi-glace, mustard, Coffee Rub, and vinegar and simmer for 3 minutes. Remove the saucepan from the heat and gently stir in the butter until melted. Cover and keep the sauce warm until ready to use. Check the consistency of the sauce before serving. If it is too thick, stir in hot water, 1 teaspoon at a time, as needed to reach the desired consistency.

WHOLE BEEF TENDERLOIN
WITH CUMBERLAND SAUCE

Cumberland sauce is traditionally served with game meats. Historically, the recipe dates back to the 1700s. We like the way it pairs with smoked beef tenderloin. This recipe is great for the holidays because it serves a number of people, and lends itself to a large buffet or party. It can be served hot or at room temperature.

½ cup Steak Rub (page 54)

1 (5½- to 6½-pound) whole beef tenderloin, silver skin removed, trussed

Cumberland Sauce (page 58)

1 cup apple juice, in a spray bottle, for the grill

Prepare the Steak Rub.

Season the tenderloin on all sides with the Steak Rub. Let it sit at room temperature for 1 hour.

Prepare the Cumberland Sauce before you grill.

When you are ready to cook, heat the grill to 400°F, using the 2-Zone setup (see 2-Zone Cooking, page 22).

Place the tenderloin on the hot side of the grill, close the lid, and cook for 20 minutes, rolling the tenderloin a quarter turn every 5 minutes and spraying with apple juice to moisten at every turn.

Move the tenderloin to the cool side of the grill, close the lid, and cook for another 10 to 20 minutes, or until a meat thermometer placed in the thickest part of the tenderloin reads an internal temperature of 125°F. Transfer to a platter or a cutting board and let the tenderloin rest for 10 to 15 minutes before carving.

Check the consistency of the Cumberland Sauce before serving. If it has thickened too much, stir in hot water, 1 teaspoon at a time, as needed to reach a desired consistency.

Slice the tenderloin across the grain and serve with the Cumberland Sauce on the side.

SMOKED BEEF RIBS
WITH STEAK SAUCE

MAKES 4 TO 6 SERVINGS

These ribs are versatile and can be cooked to fork-tender, or cooked to a lower temperature to achieve the texture of a steak.

½ cup Celery Seed Rub (page 54)

2 cups Steak Sauce (page 65)

2 (2- to 2½-pound) racks beef ribs

½ cup apple juice, in a spray bottle, for the grill

Prepare the Celery Seed Rub and the Steak Sauce.

Dust the ribs evenly on all sides with the Celery Seed Rub. Let them sit at room temperature for 1 hour before cooking.

When you are ready to cook, heat the grill to 375°F, using the 2-Zone setup (see 2-Zone Cooking, page 22).

Place the ribs meat-side down on the cool side of the grill. Close the lid and cook for 1 hour, then spray with apple juice to moisten. Cook for 1 hour more and spray again with the apple juice. Turn the ribs meat-side up, spray with apple juice, and cook for 1 hour more, or until the meat is tender and a meat thermometer placed in the thickest part of the ribs reads an internal temperature of 198°F–205°.

Separate the ribs by slicing between the bones, and serve them with the Steak Sauce on the side.

HANGER STEAK

WITH TWICE-FRIED STEAK FRIES AND MALT VINEGAR MAYONNAISE

MAKES 4 TO 6 SERVINGS

What makes these twice-fried potatoes easy to make at home is the shallow-frying technique. The malt vinegar mayonnaise is a combination of the way fries are served in England (with vinegar) and France (with mayonnaise). This condiment goes well with both the fries and the steak. The purpose of frying twice is to first blanch the potatoes in the hot oil, then crisp them, creating a creamy interior and crunchy exterior.

3 large Idaho potatoes, halved and cut lengthwise into 12 wedges each

2 tablespoons Steak Rub (page 54)

1½ cups Malt Vinegar Mayonnaise (recipe follows)

1 to 2 cups canola oil

2 (1- to 1½-pound) hanger steaks

1½ teaspoon smoked salt (see Source Guide, page 279)

Soak the potatoes in cold water for at least 4 hours or up to overnight.

Drain the potatoes and transfer to a wire rack to dry at room temperature.

Prepare the Steak Rub and the Malt Vinegar Mayonnaise.

Preheat the oven to 200°F. Line a large baking sheet with paper towels.

In a large cast-iron skillet over medium heat, heat ½ inch of canola oil to 325°F, using a deep-fry thermometer to check and maintain the temperature. Fry the potatoes in batches of 6 to 8 wedges for 5 minutes, turning occasionally if the potatoes are not fully submerged in the oil. To test for doneness, insert a toothpick into the thickest part of a wedge.

The potatoes are done when tender. Use a slotted spoon to carefully transfer the wedges to the paper towel–lined baking sheet to drain. Repeat the process until all the wedges have been fried, then turn off the heat, but leave the skillet of oil on the stove.

Dust the steaks evenly with the Steak Rub and let them sit at room temperature for 15 to 30 minutes before cooking.

Line a medium bowl and a large casserole dish with paper towels. Heat the oil in the skillet over medium-high heat to 400°F, again using a deep-fry thermometer to check and maintain the temperature. Fry the potatoes in batches of 6 to 8 wedges for 3 to 4 minutes, turning occasionally if the potatoes are not fully submerged in the oil. The potatoes are done when they are a deep golden brown. Use a slotted spoon to transfer the potatoes to the paper towel–lined bowl and toss them with a pinch of smoked salt. Turn the seasoned potatoes out onto the paper towel–lined casserole dish. Repeat the process until all the wedges have been fried twice. Transfer the casserole dish to the oven to keep warm until the steaks are ready to serve.

(continued)

When you are ready to cook, heat the grill to 400°F, using the direct grilling method (see Direct Cooking or Grilling, page 18).

Place the steaks directly over the heat and cook for 3 minutes, then rotate them 90 degrees and cook for another 3 minutes. Flip the steaks and cook for 3 minutes, then rotate them 90 degrees and cook for 3 additional minutes, or until a meat thermometer placed in the thickest part of the steak reads an internal temperature of 125°F (medium-rare). Let them rest at room temperature for 5 minutes before slicing.

Slice the steaks ¼ to ½ inch thick across the grain. Serve the sliced steak and fried potato wedges with the Malt Vinegar Mayonnaise as a dipping sauce for both.

MALT VINEGAR MAYONNAISE

MAKES 1½ CUPS

1 cup Duke's Mayonnaise, or your favorite brand

¼ cup malt vinegar

1 teaspoon Dijon mustard

2 tablespoons minced cornichons or sweet gherkins

1 tablespoon minced capers

1 teaspoon lemon zest

½ teaspoon granulated garlic

¼ teaspoon hot sauce, your choice of brand

1 tablespoon chopped fresh chives

1 tablespoon chopped fresh flat-leaf parsley

In a small bowl, combine the mayonnaise, vinegar, mustard, cornichons, capers, lemon zest, garlic, and hot sauce. Gently fold in the chives and parsley. Refrigerate in an airtight container until ready to use, up to 5 days.

NEW YORK STRIP

WITH BROWN BUTTER–BACON SAUCE AND BALSAMIC DRIZZLE

MAKES 4 SERVINGS

The first time I made this recipe, I was competing in the Kingsford Invitational in New York City as part of the One Bite challenge, with a winner-take-all $5,000 prize. I had to present and explain my dish to the judges while they tasted it in front of me. I could tell they liked it. When my team won, one of the judges, Ed Mitchell, a pitmaster from North Carolina, told me, "Tuffy, you're one tough dude." I took it as a compliment.

The balsamic drizzle added to the steaks just before serving lends a brightness that cuts through the fat in the brown butter–bacon sauce.

2 teaspoons kosher salt

1 teaspoon freshly ground black pepper

4 (8- to 10-ounce) New York strip steaks

8 tablespoons (1 stick) salted butter

½ cup finely diced bacon

½ cup balsamic vinegar

Combine the salt and pepper and season the steaks evenly on both sides. Let them sit at room temperature for 30 minutes to 1 hour before cooking.

Meanwhile, in a small nonstick sauté pan, melt 1 tablespoon of the butter over medium-low heat. Add the bacon and cook for 5 to 7 minutes, or until the fat is three-fourths rendered but the bacon is not yet crispy. Add the remaining 7 tablespoons butter and cook, stirring often, for 3 to 5 minutes, until the butter smells nutty and turns brown. Transfer the sauce to a heatproof container, cover loosely with plastic wrap or aluminum foil, and set aside until ready to use.

Clean the sauté pan and return it to medium-low heat. Add the vinegar and cook, stirring continuously, for 5 to 7 minutes, until the vinegar has reduced by half. Be careful not to over-reduce the vinegar, as this will make it bitter. Cover and set aside until ready to use.

When you are ready to cook, heat the grill to 400°F, using the direct grilling method (see Direct Cooking or Grilling, page 22).

Place the steaks directly over the heat and cook for 4 minutes, then rotate them 90 degrees and cook for another 4 minutes. Flip the steaks and cook for 4 minutes, then rotate them 90 degrees and cook for an additional 4 minutes, or until a meat thermometer placed in the thickest part of the steak reads an internal temperature of 125°F (medium-rare). Remove from the heat and let the steaks rest for 5 minutes before serving.

To plate, top each steak with 1½ to 2 tablespoons of the bacon and brown butter mixture and drizzle each with 1½ teaspoons of the balsamic reduction. Pass any additional sauces around the table.

SKIRT STEAK FAJITAS

A good time to warm the tortillas is while your meat is just off the grill and resting. It's a quick process: Place all your tortillas in stacks of two on the grill, warm them 5 seconds, then flip the stacks, and warm another 5 seconds. Transfer to a sheet of aluminum foil and wrap the stack to keep them warm until you're ready to eat.

Remember to make your marinade the night before you plan to cook.

---

1 cup soy sauce

½ cup fresh lemon juice

¼ cup minced garlic

¼ cup minced shallot

¼ cup minced jalapeño

¼ cup red wine vinegar

½ cup pickle juice from Bread-and-Butter Pickles (page 74)

¾ teaspoon kosher salt

2¼ teaspoons freshly ground black pepper

1½ pounds skirt steak

3 bell peppers, cut into ¼-inch-thick strips

1 red onion, cut into ¼-thick-thick strips

1 tablespoon canola oil

¼ teaspoon kosher salt

¼ teaspoon freshly ground black pepper

2 cups Cool Smoke Salsa (page 58) or your favorite brand

8 (6-inch) flour tortillas

1½ cups packed fresh cilantro leaves

2 avocados, pitted, peeled, and diced

2 limes, cut into wedges

The day before you plan to cook, make the marinade. In a small bowl, combine the soy sauce, lemon juice, garlic, shallot, minced jalapeño, vinegar, pickle juice, salt, and black pepper. Cover and refrigerate the marinade overnight.

The next day, place the skirt steak in a shallow casserole dish. Pour enough cold marinade through a strainer over the skirt steak to completely cover. Refrigerate for 1 hour, turning the steak after 30 minutes.

In a large bowl, toss the bell peppers and red onion with the canola oil. Season with the salt and black pepper and toss again. Place the peppers and onions in a grill basket and set aside. Make the Cool Smoke Salsa.

Remove the steak from the marinade and pat dry. When you are ready to cook, heat the grill to 500°F, using the direct grilling method (see Direct Cooking or Grilling, page 22).

Place the grill basket with the peppers and onions directly over the heat, close the lid, and cook for 5 minutes. Set aside.

Place the skirt steak directly over the heat, close the lid, and cook for 5 minutes, then flip and cook for another 3 to 5 minutes, or until a meat thermometer placed in the thickest part of the steak reads an internal temperature of 123°F (medium-rare). Remove from the heat and let the meat rest for 5 minutes.

Slice the steak across the grain. Divide the steak slices and pepper-and-onion mixture evenly among the tortillas, and garnish each with Cool Smoke Salsa, cilantro, and avocado. Serve with the lime wedges on the side.

THIS CHAPTER INCLUDES RECIPES FOR SMOKING AND
grilling chicken, turkey, game hen, duck, dove, and quail. All
these birds, except the dove, can be purchased at groceries,
specialty shops, or online (see Source Guide, page 279). My
Competition Chicken Thighs Cool Smoke Style (page 174) uses
chicken thighs, which are very popular on the competition circuit because they will retain some moisture if they happen to be
overcooked a bit. Chicken is one meat that people prefer to be
cooked through—many do not like to see any pink color in the
cooked flesh. Actually, a blush of color at the joints is normal,
and is not an indication that your chicken is undercooked. Two
good recipes to use as a test are Grilled Whole Chicken with
Lemon and Pepper (page 165) and Upright Chicken with Fennel
Pollen Rub (page 168). I have called for internal meat temperatures in the chicken recipes that will cook the meat throughout.
When you test the bird for doneness, check at the thickest part
of the thigh, and don't worry if you see a little pink.

Game birds are much better to eat when the meat is not
cooked through, so the cooking times and internal temperatures specified in those recipes will achieve your best results.
By not cooking game birds to well-done, the meat will have a
better chew and a less gamey flavor. This is best demonstrated
by these dishes: Dove Breast with Crispy Bacon and Chipotle
White Sauce (page 176), Goose Pastrami with Sautéed Cabbage,
Sun-Dried Cherries, and Spiced Pecans (page 184), and Grilled
Goose Breast (page 187).

Poultry tends to be more delicate than other meat, so be
careful not to oversmoke the birds, and allow the natural flavor
of the meat to stand out.

TARRAGON AND ALEPPO CHICKEN LEG QUARTERS

MAKES 6 TO 8 SERVINGS

Chicken leg quarters are dark meat, which are perfect for cooking on the grill because the meat stays moist even when it's slightly overcooked. The brine for this dish is similar to the chicken brine I use for competition barbecue (see page 70). Substitute fresh tarragon for the thyme, which pairs well with the fruity, gentle heat of the Aleppo pepper in the sauce.

3 quarts Chicken Brine (page 70), made with tarragon in place of thyme

6 chicken leg quarters

½ bunch tarragon

½ cup Tarragon and Aleppo Rub (page 50)

3 cups Tarragon and Aleppo White Sauce (page 60)

Prepare the Chicken Brine 24 to 48 hours before you plan to grill and refrigerate.

About 4 hours before you want to grill, rinse the chicken leg quarters and place in a large 6- to 8-quart plastic or stainless-steel container. Holding a strainer over the container, pour in enough Chicken Brine to just cover the chicken quarters. Cover the container with a lid or plastic wrap and refrigerate for 3 hours.

After 3 hours, remove the chicken quarters and pat completely dry with paper towels. Discard the brine. Refrigerate the chicken quarters until you are ready to grill.

Prepare the Tarragon and Aleppo Rub.

Remove the chicken from the refrigerator 1 hour before you are ready to grill, and dust thoroughly with the Tarragon and Aleppo Rub.

Let the chicken sit, uncovered, at room temperature for 1 hour.

Prepare the Tarragon and Aleppo White Sauce.

When you are ready to grill, heat the grill to 400°F, using the 2-Zone setup (see 2-Zone Cooking, page 22). Place the chicken quarters on the hot side of the grill, close the lid, and cook for 15 minutes, then flip and cook for another 15 minutes. Repeat this process for a total cooking time of 1 hour. The chicken is done when a meat thermometer placed into the thickest part of the leg reads 165°F.

Transfer the chicken quarters to a pan or platter and brush them on all sides with 2 cups of the Tarragon and Aleppo White Sauce. Transfer the chicken quarters to the cool side of the grill, close the lid, and cook for 5 minutes on each side to set the sauce.

Serve the chicken with the remaining 1 cup Tarragon and Aleppo White Sauce on the side, or drizzle it over the meat before serving.

SPICE-RUBBED CHICKEN WINGS
WITH CELERY SEED WHITE SAUCE

MAKES 6 TO 8 SERVINGS

What really gives these chicken wings their zip is the tanginess of the Celery Seed White Sauce. They are a refreshing change from the more common barbecued or Buffalo-style wings.

¼ cup Poultry Rub (page 49)
1½ cups Celery Seed White Sauce (page 66)
24 whole chicken wings

Prepare the Poultry Rub and the Celery Seed White Sauce.

Sprinkle the chicken wings liberally on all sides with the Poultry Rub and let them sit at room temperature for 1 hour before grilling.

When ready to cook, heat the grill to 400°F using the direct grilling method (see Direct Cooking or Grilling, page 22).

Place the wings on the grill directly over the heat and cook for 30 minutes, using tongs to flip them every 6 minutes. The wings are done when a meat thermometer placed into the thickest part of the meat reads an internal temperature of 175°F.

Transfer the wings to a large rimmed baking sheet. Brush the wings on all sides with ¾ cup of the Celery Seed White Sauce. Remove from the baking sheet and return them to the grill for 5 minutes to set the sauce, being careful not to burn the chicken. Transfer to a serving platter, drizzle with some of the remaining sauce, and pass the rest around the table. Serve hot.

CHICKEN WINGS
WITH CARAMEL BARBECUE SAUCE

Cooked on the grill instead of in a deep fryer, these wings are easier and less messy to make, and have a great smoky flavor. The brine in this recipe really accentuates the chicken, and the rub and sauce add that traditional barbecue taste we love.

3 quarts Chicken Brine (page 70)

¼ cup Cool Smoke Rub (page 49)

1 cup plus 2 tablespoons Cool Smoke Barbecue Sauce (page 57)

24 whole chicken wings

¼ cup plus 2 tablespoons Caramel Simple Syrup (page 74)

Prepare the Chicken Brine 24 to 48 hours before you plan to grill, and refrigerate.

Prepare the Cool Smoke Rub and the Cool Smoke Barbecue Sauce.

The next day, place the chicken wings in a 6- to 8-quart plastic container. Pour enough cold Chicken Brine through a large strainer onto the chicken wings to completely cover the wings. Refrigerate the brined wings for 2 hours, then remove the chicken from the brine and transfer to paper towels to dry thoroughly. Season the wings on all sides with the Cool Smoke Rub and let them sit for 1 hour at room temperature before cooking.

Prepare the Caramel Simple Syrup.

Combine 1 cup of the Cool Smoke Barbecue Sauce with the Caramel Simple Syrup, and reserve ¾ cup of this mixture for use on the grill. Set the rest aside for serving.

When you are ready to cook, heat the grill to 400°F, using the direct grilling method (see Direct Cooking or Grilling, page 22).

Place the wings on the grill directly over the heat and cook for 30 minutes, using tongs to flip them every 6 minutes. The wings are done when a meat thermometer placed into the thickest part of the meat reads an internal temperature of 175°F.

Transfer the wings to a rimmed baking sheet and brush them on all sides with the Caramel Simple Syrup–Cool Smoke Barbecue Sauce mixture. Remove from the baking sheet and return them to the grill for 5 minutes more to set the sauce, being careful not to burn the chicken. Transfer to a serving platter, drizzle with the reserved Caramel Simple Syrup–Cool Smoke Barbecue Sauce mixture, and serve hot.

GRILLED WHOLE CHICKEN
WITH LEMON AND PEPPER

MAKES 2 TO 4 SERVINGS

The lemon pepper compound butter, rubbed between the skin and the meat, is the trick to getting more flavor into the chicken, while also crisping the skin.

6 quarts Chicken Brine (page 70)

1 (3½- to 4-pound) whole chicken

¼ cup plus 2 teaspoons Lemon Pepper Rub (page 53)

2 tablespoons salted butter, at room temperature

1 (12-ounce) bottle or can of beer, your choice

1 cup Lemon Spray (page 69), in a spray bottle, for the grill

Prepare the Chicken Brine 24 to 48 hours before you plan to grill, and refrigerate.

The morning you plan to cook, rinse the chicken and place in an 8-quart plastic or stainless-steel container. Holding a strainer over the container, pour in enough chilled Chicken Brine to completely cover the whole chicken. Cover with a lid or plastic wrap and refrigerate for 8 hours or up to overnight.

Once brined, remove the chicken and pat completely dry with paper towels, then return it to the refrigerator until ready to grill. Prepare the Lemon Pepper Rub.

In a small bowl, combine the butter and 2 teaspoons of the Lemon Pepper Rub and mix until smooth. One hour before you are ready to grill, remove the chicken from the refrigerator and rub 1 tablespoon of the seasoned butter between the chicken breasts and the skin, sliding your fingers beneath the skin to gently separate it from the meat. Rub the remaining

1 tablespoon seasoned butter over the entire surface of the chicken. Sprinkle the whole chicken, inside and out, with the remaining ¼ cup Lemon Pepper Rub.

Either drink half the beer (if you like) and leave the rest in the can, or discard the beer and fill the can halfway with water.

Place the seasoned whole chicken atop the beer can, legs first, and insert the beer can inside the cavity of the chicken so it stands upright on the can. Set the chicken aside to rest at room temperature for 1 hour before cooking. Prepare the Lemon Spray.

When you are ready to cook, heat the grill to 400°F, using the 2-Zone setup (see 2-Zone Cooking, page 22). Stand the beer can chicken on the cool side of the grill, with its back toward the hot side and the breast toward the cool side. Close the lid and cook for 30 minutes, then spray the entire chicken with Lemon Spray to moisten. Turn the chicken so the breast is facing the hot side of the grill and cook for 60 to 90 minutes more, spraying the chicken every 15 minutes to moisten. The chicken is done when a meat thermometer placed in the thickest part of the breast reaches 170°F, and the thickest part of the thigh reaches 165°F.

Set the chicken aside to cool for 10 to 15 minutes before carefully removing the can and carving the bird.

SMOKED CHICKEN
WITH GRAPES, SPICED PECANS, AND ARUGULA

MAKES 4 SERVINGS

This is a meal-size salad—a great dinner to make using leftover Grilled Lemon Pepper Whole Chicken. There are a lot of things I like about this dish—it's quick and easy to make on a hot day, and you don't have to turn on your oven. I really like no-cook, cold dinners during the summer months.

2 cups pulled meat from Grilled Whole Chicken with lemon and Pepper (page 165)

½ cup Spiced Pecans (page 73)

½ cup Tarragon and Aleppo White Sauce (page 60)

½ cup halved grapes

¼ cup small-dice celery

4 cups arugula

½ teaspoon kosher salt

¼ teaspoon cracked black pepper

Prepare the Grilled Lemon Pepper Whole Chicken, Spiced Pecans, and Tarragon and Aleppo White Sauce.

In a medium bowl, combine the chicken, grapes, celery, Spiced Pecans, and arugula and gently toss. Season with the salt and pepper and toss again. Add the Tarragon and Aleppo White Sauce and toss gently to coat. Serve immediately.

UPRIGHT CHICKEN
WITH FENNEL POLLEN RUB

MAKES 2 TO 4 SERVINGS

A whole chicken is the essence of Sunday supper at our house; it's the meal that brings the entire family together at the kitchen table. An inexpensive dish, this chicken, cooked well, is a delicacy. I love the way the house smells when a chicken is roasting—as do our three dogs. For them, it means a little something extra in their bowls.

As a chef, I love the challenge that cooking a whole chicken presents: attaining the perfect doneness of the dark meat while not overcooking the breast. By cooking the bird in a standing, beer-can-chicken style, I am able to manipulate the entire chicken during the cooking process to ensure that both the dark and white meat are cooked perfectly.

6 quarts Fennel Sage Brine (page 70)

1 (3½- to 4-pound) whole chicken

¼ cup plus 2 teaspoons Fennel Pollen Rub (page 49)

2 tablespoons salted butter, at room temperature

1 (12-ounce) bottle or can beer, your choice

1 cup pineapple juice, in a spray bottle, for the grill

Prepare the Fennel Sage Brine 24 to 48 hours before you plan to grill, and refrigerate.

Rinse the chicken and place in a large 8-quart plastic or stainless-steel container. Holding a strainer over the container, pour in enough chilled Fennel Sage Brine to completely cover the whole chicken. Cover with a lid or plastic wrap and refrigerate for 8 hours or up to overnight.

Once brined, remove the chicken and pat completely dry with paper towels, then refrigerate until ready to grill.

Prepare the Fennel Pollen Rub.

In a small bowl, combine the butter and 2 teaspoons of the Fennel Pollen Rub and mix until smooth.

One hour before you are ready to grill, remove the chicken from the refrigerator and rub 1 tablespoon of the seasoned butter between the chicken breasts and the skin, sliding your fingers beneath the skin to gently separate it from the meat. Rub the remaining 1 tablespoon seasoned butter over the entire surface of the chicken. Sprinkle the whole chicken, inside and out, with the remaining ¼ cup Fennel Pollen Rub.

Either drink half the beer (if you like) and leave the rest in the can, or discard the beer and fill the can halfway with water.

Place the seasoned whole chicken atop the beer can, legs first, and insert the beer can inside the cavity of the chicken so it stands upright on the can. Set the chicken aside to rest at room temperature for 1 hour before cooking.

When you are ready to cook, heat the grill to 400°F, using the 2-Zone setup (see 2-Zone Cooking, page 22).

Stand the beer can chicken on the cool side of the grill, with its back toward the hot side and the breast toward the cool side. Close the lid and cook for 30 minutes, then spray the entire chicken with pineapple juice to moisten. Turn the chicken so the breast is facing the hot side of the grill and cook for 60 to 90 minutes more, spraying the chicken every 15 minutes to moisten. The chicken is done when a meat thermometer placed in the thickest part of the breast reaches 170°F, and the thickest part of the thigh reaches 165°F.

Set the chicken aside to cool for 10 to 15 minutes before carefully removing the can and carving the bird.

SPATCHCOCKED GAME HEN
WITH SPICY APRICOT GLAZE

The spatchcock process of removing the backbone of the hen helps to shorten the cooking time and assists in even cooking. Placing the dark meat toward the hotter part of the fire and the breast meat to the cooler part ensures that the dark and the white meat will be cooked to the proper doneness.

3 quarts Chicken Brine (page 70)

4 game hens

Game Hen Rub (recipe follows)

3 tablespoons salted butter, at room temperature

1 cup Spicy Apricot Glaze (recipe follows)

1 cup Apple Spray (page 69), in a spray bottle, for the grill

Prepare the Chicken Brine 24 to 48 hours before you plan to brine, and refrigerate.

Rinse the hens and place in an 8-quart plastic or stainless-steel container. Holding a strainer over the container, pour in enough chilled Chicken Brine to completely cover the game hens. Cover with a lid or plastic wrap and refrigerate for 3 hours.

Prepare the Game Hen Rub and the Spicy Apricot Glaze.

In a small bowl, combine the butter and 1 tablespoon of the Game Hen Rub and mix until smooth.

Once brined, remove the hens and pat completely dry with paper towels. Using poultry shears, spatchcock the hens, remove the backbones and lay the hens flat. Rub the seasoned butter over and under the skin of the hens, sliding your fingers beneath the skin to gently separate it from the meat. Dust both sides of each game hen evenly with 1 tablespoon of the Game Hen Rub. Let the hens rest for 1 hour at room temperature before grilling.

When you are ready to cook, heat the grill to 400°F, using the direct grilling method (see Direct Cooking or Grilling, page 22).

Place the game hens skin-side down over the heat, close the lid, and cook for 10 minutes. Spray with the Apple Spray to moisten, rotate the birds 90 degrees, and cook for an additional 10 minutes. Spray again and flip the birds so they are skin-side up. Spray the skin side to moisten and cook for an additional 10 minutes, or until a meat thermometer placed in the thickest part of the breast reads 170°F, and the thickest part of the thigh reaches 165°F.

Transfer the game hens to a baking sheet and brush both sides with the Spicy Apricot Glaze. Remove from the pan and return the hens to the grill, skin-side up, and cook for 5 minutes to set the glaze. Transfer the birds to a platter

(continued)

GAME HEN RUB

MAKES ABOUT ½ CUP

6 tablespoons kosher salt

1 tablespoon Espelette pepper (see Source Guide, page 279)

1 tablespoon cracked black pepper

1½ teaspoons ground coriander

1½ teaspoons granulated garlic

Combine all the ingredients in a small bowl and mix thoroughly. Reserve 1½ teaspoons for the Spicy Apricot Glaze (recipe follows) and use the rest for the hens.

SPICY APRICOT GLAZE

MAKES ABOUT 1 CUP

½ cup apricot preserves

¼ cup chicken stock

⅛ cup minced jalapeño

1½ teaspoons Game Hen Rub (page 172)

½ teaspoon fresh lemon juice

Combine all the ingredients in a small bowl and stir until well incorporated. Refrigerate in an airtight container until ready to use.

GRILLED CHICKEN BREAST
WITH CHIMICHURRI

MAKES 4 SERVINGS

Chimichurri sauce is typically served with grilled beef, but the herbaceous spiciness goes great with chicken, too. Because the acidity from the red wine vinegar complements the flavors of the grill, you can also pair it with grilled meat, seafood, and vegetables.

2 cups Chimichurri (page 57)

4 (8-ounce) boneless, skin-on chicken breasts

2 tablespoons plus 2 teaspoons Lemon Pepper Rub (page 53)

Prepare the Chimichurri.

In a large bowl, combine the chicken breasts and 1 cup of the Chimichurri (refrigerate the remaining Chimichurri until ready to serve). Toss to thoroughly coat the breasts. Cover the bowl with plastic wrap and refrigerate for 4 to 8 hours.

Prepare the Lemon Pepper Rub.

When you are ready to grill, evenly dust both sides of each chicken breast with the Lemon Pepper Rub.

Heat the grill to 400°F, using the direct grilling method setup (see Direct Cooking or Grilling, page 22).

Place the seasoned chicken breasts skin-side down on the hot grill grate. Cook for 4 minutes, then rotate each breast 90 degrees and cook for 4 minutes more. Flip the breasts skin-side up and cook for 4 minutes, then rotate the breasts 90 degrees and cook for 4 minutes more, or until a meat thermometer placed in the thickest part of the breast reads an internal temperature of 160°F.

Let the chicken rest for 5 minutes before serving. Top each breast with 2 tablespoons of the Chimichurri, and pass the remaining sauce around the table.

COMPETITION CHICKEN THIGHS
COOL SMOKE STYLE

MAKES 6 TO 8 SERVINGS

Chicken thighs are the preferred cut to use in competition barbecue because they don't dry out as easily as chicken breasts on the grill or in the smoker. "Bite-through" skin is an important element in judging competition barbecue. Perforating the skin with a Jaccard or meat tenderizer (see Tools, page 12)—which punches numerous little holes on the surface—before grilling enables the skin to tear easily into bite-size portions.

8 bone-in, skin-on chicken thighs

3 quarts Chicken Brine (page 70)

1 cup Cool Smoke Rub (page 49)

4 cups Cool Smoke Barbecue Sauce (page 57)

12 tablespoons (1½ sticks) salted butter, cut into ½-inch-thick slices

1 cup pineapple juice, in a spray bottle, for the grill

Clean the chicken thighs and place skin-side down on a clean cutting board. Use a sharp knife to trim away any excess skin so that the thighs are uniformly square. Remove any exposed silver skin or tendons. Flip the thighs skin-side up and use a Jaccard to pierce the skin every ¼ inch.

Prepare the Chicken Brine.

Place the chicken thighs in a 6- to 8-quart lidded plastic container. Pour enough cold Chicken Brine through a strainer over the thighs to completely cover. Refrigerate for 2 hours, then remove the chicken and pat dry thoroughly with paper towels. Discard the brine.

Prepare the Cool Smoke Rub and the Cool Smoke Barbecue Sauce.

Dust the chicken thighs evenly on all sides with ¾ cup of the Cool Smoke Rub. Use your hands to shape the thighs uniformly by stretching and tucking the skin underneath the meat, so that each thigh resembles a tight bundle.

Place the bundles in a 9 x 12 x 3-inch disposable aluminum pan. Place the pats of butter evenly between each bundle. Dust the top of each chicken thigh with a light coating of Cool Smoke Rub, and let them sit for 1 hour at room temperature before cooking.

When you are ready to cook, heat the smoker to 325°F pit temperature (see Smoke, page 25). Place the pan of chicken thighs, uncovered, on the heated grate of the smoker. Close the lid and cook the thighs for 1 hour, spraying them with pineapple juice every 20 minutes to moisten. After 1 hour, flip each thigh so that it is skin-side down and spray each again with pineapple juice to moisten. Cook for another 20 minutes, then turn the thighs skin-side up. Dust lightly with the Cool Smoke Rub overall and cook for an additional 20 minutes, or until a meat thermometer placed in the thickest part of the thigh reads an internal temperature of 180°F.

During the last 20 minutes of cooking, warm the Cool Smoke Barbecue Sauce in a saucepan over low heat.

When the thighs have reached 180°F, remove the pan from the smoker. Use tongs to individually dip each thigh into the warm barbecue sauce. Tap the tongs on the side of the saucepan to remove excess sauce from each thigh, and transfer the chicken to a wire rack. When all the thighs are sauced, place the wire rack in the smoker for 10 minutes to set the sauce. Allow the thighs to rest 5 minutes at room temperature before serving.

DOVE BREAST

WITH CRISPY BACON AND CHIPOTLE WHITE SAUCE

MAKES 6 TO 8 SERVINGS

Unless you're a hunter, doves are only available through friends who hunt. Dove season is a group activity and opening day is in September. Basically, the best part of the bird is the breast, which is best when cooked quickly on the grill—it's important not to over-cook them. The shishito peppers in this recipe are mild, but you'll find an occasional one that's really fiery, so hold on to your britches! They add a wonderful brightness to game meat.

1¼ cups Chipotle White Sauce (page 63)

12 bacon slices

1 tablespoon Cool Smoke Rub (page 49)

12 dove breasts, split in half

24 shishito peppers, or 12 Hatch chiles (available at most specialty groceries)

1 tablespoon olive oil

Kosher salt and freshly ground black pepper

Prepare the Chipotle White Sauce.

Preheat the oven to 350°F.

Cover a baking sheet with aluminum foil and arrange the bacon on it. Bake for 9 to 12 minutes, until the fat has mostly rendered but the bacon is not yet crisp. Set the bacon aside to cool slightly, then cut each strip in half crosswise on an angle.

Prepare the Cool Smoke Rub.

Use a sharp knife to halve each dove breast vertically. Season each breast half with ¼ teaspoon of the Cool Smoke Rub and wrap with a half slice of bacon; secure the bacon with a toothpick.

When you are ready to cook, heat the grill to 400°F, using the direct grilling method (see Direct Cooking or Grilling, page 22).

Toss the shishito peppers in a bowl with the olive oil and season them to taste with salt and black pepper. Place the peppers on the grill, directly over the heat, and cook for 6 minutes, or until the skin blisters. Use tongs to flip the peppers, and cook for an additional 6 minutes, or until the skin is evenly blistered. Transfer the peppers to a large, clean bowl and set aside.

Place the wrapped dove breasts on the grill, directly over the heat, and cook for 4 minutes. Flip the breasts and cook for an additional 4 minutes for medium-rare meat, or until a meat thermometer placed in the thickest part of a breast reads an internal temperature of 140°F. Transfer the dove breasts to a rimmed baking sheet and brush each breast all over with Chipotle White Sauce.

Remove the breasts from the baking sheet and return them to the grill. Cook for a final 3 minutes to set the sauce. Add the cooked breasts to the bowl with the peppers and toss with ½ cup Chipotle White Sauce to coat. Transfer to a platter and serve immediately.

SMOKED WHOLE TURKEY

WITH FENNEL SAUSAGE STUFFING AND HERB GRAVY

MAKES 8 TO 12 SERVINGS

There are many things to like about preparing this dish for an outdoor turkey day feast: cooking outdoors, the delicate floral flavors of fennel pollen, the savory sausage stuffing, and the light herb gravy. To achieve the best smoked turkey, take care not to overcook the meat, ensuring the smoke is a background flavor to the natural taste of the turkey itself.

6½ quarts Fennel Sage Brine (page 70)

1 (12- to 14-pound) turkey

Herb Gravy (page 64)

6 tablespoons plus 4 teaspoons Fennel Pollen Rub (page 49)

4 tablespoons (½ stick) salted butter, at room temperature

2½ cups Lemon Spray (page 69), in a spray bottle, for the grill

Fennel Sausage Stuffing (page 248)

Up to two days before you plan to grill, prepare the Fennel Sage Brine and refrigerate for 24 to 48 hours.

The day before you plan to grill, rinse the whole turkey and place in a large 16-quart plastic or stainless-steel container. Holding a strainer over the container, pour in enough chilled Fennel Sage Brine to completely cover the whole turkey. Cover with a lid or plastic wrap and refrigerate for 12 hours or up to overnight.

Prepare the Herb Gravy and refrigerate until ready to use.

Once brined, remove the turkey and pat completely dry with paper towels. Place the turkey on a wire rack and return it to the refrigerator, uncovered, for 2 hours to dry.

Prepare the Fennel Pollen Rub.

In a small bowl, combine the butter and 4 teaspoons of the Fennel Pollen Rub and mix thoroughly until smooth.

Remove the turkey from the refrigerator 1 hour before you plan to grill. Rub 2 tablespoons of the seasoned butter between the turkey breasts and the skin, sliding your fingers beneath the skin to gently separate it from the meat. Rub the remaining 2 tablespoons seasoned butter over the entire skin of the turkey. Dust the turkey evenly, inside and out, with the remaining 6 tablespoons Fennel Pollen Rub and let it sit for 1 hour at room temperature before cooking.

Prepare the Lemon Spray.

When you are ready to cook, heat the grill to 350°F, using the 2-Zone setup (see 2-Zone Cooking, page 22).

Place the turkey breast-side up on the cool side of the grill, with the breast toward the cool side and the legs toward the hot side. Close the lid and cook for 2½ to 3 hours, spraying with Lemon Spray to moisten and turning a quarter turn every 30 minutes. The turkey is done when a meat thermometer placed in the thickest part of the breast reads a temperature

of 170°F, and the thickest part of the thigh reaches 165°F. Let the turkey rest at room temperature for approximately 30 minutes before serving.

While the turkey is on the grill, prepare the Fennel Sausage Stuffing. Bake the stuffing and rewarm the Herb Gravy in a small saucepan over low heat while the turkey is resting.

Serve with the Fennel Sausage Stuffing and Herb Gravy.

CITRUS-BRINED TURKEY BREAST

WITH BLOOD ORANGE AND CRANBERRY CHUTNEY

MAKES 8 TO 10 SERVINGS

Turkey breasts are nice because they are a more manageable cut of meat than whole turkeys, and they still feed a good number of people. Because they tend to dry out easily, I like to use a citrus brine. This brings flavor and moisture to the breast, which makes this dish a standout.

6½ quarts Citrus Brine (see next page)

1 (8- to 10-pound) bone-in turkey breast

1 quart Blood Orange and Cranberry Chutney (see page 66)

3 tablespoons plus 2 teaspoons Poultry Rub (page 49)

2 tablespoons salted butter, at room temperature

Place the turkey breast skin-side down in a 16-quart plastic container. Pour enough of the strained Citrus Brine over the turkey breast to completely cover and reserve another 2 cups of the strained brine to fill a spray bottle. Refrigerate the brined turkey breast for 8 hours or up to overnight.

When brined, remove the turkey breast and pat dry with paper towels. Transfer to a plate or platter and refrigerate again until you are ready to grill.

Prepare the Blood Orange and Cranberry Chutney and the Poultry Rub.

One hour before you grill, combine the butter and 2 teaspoons of the Poultry Rub in a small bowl and mix until smooth. Rub 1 tablespoon of the seasoned butter between the turkey breast and the skin, sliding your fingers beneath the skin to gently separate it from the meat. Rub the remaining 1 tablespoon seasoned butter over all sides of the turkey breast. Dust with the remaining 3 tablespoons Poultry Rub and let the breast sit for 1 hour at room temperature.

When you are ready to cook, heat the grill to 400°F, using the 2-Zone setup (see 2-Zone Cooking, page 22).

Place the seasoned turkey breast on the cool side of the grill, with the neck positioned toward the hot side. Close the lid and cook for 30 minutes, then spray the turkey breast with the reserved Citrus Brine to moisten. Cook for 2 to 2½ hours more, spraying the breast with the Citrus Brine and rotating it 180 degrees every 15 minutes. The breast is done when a meat thermometer placed in the thickest part of the meat reads 160°F.

Transfer the turkey breast to a platter to rest for 10 to 15 minutes at room temperature before serving. Serve with the Blood Orange and Cranberry Chutney on the side.

TURKEY AND BRIE SANDWICH

MAKES 4 SANDWICHES

If you happen to have anything left from the Citrus Brined Turkey Breast, the tartness of the Blood Orange and Cranberry Chutney and Brie, layered with the smoked flavor of the turkey, will make you forget you're eating leftovers.

1 pound Citrus-Brined Turkey Breast (page 180), sliced

½ cup Blood Orange and Cranberry Chutney (page 66)

1 large French baguette, cut in half lengthwise

⅓ cup Duke's Mayonnaise, or your favorite brand

1 cup arugula

8 ounces Brie cheese, sliced into 8 (¼-inch-thick) pieces

Kosher salt and cracked black pepper

Prepare the Citrus-Brined Turkey and Blood Orange and Cranberry Chutney if you don't have any left over.

Cut the baguette in half lengthwise. Spread the mayonnaise equally over the top and bottom halves of the baguette. Spread the Blood Orange and Cranberry Chutney evenly over the bottom half of the baguette. Top the chutney with the arugula. Layer the turkey slices, then the Brie, over the arugula. Season with salt and pepper, and top with the remaining baguette half. Cut into four equal sandwiches and serve immediately.

CITRUS BRINE

MAKES ABOUT 6½ QUARTS

2 quarts orange juice, any kind is ok

1⅛ cups kosher salt

1 cup packed light brown sugar

5 bay leaves

10 star anise pods

4 cinnamon sticks

1 cup coarsely chopped yellow onion

1 bunch fresh thyme

2 whole guajillo peppers, cut into strips (using scissors)

3 tablespoons whole black peppercorns

In an 8-quart container, combine the orange juice, salt, sugar, and 4 quarts water and stir until the salt and sugar have dissolved. Add the bay leaves, star anise, cinnamon sticks, onion, thyme, peppers, and black peppercorns, stir, cover, and refrigerate for 24 hours.

GOOSE PASTRAMI

WITH SAUTÉED CABBAGE, SUN-DRIED CHERRIES, AND SPICED PECANS

MAKES 4 TO 6 SERVINGS

My hunter friends often tell me they love duck, but don't care much for goose meat; however, this dish is one of our favorites. The Goose Rub brings robust flavors to the meat.

While this dish takes 4 days to prepare, don't worry—it's simple to make. Most of that time is refrigeration. The key to cooking is to adhere to the specified 138°F for medium-rare doneness—it will be more tender and have a less gamey taste.

¼ cup Goose Rub (page 53)

½ teaspoon pink curing salt

2 (1- to 1½-pound) goose breasts

2 tablespoons coarsely cracked black pepper

2 tablespoons coarsely cracked coriander seeds

2 teaspoons granulated garlic

½ cup Apple Spray (page 69), in a spray bottle, for the grill

Sautéed Cabbage, Sun-Dried Cherries, and Spiced Pecans (page 217)

Four days before you plan to cook, prepare the Goose Rub. Combine the Goose Rub and the pink curing salt in a small bowl.

Cut four 12-inch lengths of plastic wrap and lay them side by side on a clean work surface. Place each breast on a separate length of plastic wrap. Using all the Goose Rub–pink salt mixture, dust both sides of each breast. Tightly wrap each breast in the plastic wrap, then double wrap them with the remaining lengths of plastic. Refrigerate for 24 hours, then flip the wrapped breasts and refrigerate for another 24 hours.

On the third day, unwrap the breasts and rinse with cold water, then pat them dry with paper towels.

In a shallow medium bowl, combine the pepper, coriander, and granulated garlic. Sprinkle both sides of the breasts with this mixture, patting to ensure uniform coverage. Place the breasts, uncovered, on a wire rack in the refrigerator for 48 hours.

When you are ready to cook, heat the grill to 200°F, using the 2-Zone setup (see 2-Zone Cooking, page 22).

Prepare the Apple Spray.

Prepare the Sautéed Cabbage, Sun-Dried Cherries, and Spiced Pecans. Let it stand at room temperature until ready to serve. (If you prefer it warmer, reheat just before serving.)

Place the breasts on the cool side of the grill, close the lid, and cook for 30 minutes, spraying every 15 minutes with Apple Spray to moisten. Flip the breasts and cook for an additional 30 minutes, spraying again every 15 minutes. The meat is done when a meat thermometer placed in the thickest part of the breast reaches an internal temperature of 138°F.

Slice the breasts very thin, and serve them hot or cold with the Sautéed Cabbage, Sun-Dried Cherries, and Spiced Pecans.

SMOKED AND LACQUERED DUCK

MAKES 4 TO 6 SERVINGS

I made this dish the first time while working with chef David Harmon at Millie's in Richmond, Virginia, years ago, and I still love it. The saltiness of the soy in the marinade coupled with the lime and the heat of the smoker creates a glaze that lacquers the skin, producing an intense, crispy bite.

Duck Marinade (recipe follows)

1 (5½- to 6-pound) duck

¼ cup Duck Rub (page 50)

1 (12-ounce) bottle or can beer, your favorite brand

1 cup white grape juice, in a spray bottle, for the grill

Prepare the Duck Marinade 2 days before you plan to cook, and refrigerate.

The day before you plan to cook, rinse the duck and place it breast-side down in an 8-quart plastic or stainless-steel container. Holding a strainer over the container, pour in enough chilled Duck Marinade to completely cover the duck. Cover with a lid or plastic wrap and refrigerate for 5 hours. After 5 hours, flip the duck breast-side up and brine for an additional 5 hours, for a total brining time of 10 hours.

Prepare the Duck Rub.

The day you plan to grill, remove the duck from the marinade and pat the duck completely dry with paper towels. Season it inside and out with the Duck Rub.

Either drink half the beer (if you like) and leave the rest in the can, or discard the beer and fill the can halfway with water.

Place the seasoned whole duck atop the beer can, legs first, and insert the beer can inside the cavity of the duck so that it stands upright on the can. Let the duck rest for 1 hour at room temperature before cooking.

When you are ready to cook, heat the grill to 500°F, using the 2-Zone setup (see 2-Zone Cooking, page 22).

Stand the beer can duck on the cool side of the grill, with its back toward the hot side and the breast toward the cool side. Close the lid and cook for 30 minutes, then spray the whole duck with white grape juice to moisten and turn the duck so the breast is facing the hot side of the grill. Cook for 1 hour more, spraying the duck every 15 minutes, until a meat thermometer placed in the thickest part of the breast meat reads 135°F and the thigh meat is 140°F.

Remove the duck from the grill and let it rest for 10 to 15 minutes before carefully removing the beer can and carving the duck.

DUCK MARINADE

MAKES 2½ QUARTS

8 cups white grape juice

2 cups soy sauce

6 bay leaves

12 garlic cloves, thinly sliced

2 tablespoons crushed coriander seeds

2 tablespoons crushed black peppercorns

20 whole cloves

2 (4-inch-long) dried guajillo peppers, cut into thin strips (using scissors)

1 lime, sliced into thin rounds

Combine all the ingredients in a large bowl or 3-quart plastic container and cover. Refrigerate for 24 hours before using.

GRILLED GOOSE BREAST

MAKES 2 TO 4 SERVINGS

Other than shooting and cleaning the goose, this is one of the simplest recipes in the book. As with all goose recipes, avoiding overcooking.

4 tablespoons Goose Rub (page 53)

½ cup Apple Spray (page 69), in a spray bottle, for the grill

2 (1- to 1½-pound) goose breasts

2 tablespoons salted butter, melted

Prepare the Goose Rub and Apple Spray.

When you are ready to cook, heat the grill to 400°F, using the direct grilling method (see Direct Cooking or Grilling, page 22).

Brush all sides of the goose breasts with the melted butter. Dust each goose breast evenly with 2 tablespoons of the Goose Rub, using 1 tablespoon per side. Let the breasts sit for 30 minutes, uncovered, at room temperature.

Place the breasts directly over the heat and cook for 5 minutes, then rotate them 90 degrees and spray with Apple Spray to moisten. Cook for another 5 minutes, then spray again and flip the breasts over. Spray again and cook for an additional 5 minutes, or until a meat thermometer placed in the thickest part of the breast reads an internal temperature of 138°F.

Transfer to a cutting board or platter and let the meat rest for 5 minutes. Slice thinly to serve.

CHICKEN-FRIED QUAIL
WITH SAUSAGE GRAVY

MAKES 4 TO 6 SERVINGS

I like to have an occasional fried dish. Because this quail is panfried, it's not very greasy. The nice crunch of the breading gives the delicate meat a more substantial chew; plus, the heat from the sausage in the gravy provides a good kick.

3 cups Sausage Gravy (page 61)

3 tablespoons Quail Rub (page 49)

4 large eggs

1 cup all-purpose flour

1 cup canola oil

6 (4-ounce) quail, backbones removed

Prepare the Sausage Gravy. Cover and keep warm until ready to serve.

Prepare the Quail Rub.

When you are ready to cook the quail, crack the eggs into a medium bowl and whisk to combine.

In a separate shallow bowl, stir together the flour and 2 tablespoons of the Quail Rub.

Dust each quail evenly with ½ teaspoon of the Quail Rub.

Dredge each quail in the seasoned flour to coat completely. Shake off any excess flour, and dip the quail into the egg to coat. Shake off excess egg, and return the quail to the bowl of seasoned flour, dredging to coat completely. Set aside until the oil is hot.

In a 12-inch cast-iron skillet, heat the canola oil over medium heat. When the oil is hot but not smoking, carefully place 3 quail breast-side down in the pan and cook for 5 minutes, until golden brown. Use tongs to flip the quail and cook for another 5 minutes, until golden brown. Carefully transfer the quail to a paper towel–lined platter to drain. Repeat the process with the remaining quail.

To serve, top each quail with ¼ cup of the Sausage Gravy and pass the remaining gravy around the table.

SEAFOOD
AND OTHER MEATS

SOME SEAFOOD IS PERFECT FOR THE GRILL OR SMOKER, but, much like poultry, fish tend to be more delicate in flavor and require less smoke. The recipes in this chapter are designed so the smoke from the grill or smoker is mild and doesn't overwhelm the taste of the seafood.

Some fish, such as the Salmon with Cucumber Yogurt Sauce (page 199), are better suited for the grill than others because they are not too fragile to handle and don't overcook quickly. Salmon is generally a sturdy, thick-cut piece of fish with a high fat content that requires a longer cooking time, which allows for the flavors of the grill to be imparted.

We have included four venison recipes that were developed using wild game, but it's important to note that venison may be purchased online (see Source Guide, page 279) and at specialty shops, so if you're not a hunter, don't worry. While testing our game recipes, we found that the wild venison tasted much better when the meat was not cooked too long. A good example of this is the Smoked Venison Stew (page 212). When we first made this, we let the venison simmer too long in the stew. The end product was very tough. You will see in the instructions that after adding the (precooked) venison to the stew, it is vital that it only simmer until the meat is just warmed through, 2 to 3 minutes. The result is a much better chew, without the strong mineral or gamey taste that many people do not prefer. The heat and timeline guides for these recipes will help you achieve a tender meat with a pleasant taste, without overcooking.

And I can't help but point you to our take on a traditional dish, Smoked Venison Stroganoff (page 210). The venison adds a depth of flavor that takes this dish beyond the ordinary.

BLACKENED ROCKFISH

MAKES 4 SERVINGS

Blackened fish was a popular dish in the eighties, and as a chef, I haven't thought about blackening seafood since that time. This Virginia rockfish—a local nickname for striped bass—is a favorite catch that I've fished for decades. I recently realized that the Cool Smoke Rub had many of the elements of a blackening seasoning, so we tried it and it's great.

½ cup Cool Smoke Rub (page 49)

4 (6-ounce) skinless rockfish (striped bass) fillets, or substitute grouper or redfish

1 tablespoon unsalted butter, melted

2 tablespoons canola oil

Juice of ½ lemon

Prepare the Cool Smoke Rub.

Brush both sides of the rockfish with the melted butter and dust each fillet with 2 tablespoons of the Cool Smoke Rub (use 1 tablespoon on each side).

In a large cast-iron skillet, heat the canola oil over medium-high heat. When the oil begins to smoke, place the rockfish flesh-side down in the pan. Cook for 3 minutes, then carefully flip and cook for an additional 3 minutes, or until just cooked through.

Transfer the rockfish to a plate and top with the lemon juice. Serve immediately.

GRILLED OYSTERS
WITH THREE SAUCES

MAKES 4 SERVINGS

You'll need a good oyster knife. Please don't use a sharp knife, or you'll cut yourself. When the oysters are on the grill, check them frequently. As you see them pop open slightly, use a towel or tongs to remove them from the grill, let them cool enough to handle, and use an oyster knife to open them completely, being careful to retain the oyster liquor. If you leave them on the grill until they've all opened, many of the oysters will be overcooked. Place the oysters, opened, on a towel-lined platter or pan to serve.

Pineapple Mignonette (recipe follows)

Cocktail Sauce (recipe follows)

Spicy Butter (recipe follows)

24 fresh large oysters, unshucked, scrubbed

Prepare the Pineapple Mignonette and Cocktail Sauce.

When you are ready to cook, heat the grill to 400°F, using the direct grilling method (see Direct Cooking or Grilling, page 22).

Prepare the Spicy Butter just before you cook the oysters. Place the oysters, cup-side down, on the grill. Close the grill lid and cook for 3 to 4 minutes, then check to see if the oysters have begun to open. Remove any oysters that have begun to open and shuck them using an oyster knife. Serve immediately on the half shell with the trio of sauces on the side.

COCKTAIL SAUCE

MAKES ABOUT ¼ CUP

¼ cup Chili Catsup (page 65)

1 teaspoon prepared horseradish

Combine the catsup and horseradish in a small bowl, cover, and refrigerate until ready to use. Will keep refrigerated for up to 5 days

PINEAPPLE MIGNONETTE

MAKES ABOUT ½ CUP

¼ cup rice vinegar

1½ tablespoons minced shallot

1½ tablespoons minced pineapple

1½ tablespoons minced jalapeño

½ teaspoon coarsely ground black pepper

⅛ teaspoon kosher salt

Combine all the ingredients in a small bowl, cover, and refrigerate until ready to use. Can be made the day before.

SPICY BUTTER

MAKES ¼ CUP

2 tablespoons unsalted butter, melted

2 tablespoons hot sauce, your favorite brand

In a small bowl or a cup, whisk the ingredients together just prior to serving with the oysters.

GRILLED SHRIMP, SCALLOPS, AND MUSSELS

WITH LINGUINE

MAKES 6 SERVINGS

Ask your fishmonger to clean the seafood as specified in the ingredients list. It's critical not to overcook seafood, which is really easy to do with scallops and shrimp. Carefully follow these grilling times and you'll achieve the best results.

2 tablespoons plus 2 teaspoons Tarragon and Aleppo Rub (page 50)

1 teaspoon canola oil

2 cups diced bacon (from 26 to 28 slices)

½ cup minced shallots

½ cup dry white wine

2 cups heavy cream

2 teaspoons lemon zest

2 tablespoons kosher salt

18 large shrimp, peeled and deveined

12 sea scallops, abductor mussel removed

24 mussels, scrubbed and debearded

3 tablespoons unsalted butter

Nonstick cooking spray

12 ounces uncooked linguine

1½ cups frozen petite peas, defrosted

2 teaspoons chopped fresh tarragon

2 tablespoons chopped fresh chives

2 tablespoons chopped fresh flat-leaf parsley

Prepare the Tarragon and Aleppo Rub.

In a 3-quart saucepan, heat the canola oil over medium heat. Add the bacon and cook, stirring often with a wooden spoon, for 3 to 5 minutes,

until crisp. Reduce the heat to low, remove the bacon using a slotted spoon, and drain on paper towels. Discard all but 2 teaspoons of the rendered bacon fat from the pan.

Return the bacon to the pan and add the shallots and half the Tarragon and Aleppo Rub. Cook, stirring often, for 3 minutes, or until the shallots are translucent. Increase the heat to medium, pour in the wine, and cook for 3 to 5 minutes, or until the wine has reduced to about ⅛ cup. Add the cream and simmer for 5 minutes, or until the sauce thickens enough to coat the back of the wooden spoon. Remove from the heat and stir in the lemon zest. Cover and set aside.

Bring 4 to 6 quarts water and the salt to a boil in a large stockpot for the pasta. When the water comes to a rapid boil, cover and reduce the heat to medium.

When you are ready to cook the seafood, heat the grill to 400°F, using the direct grilling method (see Direct Cooking or Grilling, page 22).

Dust the shrimp and scallops with 1 tablespoon of the Tarragon and Aleppo Rub.

(continued)

Place the mussels on a piece of foil with the edges turned up to form a boat. Dust them with the remaining 1 teaspoon Tarragon and Aleppo Rub and top with the butter, cut into pieces.

Spray the grill grates with nonstick spray. Place the scallops and the foil packet of mussels on the grill, close the lid, and cook for 2 minutes. Add the shrimp to the grill, close the lid again, and cook for an additional 2 minutes. Use tongs to carefully flip the scallops and shrimp, close the lid, and cook for 2 minutes more.

Remove the shrimp from direct heat and place them on top of the mussels. Close the grill lid and cook for 2 minutes more. Add the scallops atop the shrimp and mussels, and transfer the foil packet to a plate. Draw the edges of the foil together so that the seafood stays warm but the packet is not completely sealed. Leave the shrimp, scallops, and mussels in the foil packet until ready to serve.

Return the water to a rapid boil and drop in the linguine. Cook, stirring occasionally to prevent sticking, for 8 to 10 minutes, until the pasta is al dente. Reserve ½ cup of the pasta water, then drain the pasta.

Add the pasta, peas, tarragon, chives, and parsley to the pot with the pasta sauce and toss to combine. If the sauce is too thick, add the reserved pasta water, 1 tablespoon at a time, to thin it.

Remove the seafood from the foil packet and discard the melted butter. Transfer the pasta to a serving platter, top with the seafood, and serve immediately.

SALMON
WITH CUCUMBER YOGURT SAUCE

MAKES 4 SERVINGS

Salmon is a perfect fish for grilling because of its high fat content, which provides moisture in cooking. Because it's not a fragile fish, it stands up to the heat of the grill well. If you like smoked salmon, you'll enjoy smoking this on the grill.

¼ cup plus 1 teaspoon Dill Rub (page 53)
4 (6-ounce) skin-on salmon fillets
Cucumber Yogurt Sauce (recipe follows)
Nonstick cooking spray

The day before you plan to grill, prepare the Dill Rub.

Lay out eight 12 x 12-inch pieces of plastic wrap on your work surface. Holding a portion of salmon over the plastic wrap, dust each evenly on all sides with 1 tablespoon of the Dill Rub. Wrap each portion of salmon tightly with two sheets of plastic wrap and refrigerate for 12 hours.

About 30 minutes before you plan to grill, make the Cucumber Yogurt Sauce.

When you are ready to cook, heat the grill to 400°F, using the direct grilling method (see Direct Cooking or Grilling, page 22).

Spray the grill grates with nonstick spray and place the salmon portions skin-side down directly on the grill. Close the lid and cook for 5 minutes, then turn the salmon, close the lid, and cook for an additional 5 minutes.

Serve each portion with 1 to 2 tablespoons of the Cucumber Yogurt Sauce and pass the remaining sauce around the table.

CUCUMBER YOGURT SAUCE

MAKES A GENEROUS 1½ CUPS

1 teaspoon Simple Syrup (page 74)
¾ cup sour cream
1 tablespoon plus 1 teaspoon fresh lemon juice
¼ teaspoon granulated garlic
2 tablespoons chopped fresh cilantro
¾ cup finely diced English cucumber

Prepare the Simple Syrup.

Combine the sour cream, lemon juice, garlic, Simple Syrup, cilantro, and cucumber in a small bowl. Cover and refrigerate until ready to use. Will keep refrigerated for 2 to 3 days.

HERB-STUFFED TROUT
WITH SAVORY ALMOND GRANOLA

MAKES 6 SERVINGS

Trout amandine is a classic French dish. This recipe adds a smoking-with-fire twist to the original, plus a rustic touch with the Savory Almond Granola garnish.

1 cup Savory Almond Granola (recipe follows)

6 tablespoons (¾ stick) unsalted butter

1 tablespoon canola oil

4 cups sliced leeks (halved lengthwise, then sliced crosswise into ¼-inch-thick half-moons)

½ cup thinly sliced shallots

1 tablespoon thinly sliced garlic cloves

4 sprigs fresh thyme

1 tablespoon plus 1 teaspoon kosher salt

1 teaspoon cracked black pepper

1 tablespoon minced fresh chives

1 tablespoon chopped fresh flat-leaf parsley

6 (12- to 16-ounce) head-on rainbow trout, butterflied

Nonstick cooking spray

Juice of 1 lemon

Prepare the Savory Almond Granola.

In a large sauté pan, melt 1 tablespoon of the butter with the canola oil over medium-low heat. Add the leeks, shallots, garlic, and thyme and cook, stirring often, for 10 minutes, until the leeks are soft and translucent. Stir in 1 teaspoon of the salt and ⅛ teaspoon of the pepper. Remove the pan from the heat and fold in the chives and parsley. Set aside until ready to serve.

Place the butterflied trout skin-side down on a rimmed baking sheet. Melt 4 tablespoons of the butter and brush the flesh of the trout with half the melted butter, then dust with ½ teaspoon of the salt and ⅛ teaspoon of the pepper.

Remove the thyme sprigs from the stuffing mixture. Spread a thin layer of the leek stuffing on the right half of each trout. Fold the other side of the trout over the filling, brush the outside of each fish with half the remaining melted butter, and season with a pinch each of salt and pepper. Carefully turn and brush each on the opposite side with the remaining butter, and season with a pinch each of salt and pepper. Set aside at room temperature while you prepare the grill.

When you are ready to cook, heat the grill to 400°F, using the direct grilling method (see Direct Cooking or Grilling, page 22).

Spray the grill grates with nonstick spray. Carefully place each stuffed trout directly on the grill, close the lid, and cook for 4 minutes. Use a long metal spatula to carefully roll each trout over their backbone onto the other side (this way, the stuffing won't fall out). Close the lid again and cook for an additional 4 minutes, or until the flesh nearest the backbone is white and opaque. Carefully transfer the trout to a serving platter.

(continued)

Garnish the platter of fish with the lemon juice and 1 tablespoon melted butter. Sprinkle the Savory Almond Granola evenly over the fish and serve immediately.

SAVORY ALMOND GRANOLA

MAKES 2 CUPS

4 tablespoons (½ stick) unsalted butter, melted

1 tablespoon sugar

1 teaspoon granulated garlic

1 teaspoon kosher salt

½ teaspoon chipotle chile powder (available in most major groceries)

½ teaspoon smoked paprika

1½ cups whole skin-on almonds, coarsely chopped

½ cup rolled oats

2 egg whites

Preheat the oven to 300°F. Line a large baking sheet with a silicone baking mat or parchment paper.

In a large bowl, stir together the melted butter, sugar, garlic, salt, chipotle powder, and smoked paprika until well combined. Add the almonds and oats and toss to thoroughly coat.

In a small bowl, whisk the egg whites until they hold soft peaks. Gently fold the egg whites into the almond-oat mixture until just combined. Spread the granola over the prepared baking sheet in an even layer.

Bake the granola for 30 to 45 minutes, stirring every 10 minutes, until golden brown. Let the granola cool to room temperature on the baking sheet. Transfer the cooled granola to an airtight container and store at room temperature for up to 2 weeks.

MARINATED VENISON BACKSTRAP

MAKES 2 SERVINGS

The backstrap refers to the loin, the most tender cut of venison. This cut in particular is best cooked to rare or medium-rare. If venison is overcooked, the gamey flavors become more pronounced. Cumberland Sauce (page 58), a classic condiment created for game meats, pairs well with this dish.

1 tablespoon Venison Rub (page 54)

Venison Marinade (recipe follows)

1 (1-pound) venison backstrap (see Source Guide, page 279)

Prepare the Venison Rub and the Venison Marinade.

Place the venison in a resealable plastic bag, add the Venison Marinade, seal the bag, and turn until the marinade is distributed over all the meat. Refrigerate for 4 hours, then remove the meat from the plastic bag and discard any solids clinging to the venison. Season the venison with the Venison Rub and let it sit at room temperature for 30 minutes before grilling.

When you are ready to cook, heat the grill to 400°F, using the direct grilling method (see Direct Cooking or Grilling, page 22).

Place the venison directly on the grill and cook for 4 minutes, then flip it and cook for another 4 to 6 minutes, or until a meat thermometer placed in the thickest part of the backstrap reads an internal temperature of 126°F. Remove from the heat and let the venison rest for 5 minutes before slicing.

VENISON MARINADE

MAKES ABOUT ¾ CUP

½ cup olive oil

¼ bunch parsley, stems only

2 garlic cloves, thinly sliced

1½ teaspoons whole pink peppercorns, crushed using a mallet or the flat side of a knife

1½ teaspoons whole black peppercorns, crushed using a mallet or the flat side of a knife

1 teaspoon coriander seeds, crushed using a mallet or the flat side of a knife

1½ teaspoons juniper berries, crushed using a mallet or the flat side of a knife

Combine all the ingredients in a small bowl.

RACK OF LAMB
WITH BALSAMIC DRIZZLE

When the weather starts to warm up in spring, people like to fire up their grills. This just happens to coincide with lamb season. Lamb is best cooked rare to medium-rare. Position the bones curve-side up on the cooler part of the grill so they don't burn, or cover them with foil.

¼ cup Poultry Rub (page 49)

2 racks lamb, trimmed (ask your butcher to do this)

½ cup balsamic vinegar

Prepare the Poultry Seasoning.

Season the lamb evenly on all sides with the Poultry Seasoning and let it sit, uncovered, at room temperature for 30 minutes.

While the lamb is resting, in a small nonstick pan, heat the vinegar over medium-low heat, stirring, for 5 to 7 minutes, until the vinegar has reduced by half. Be careful not to overreduce the vinegar, as this will make it bitter. Set aside until ready to serve.

When you are ready to cook the lamb, heat the grill to 400°F, using the direct grilling method (see Direct Cooking or Grilling, page 22).

Place the lamb directly on the grill and cook for 5 minutes, then flip it and cook for 5 to 7 minutes more, or until a meat thermometer placed in the thickest part of the meat reads an internal temperature of 126°F. Remove the lamb from the heat and let it rest for 5 minutes before carving.

Slice the lamb between the bones and transfer the meat to a platter. Drizzle with the balsamic reduction and serve immediately.

HALIBUT
WITH PISTACHIO, LEMON, AND HERBS

The flavors in this dish are reminiscent of gremolata, a traditional Italian herb garnish of lemon, garlic, and parsley. By using granulated garlic as opposed to fresh garlic, you are able to grill the fish without burning the garlic. We like the combination of the delicate halibut with the crunchiness of the pistachios.

½ cup chopped toasted pistachios

2 tablespoons chopped fresh flat-leaf parsley

1 teaspoon lemon zest

2 tablespoons plus 1 teaspoon olive oil

2⅛ teaspoons salt

4 (6-ounce) portions halibut, skin removed

½ teaspoon cracked black pepper

Scant ⅛ teaspoon granulated garlic

Nonstick cooking spray

½ lemon

In a small bowl, combine the pistachios, parsley, lemon zest, 2 tablespoons of the olive oil, and ⅛ teaspoon of the salt. Cover and refrigerate until ready to use.

Brush the halibut portions with the remaining 1 teaspoon olive oil.

In a separate small bowl, combine the remaining 2 teaspoons salt, the pepper, and the granulated garlic. Season the halibut evenly on both sides with this mixture.

When you are ready to cook, heat the grill to 400°F, using the direct grilling method (see Direct Cooking or Grilling, page 22).

Spray the grill grates with nonstick spray and place the halibut portions directly on the grill. Close the grill lid and cook for 5 minutes, then carefully flip the halibut, close the lid, and cook for 5 minutes more.

Transfer to a platter and top each portion with one-quarter of the pistachio mixture and a squeeze of lemon juice. Serve immediately.

SMOKED VENISON MEAT LOAF
WITH CHILI CATSUP

MAKES 6 TO 8 SERVINGS

If you are a hunter, ask your processor for an 80/20, or 75/25, meat-to-fat ratio for this dish. By grinding the lean, tough cuts of venison, your end product will be far more tender.

1 tablespoon olive oil

½ cup finely diced green bell pepper

½ cup finely diced yellow onion

½ cup finely diced celery

2 tablespoons Fennel Garlic Rub (page 53)

2 cups ground venison (1 pound)

1 cup fine bread crumbs

2 large eggs

2 tablespoons Worcestershire sauce

1½ cups Chili Catsup (page 65)

In a small sauté pan, heat the olive oil over medium-low heat. Add the bell pepper, onion, and celery and cook, stirring, for 3 to 5 minutes, until soft. Transfer the vegetables to a large bowl to cool to room temperature.

Prepare the Fennel Garlic Rub.

When the veggies are cool, add the ground venison, bread crumbs, Fennel Garlic Rub, eggs, and Worcestershire to the bowl. Use your hands to gently mix until all the ingredients are well incorporated.

When you are ready to cook, heat the grill to 300°F, using the 2-Zone method (see 2-Zone Cooking, page 22). Line a baking sheet with aluminum foil.

Use your hands to shape the ground venison mixture into an 8 x 5 x 2-inch loaf and place it on the lined baking sheet.

Place the baking sheet on the cool side of the grill and cook for 1 hour, or until a meat thermometer placed in the middle of the meat loaf reads an internal temperature of 155°F. Remove from the heat and set the meat loaf aside to rest for 5 minutes.

Prepare the Chili Catsup.

To serve, top the meat loaf with ¾ cup of the Chili Catsup and pass the remaining sauce around the table.

SMOKED VENISON STROGANOFF

Everybody loves beef stroganoff, a quintessential comfort dish. The smoked venison in this recipe adds an interesting twist to a classic.

---

1 tablespoon plus 1 teaspoon Venison Rub (page 54)

2 pounds venison roast or quarter, cut into 1-inch cubes

½ cup apple juice, in a spray bottle, for the grill

¼ cup canola oil

8 cups quartered or sliced cremini mushrooms

2 cups finely diced yellow onion

4 tablespoons (½ stick) butter, at room temperature

¼ cup thinly sliced garlic

2 teaspoons kosher salt

1 teaspoon freshly ground black pepper

1 cup cognac

1 pound dried egg noodles, cooked according to the package directions

3 cups chicken stock

½ cup Dijon mustard

1 teaspoon smoked paprika

¾ cup sour cream

2 tablespoons fresh lemon juice

¼ cup chopped fresh flat-leaf parsley

Prepare the Venison Rub.

Cover a rimmed baking sheet with parchment paper or aluminum foil.

Arrange the cubed venison on the baking sheet in one layer with all the cubes touching. Dust the meat with ½ tablespoon of the Venison Rub, then use your hands to flip the venison cubes over and dust again with

another ½ tablespoon of the Venison Rub. Transfer the seasoned cubes to a wire rack.

When you are ready to cook, heat the smoker to 300°F pit temperature (see Smoke, page 25). Alternatively, heat a grill to 300°F, using the 2-Zone setup (see 2-Zone Cooking, page 22).

Place the wire rack of venison in the smoker or on the cool side of the grill. Close the lid and cook for 30 to 40 minutes, spraying the meat with apple juice every 15 minutes to moisten. The venison is done when a meat thermometer placed in the thickest part reads an internal temperature of 135°F. Remove the venison from the smoker or grill and set aside to cool to room temperature. Slice the cooled cubes into thirds and set aside.

In a heavy-bottomed 4-quart saucepan, heat the canola oil over medium-high heat. Add the mushrooms and cook, stirring often with a wooden spoon, for 5 to 7 minutes, until golden. Reduce the heat to medium, add the onion, and cook, stirring often, for 3 to 5 minutes more, until the onion is soft. Add the butter, garlic, salt, and pepper and cook, stirring, for 1 minute, then remove the pot from heat and deglaze with the cognac, using a wooden spoon to scrape up and incorporate any browned bits from the bottom of the pan. Return the pot to medium heat and cook, stirring often, for 3 to 5 minutes, or until the cognac has reduced to ⅓ cup.

(continued)

Meanwhile, prepare the egg noodles according to the package directions.

When the cognac has reduced, add the stock, mustard, remaining 1 teaspoon Venison Rub, and the smoked paprika to the saucepan and cook for 8 to 10 minutes, or until the sauce thickens enough to coat the back of the wooden spoon. Remove from the heat and fold in the sliced venison, sour cream, lemon juice, and parsley.

Toss with the egg noodles and serve immediately.

SMOKED VENISON STEW

MAKES 6 TO 8 SERVINGS

Having tested this recipe many times, the most important thing we learned is to add the smoked venison to the finished stew base. If you cook the venison in the stew base, it will be too tough.

1 cup dried pinto beans

2 teaspoons Smoked Chili Powder (page 50)

2 pounds venison roast or quarter, cut into 1-inch cubes

1 tablespoon plus 2 teaspoons kosher salt

½ cup apple juice, in a spray bottle, for the grill

1 tablespoon canola oil

1½ cups medium-dice yellow onion

1½ cups medium-dice green bell pepper

1½ cups medium-dice celery root

¼ cup minced jalapeño

1 tablespoon thinly sliced garlic

1 teaspoon freshly ground black pepper

½ teaspoon ground cinnamon

1 teaspoon unsweetened cocoa powder

1 (14.5-ounce) can whole peeled tomatoes, coarsely chopped, juice reserved

5 cups chicken stock

The day before you plan to cook, place the pinto beans in a medium bowl or pot with 1 quart water, and let them soak overnight, uncovered.

The next day, drain and rinse the beans, discarding any broken ones or stones. Set aside until ready to use.

Prepare the Smoked Chili Powder.

Cover a rimmed baking sheet with parchment paper or aluminum foil. Arrange the cubed venison on the baking sheet in one layer with all the cubes touching. Dust the meat with ½ teaspoon of the Smoked Chili Powder and ½ teaspoon of the salt, then use your hands to flip the venison cubes over and dust again with ½ teaspoon of the Smoked Chili Powder and ½ teaspoon of the salt. Transfer the seasoned cubes to a wire rack.

When you are ready to cook, heat the smoker to 300°F pit temperature (see Smoke, page 25). Alternatively, heat a grill to 300°F, using the 2-Zone setup (see 2-Zone Cooking, page 22).

Place the wire rack of venison in the smoker or on the cool side of the grill and cook for 30 to 40 minutes, spraying the meat with apple juice every 15 minutes to moisten. The venison is done when a meat thermometer placed in the thickest part of the meat reads an internal temperature of 135°F. Remove the wire rack from the smoker or grill and set the venison aside to cool to room temperature. Slice the cooled cubes into thirds and set aside.

In a heavy-bottomed 4-quart pot, heat the canola oil over medium-low heat. Add the onion, bell pepper, celery root, and jalapeño and cook, stirring often with a wooden spoon, for 5 minutes. Stir in the garlic and season with the remaining 1 tablespoon plus 1 teaspoon salt, the black pepper, cinnamon, and cocoa powder, and cook, stirring continuously, for 3 minutes. Stir in the tomato, stock, and the drained pinto beans and simmer 60 to 75 minutes, uncovered, until the beans are tender.

Remove from the heat, cover, and let the stew rest for 1 hour.

Return the pot to medium-low heat, add the cubed venison, and gently simmer for 2 to 3 minutes, until the stew is warmed through. Taste and adjust the seasoning as necessary, and serve in bowls.

SIDE DISHES SERVED WITH BARBECUE ARE OFTEN LIMITED
to the traditional—potato salad, coleslaw, and baked beans, all
of which I love. When I was working on the first menu for our
barbecue restaurant, I decided to offer more side dishes to
complement the meats. This chapter is packed with fresh twists
on classic dishes—and some bound-to-be-favorite new recipes.
You will find that the traditional recipes in this chapter are all a
little unique (see Grilled Potato Salad, page 223) and add some
new flavors to old favorites.

A lot of great regional and seasonal dishes pair well with barbecue, and I've included many of those for you. Because stone
fruit and ears of corn are best eaten fresh during the summer
months, the Farro and Stone Fruit Salad (page 221) and Grilled
Corn on the Cob (page 227) will be best enjoyed during the
summer. For fall and winter bounties, apples and root vegetables become the prime ingredients for Caramelized Applesauce
(page 233) and Roasted Root Vegetables (page 237).

All these dishes were developed to be great additions to
the meat recipes in this book. While some side dishes were
developed for a specific dish, most go well with other meats.
For example, the Sautéed Cabbage, Sun-Dried Cherries, and
Spiced Pecans (page 217) was specifically created to accompany Goose Pastrami (page 184), but it also pairs nicely with
beef or chicken.

I think these side dishes are stars, and I think you will, too.

As with all food, buy the best-quality ingredients you can
source and cook them with care.

SAUTÉED CABBAGE, SUN-DRIED CHERRIES, AND SPICED PECANS

This dish was created to accompany Goose Pastrami (page 184). The idea came from the classic combination of pastrami and sauerkraut, which I love. It's a great accompaniment to brisket, grilled goose breast, and pork chops, too.

1½ tablespoons Goose Rub (page 53)

½ cup Spiced Pecans (page 73)

2 tablespoons canola oil

½ large yellow onion, julienned

6 cups shredded cabbage

½ cup sun-dried cherries

2 tablespoons rice wine vinegar

3 tablespoons sour cream

Prepare the Goose Rub and the Spiced Pecans.

In a large sauté pan, heat the canola oil over medium heat. Add the onion and cook, stirring, for 3 to 5 minutes, until translucent. Stir in the cabbage, 1¼ tablespoons of the Goose Rub, and the cherries, and cook, stirring often, for 5 to 7 minutes, until the cabbage is slightly wilted but still a bit crunchy.

Deglaze the pan using the vinegar, scraping up any bits from the bottom. Cook, stirring occasionally, for 3 to 5 minutes more. Remove from the heat and fold in the sour cream. Stir in the Spiced Pecans, taste, and adjust the seasoning with the remaining Goose Rub, as needed. Serve immediately.

GRILLED VEGETABLE SALAD

MAKES 6 TO 8 SERVINGS

This is a perfect dish to partner with chops, steaks, or seafood when you want to make your whole meal outside on the grill, using the best of the summer produce. While I personally love this combination of vegetables, you can add or subtract available produce throughout the other seasons.

½ cup Spiced Pecans (page 73)

5 ears corn, shucked and rinsed

½ red onion, quartered, core intact

2 medium yellow squash, halved lengthwise

2 tablespoons olive oil

Kosher salt and freshly ground black pepper

2 cups large-dice tomatoes (about 2 medium)

½ cup apple cider vinegar

¼ cup fresh flat-leaf parsley leaves

2 tablespoons torn fresh basil leaves

Prepare the Spiced Pecans. These can be made the same day or earlier.

Prepare the grill for direct-heat cooking (see Direct Cooking or Grilling, page 22) and preheat to 300°F.

Lightly brush the corn, onion, and squash with the olive oil and season with salt and pepper.

Grill the corn for 3 minutes, then roll it a quarter turn and grill for 3 minutes more. Roll two more times for a total grilling time of 12 minutes, ensuring the whole ear is charred.

Meanwhile, grill the onion quarters and squash halves for 3 minutes on each side, to ensure uniform grill marks.

Set the vegetables aside on a clean surface, or a cutting board, until they are cool enough to handle.

Hold each corncob over a large bowl. Using a sharp knife, cut downward to slice the kernels from the cobs into the bowl. Slice the squash into ½-inch-thick half-moons and add those to the bowl.

In the same bowl, gently toss the corn kernels and squash with the onion quarters, tomatoes, vinegar, Spiced Pecans, parsley, and basil. Season with salt and pepper and serve immediately.

DILL COLESLAW

You can serve this chilled or at room temperature—it tastes good either way. If you make it the day before, don't add the dressing—the slaw will wilt. Just refrigerate both separately. For crunchy coleslaw, you may add the dressing just before serving, or a maximum of 1 to 2 hours before serving, and toss again just before plating.

DRESSING

1 cup Duke's Mayonnaise, or your favorite brand

¼ cup apple cider vinegar

3 tablespoons sugar

¾ teaspoon celery seeds

¾ teaspoon kosher salt

¼ teaspoon freshly ground black pepper

SLAW

6 cups julienned green cabbage (about 1¼ pounds)

½ cup julienned carrot

½ cup julienned Granny Smith apple

½ tablespoon chopped fresh dill

Kosher salt and freshly ground black pepper

Make the dressing: In a small bowl, whisk together the mayonnaise, vinegar, sugar, celery seeds, salt, and pepper and set aside.

Make the slaw: In a large bowl, combine the cabbage, carrots, apples, and dill. Add the mayonnaise dressing and toss to combine. Season with salt and pepper.

Serve chilled or at room temperature.

FARRO AND STONE FRUIT SALAD

MAKES 6 TO 8 SERVINGS

This dish can be made in advance and refrigerated. It transports well in a cooler, so it's perfect for picnics and tailgate parties. It also pairs well with the Tarragon and Aleppo Chicken Leg Quarters (page 161).

4 cups cooked and cooled farro (available at most groceries and Italian markets)

2 medium romaine lettuce hearts, halved lengthwise

2 tablespoons plus 1 teaspoon olive oil

Kosher salt and freshly ground black pepper

4 large peaches (or your choice of assorted stone fruit), pitted and sliced

¼ cup plus 1 tablespoon apple cider vinegar

½ cup roasted pistachios, coarsely chopped

2 tablespoons torn fresh basil leaves

2 tablespoons torn fresh mint leaves

2 tablespoons fresh tarragon leaves

Prepare the grill for direct-heat cooking (see Direct Cooking or Grilling, page 22) and pre-heat to 300°F. Prepare the farro according to the package instructions.

When completed, spread the hot, cooked farro out on a baking sheet in a thin layer, and let it cool to room temperature.

Lightly brush each romaine half with 1 table-spoon of the olive oil, and season with salt and pepper. Grill the romaine halves for 3 minutes on each side, turning to ensure uniform grill marks. Set aside to cool to room temperature.

In a large bowl, toss the peaches with the vinegar and set aside to marinate for about 5 minutes. In the meantime, slice the cooled romaine hearts into ¼-inch-thick pieces.

Add the farro and romaine slices to the bowl with the peaches and toss with the remaining olive oil, the pistachios, and the fresh herbs. Season with salt and pepper and serve immediately.

GRILLED POTATO SALAD
WITH SOFT-BOILED EGGS

We hold these things to be self-evident: Potato salads are always good with grilled meats. In an effort to come up with a unique version that we really love, we grilled the potatoes, onions, and scallions to give them a good char. We incorporated our own Bread-and-Butter Pickles, and finished with soft-boiled eggs, which are halved so the runny yolks help dress the salad.

1 cup Grainy Mustard Dressing (page 224), plus more for serving

3 pounds baby potatoes, mixed colors

¼ cup kosher salt, plus more as needed

5 medium eggs

1 large yellow onion, halved, with core intact

3 bunches scallions

2 tablespoons olive oil

Freshly ground black pepper

12 slices crispy cooked bacon, finely chopped

1 cup drained Bread-and-Butter Pickles (page 74) or store bought

¼ cup fresh flat-leaf parsley leaves

⅛ cup fresh dill

2 cups finely diced celery

Prepare the Grainy Mustard Dressing.

When you are ready to cook, heat the grill to 300°F using the direct grilling method (see Direct Cooking or Grilling, page 22).

Put the potatoes in a heavy-bottomed 4-quart pot and add enough cold water to cover. Stir in the salt, bring the water to a boil over high heat, then reduce the heat to maintain a simmer and cook for 5 to 8 minutes, or until the potatoes are just tender. Drain and set the potatoes aside to cool to room temperature.

While the potatoes are cooking, put the eggs in a small pot and add enough cold water to cover. Bring to a boil over medium-high heat, then remove the pot from the heat, cover, and let stand for 6 minutes. Gently drain the eggs, and use a large slotted spoon to carefully transfer them to a bowl of ice water to chill until they are cool enough to peel.

Cut the potatoes in half. Lightly brush the potatoes, onion halves, and scallions with olive oil and season to taste with salt and pepper. Grill the potatoes cut-side down over direct heat, with the grill lid open, for 10 minutes. Rotate the potatoes 45 degrees, still cut-side down, and cook for 5 minutes more to char them. Flip the potatoes and cook for 5 minutes more, for a total grill time of 20 minutes. Set aside.

Next, grill the onions and scallions. Place the onion halves cut-side down over direct heat, with the grill lid open, and cook for 3 minutes. Rotate them 45 degrees, still cut-side down, and grill for 3 minutes more to char them. Set the onions aside.

Grill the scallions for 1 minute on each side until just charred, being careful not to burn them.

(continued)

Set the vegetables aside to cool at room temperature, then slice the onions and scallions into ¼-inch-wide slices.

To assemble the salad, toss the potatoes, onions, scallions, bacon, pickles, parsley, dill, celery, and Grainy Mustard Dressing together in a large bowl. Season with salt and pepper. Transfer to a serving platter.

Peel and halve the eggs and arrange them on the platter. Serve immediately.

GRAINY MUSTARD DRESSING

MAKES 2 CUPS

½ cup plus 1 tablespoon apple cider vinegar

¼ cup plus 2 tablespoons whole-grain mustard

1 tablespoon plus 1 teaspoon honey

1 cup olive oil

Kosher salt and freshly ground black pepper

Combine vinegar, mustard, and honey in a large bowl. While whisking continuously, gradually add the olive oil and whisk until emulsified. Season with salt and pepper. Store in an airtight container in the refrigerator until ready to use, up to 1 week.

COLLARD GREENS
WITH PEPPER RELISH

MAKES 4 SERVINGS

If collard greens aren't available at the store or your farmers' market, you can substitute other greens such as kale or mustard greens. Keep in mind that your cooking time may differ according to the kind of greens you substitute. Don't skimp on the pepper relish, because the acidity brings brightness to the overall flavor of this Southern staple.

2 tablespoons Caramel Simple Syrup (page 74)

¼ cup Pepper Relish (page 58)

¼ cup olive oil

3 smoked bacon slices, cut in ¼-inch pieces

5 garlic cloves, thinly sliced

½ cup thinly sliced leeks

2 bunches collard greens (about 1 pound), washed and stemmed

½ teaspoon ground Espelette pepper (see Source Guide, page 279)

1 teaspoon kosher salt

½ teaspoon black pepper

4 ounces country ham, thinly sliced

Prepare the Caramel Simple Syrup and the Pepper Relish.

In a heavy-bottomed 4-quart saucepan or Dutch oven, heat the olive oil over medium-low heat. When the oil is hot, add the bacon and cook for 3 minutes, or until the bacon is lightly browned and slightly crispy. Reduce the heat to low and add the garlic and leeks. Cook, stirring continuously, for 3 minutes, until the garlic is a golden color. Be careful not to burn the garlic.

Add the collard greens, Espelette, and salt and stir to combine. Add 1 quart water and the Caramel Simple Syrup, stir to combine, and cook, covered, for 1 hour. The collards are done when they are tender.

Before serving, add the Pepper Relish and ham and stir to combine. Season with salt and pepper and serve immediately.

GRILLED CORN ON THE COB
WITH CHIPOTLE WHITE SAUCE

By soaking the corn overnight, it absorbs enough moisture to steam in the husk while on the grill. Additionally, the husk doesn't burn. When you take it off the grill, peel the husk back, and either remove it or leave it on as a decorative garnish or handle.

6 to 8 ears corn, with husks

1 cup Chipotle White Sauce (page 63)

¼ cup whole fresh cilantro leaves

⅛ cup fresh oregano leaves

Place the ears of corn in their husks in a lidded container with enough water to cover and refrigerate overnight.

Prepare the Chipotle White Sauce.

When you are ready to cook, heat the grill to 300°F, using the 2-Zone setup (see 2-Zone Cooking, page 22).

Place the ears of corn in their husks on the cool side of the grill and cook for 15 minutes, then flip and cook for 15 minutes more, or until the corn is tender. Remove from the grill and set aside until cool enough to handle.

Peel the husks and silk back from the ears, but do not remove them from the cobs. Brush the ears lightly with Chipotle White Sauce and place them on the cool side of the grill, positioning the husks with the silks so that they hang over the edge, away from the heat. Grill for 5 minutes, turning halfway through to cook evenly on all sides.

Transfer to a platter with the husks still on, and drizzle the corn with additional Chipotle White Sauce. Serve the remaining sauce on the side. Sprinkle each ear with cilantro and oregano and serve immediately.

GREEN BEAN SALAD
WITH SPICY ALMOND GRANOLA

MAKES 4 SERVINGS

Don't fret that the recipe for the Spicy Almond Granola makes more than you need for the green bean salad. You'll enjoy it for breakfast with yogurt and a little honey!

1 cup Spicy Almond Granola (recipe follows)

¼ cup Yogurt Dressing (recipe follows)

2 tablespoons kosher salt, plus more as needed

½ pound fresh green beans, trimmed

¼ cup dried cranberries

2 tablespoons fresh tarragon leaves

Prepare the Spicy Almond Granola and the Yogurt Dressing.

Fill a 4-quart stockpot with 2 quarts cold water, add the salt, and bring to a boil over medium-high heat. Add the green beans and cook for 3 to 5 minutes. The beans are done when they are bright green and al dente. Drain, and plunge them immediately into a bowl of ice water to cool. Once cool, drain the beans again, turn them out onto a paper towel–lined plate or platter, and pat them dry with paper towels.

In a large bowl, toss the beans with the cranberries, Yogurt Dressing, Spicy Almond Granola, and tarragon. Season with salt and serve immediately.

SPICY ALMOND GRANOLA

MAKES 4½ CUPS

8 tablespoons (1 stick) unsalted butter, melted

1 cup sugar

4 teaspoons dried tarragon

2 teaspoons freshly ground pink peppercorns

1 teaspoon Espelette pepper (see Source Guide, page 279)

1 teaspoon Maldon sea salt (see Source Guide, page 279)

3 cups whole skin-on almonds, coarsely chopped

1 cup rolled oats

3 egg whites

Preheat the oven to 300°F. Line a baking sheet with a silicone baking mat or parchment paper.

In a large bowl, stir together the melted butter, sugar, tarragon, pink peppercorns, Espelette, and sea salt. Add the almonds and oats and toss to thoroughly coat.

(continued)

In a small bowl, whisk the egg whites until they hold soft peaks. Gently fold the egg whites into the almond-oat mixture. Spread the granola out on the prepared baking sheet in an even layer, and bake for 30 to 45 minutes, stirring every 10 minutes, until golden brown.

Set the baking sheet aside and let the mixture cool to room temperature. Use your hands to break the granola into bite-size pieces. The granola may be stored in an airtight container at room temperature for up to 2 weeks.

YOGURT DRESSING

MAKES ½ CUP

¼ **cup plain Greek yogurt**

¼ **cup Duke's Mayonnaise, or your favorite brand**

¼ **teaspoon granulated garlic**

¼ **teaspoon Espelette pepper (see Source Guide, page 279)**

¼ **teaspoon freshly ground pink peppercorns**

1 **tablespoon fresh lemon juice**

1 **tablespoon chopped fresh tarragon**

Whisk together all the ingredients thoroughly in a medium bowl. Transfer to an airtight container and refrigerate until ready to use, up to 1 day.

GREEN BEAN, WHITE BEAN, AND ARUGULA SALAD

2 tablespoons plus ½ teaspoon kosher salt, plus more as needed

½ pound green beans, trimmed

⅔ cup Spiced Pecans (page 73)

1½ cups canned white beans, drained and rinsed

2 cups packed baby arugula

1 cup shaved Grana Padano or Parmesan cheese

2 garlic cloves, thinly sliced

¼ teaspoon freshly ground black pepper, plus more as needed

2 tablespoons olive oil

2 teaspoons fresh lemon juice

Fill a 4-quart stockpot with 2 quarts cold water, add 2 tablespoons of the salt, and bring to a boil over medium-high heat. Add the green beans and cook for 3 to 5 minutes. The beans are done when they are bright green and al dente. Drain, and plunge them immediately into a bowl of ice water to cool. Once cool, drain the beans again, turn them out onto a paper towel–lined plate or platter, and pat them dry with paper towels.

Prepare the Spiced Pecans.

In a large bowl, combine the green beans, white beans, baby arugula, Spiced Pecans, cheese, garlic, remaining ½ teaspoon salt, pepper, olive oil, and lemon juice. Gently toss, season with salt and pepper, and serve immediately.

RED POTATO SALAD
WITH TANGY HERB DRESSING

MAKES 4 SERVINGS

This potato salad features a dressing reminiscent of Green Goddess, which I confess is one of my all-time favorites.

¾ cup Tangy Herb Dressing (recipe follows)

1 pound small red potatoes

3 tablespoons kosher salt, plus more as needed

Freshly ground black pepper

8 cornichons, halved lengthwise and sliced on an angle

2 hard-boiled eggs, cut into large chunks

Prepare the Tangy Herb Dressing.

Put the potatoes and salt in a heavy-bottomed 3-quart pot and add enough cold water to cover. Bring to a boil over medium-high heat, then reduce the heat and simmer for 5 to 8 minutes, or until just tender. Drain and set aside to cool to room temperature.

When they are cool enough to handle, cut the potatoes into bite-size chunks and transfer them to a large bowl. Season with salt and pepper and toss with ¼ cup of the dressing to thoroughly coat.

Add the cornichons and eggs and gently toss. Cover and refrigerate for at least 1 hour before serving. When you are ready to serve, adjust the seasoning to taste and toss with the remaining dressing to taste, or pass the dressing around the table.

TANGY HERB DRESSING

MAKES ABOUT ¾ CUP

½ cup Duke's Mayonnaise, or your favorite brand

⅛ cup sour cream

¼ teaspoon kosher salt

⅛ teaspoon cracked black pepper

⅛ teaspoon cayenne pepper

1½ teaspoons fresh lemon juice

1½ teaspoons distilled white vinegar

1 tablespoon coarsely chopped fresh basil

1 tablespoon picked fresh tarragon

In a medium bowl, combine all the ingredients and stir to combine. Transfer to an airtight container and refrigerate until ready to use.

CARAMELIZED APPLESAUCE

MAKES 6 TO 8 SERVINGS

What makes this applesauce unique are the fennel pollen and caramelized apples.

Juice of 1 lemon

3 pounds tart green apples (such as Granny Smith), peeled, cored, and cut into medium chunks

½ teaspoon ground cinnamon

¼ teaspoon ground mace

¼ teaspoon freshly ground cloves

1 tablespoon plus 2 teaspoons sugar

2 teaspoons kosher salt

1½ teaspoons fennel pollen

Squeeze the lemon juice into a large bowl and add 2 quarts cold water. Place the apples in the acidulated water to keep them from browning. Drain before cooking.

In a heavy-bottomed 3-quart saucepan, combine the apples, cinnamon, mace, cloves, sugar, salt, and fennel pollen. Cover and cook over medium-low heat for 15 minutes, or until the apples have softened. Remove the lid and increase the heat to medium. Cook, stirring often and mashing the apples with a wooden spoon, for 5 to 10 minutes more, until they caramelize. Remove the pot from the heat and set aside to cool completely. Transfer the applesauce to an airtight container and refrigerate until ready to serve, up to 5 days.

MACARONI AND CHEESE
WITH SMOKED PAPRIKA

MAKES 8 TO 12 SERVINGS

This version of macaroni and cheese is not just for kids. We chose Fontina, Gruyère, and smoked cheddar cheese to create a smooth-textured sauce that is popular with adults because it is a bit more sophisticated.

Garlic and Smoked Paprika Bread Crumbs
(recipe follows)

6 tablespoons (¾ stick) unsalted butter,
plus more for greasing

5½ cups whole milk

½ cup all-purpose flour

4 tablespoons kosher salt

1 tablespoon plus 1 teaspoon mustard powder

1 teaspoon freshly ground black pepper

1 teaspoon cayenne pepper

3 cups Fontina cheese

1½ cups Gruyère cheese

1 pound cavatappi pasta

1 teaspoon olive oil

1½ cups grated smoked cheddar cheese

Prepare the Garlic and Smoked Paprika Bread Crumbs.

Preheat the oven to 375°F. Butter a 9 x 13-inch casserole dish. Bring a large pot of water to a rapid boil.

Heat the milk in a small saucepan over medium-low heat, but do not allow it to boil.

Meanwhile, in a large pot, melt the butter over medium-low heat. When the foam subsides, stir in the flour and reduce the heat to low.

Whisk continuously for 2 minutes, then begin gradually adding the hot milk as you whisk, and cook for 10 minutes, until the mixture is thick and bubbling.

Remove the pot from the heat and add 2 tablespoons of the salt, mustard powder, black pepper, cayenne, Fontina, and Gruyère. Whisk until all the ingredients are thoroughly combined and the cheeses have melted. Set aside.

Meanwhile, add the remaining 2 tablespoons salt to the boiling water. Add the pasta, stir gently, and return the water to a boil. Cook for 11 minutes, or until the pasta is not quite al dente. Drain, and rinse the pasta with cold water to halt the cooking process. Drain well again, and toss in a large bowl with the olive oil to prevent the pasta from sticking.

Fold the cooked pasta into the cheese sauce to coat. Pour the mixture into the prepared casserole. Sprinkle the smoked cheddar cheese evenly over the top and bake for 25 to 30 minutes, until the cheese is golden brown and bubbling.

Let the macaroni and cheese cool for 10 minutes, then top with the Garlic and Smoked Paprika Bread Crumbs and serve immediately.

(continued)

GARLIC AND SMOKED PAPRIKA BREAD CRUMBS

1 cup canola oil

3 large or 5 small garlic cloves

1 (26-inch) baguette, crust removed, cut into ½-inch cubes

1 tablespoon smoked paprika

1 teaspoon kosher salt

Line a small rimmed baking sheet with paper towels.

Puree the garlic cloves and oil in a blender. Strain the mixture, reserving the oil and discarding the garlic pulp.

In a large sauté pan, heat the garlic oil over medium-low heat for 1 minute, or until the oil begins to shimmer. Add the bread cubes and stir with a wooden spoon for 3 to 5 minutes, or until the bread turns a light golden brown. Transfer to the prepared baking sheet to drain and cool completely.

Transfer the cooled bread cubes to a food processor and pulse into coarse crumbs.

In a medium bowl, toss the bread crumbs with the smoked paprika and salt. Set aside until ready to use. Keeps for up to a week in a tightly sealed container.

ROASTED ROOT VEGETABLES

Serve this with your holiday turkey. The peel of the acorn squash is edible, and when left on, it makes a beautiful presentation.

2 large sweet potatoes, unpeeled, cut into 1-inch chunks

12 small red potatoes, unpeeled, halved

1 acorn squash, unpeeled, cut into ½-inch-thick half-moons

½ large red onion, cut into chunks

8 garlic cloves, smashed

24 sprigs thyme

¼ cup olive oil

2 teaspoons kosher salt

1 teaspoon freshly ground black pepper

½ teaspoon ground mace

8 tablespoons (1 stick) unsalted butter, cut into 8 pieces

Preheat the oven to 400°F.

In a large bowl, toss the sweet potatoes, red potatoes, squash, red onion, garlic, and thyme with the olive oil. Season with the salt, pepper, and mace and toss again to coat evenly.

Arrange the vegetables in a large roasting pan and top with the pieces of butter. Bake for 20 minutes, then stir with a wooden spoon, and bake for another 20 minutes, or until the vegetables are fork-tender. Transfer the vegetables to a platter and serve immediately.

ORECCHIETTE SALAD
WITH GRILLED BROCCOLI AND GRAPES

MAKES 8 TO 12 SERVINGS

If you've never tasted grilled grapes, you need to try this pasta salad. It goes especially well with the Tarragon and Aleppo Chicken Leg Quarters (page 161).

1½ cups Tarragon and Aleppo White Sauce (page 161)

1 cup Spicy Walnuts (page 73)

2 large tart apples, such as Granny Smith, peeled, cored, and cut into thin wedges

Juice of ½ lemon

2 heads broccoli, quartered

¼ white onion

1 orange, cut in half

¼ cup plus 1 teaspoon olive oil

2 tablespoons kosher salt, plus more as needed

Freshly ground black pepper

2 cups red seedless grapes

1 pound orecchiette

¼ cup fresh tarragon leaves

¼ cup torn fresh basil

Prepare the Tarragon and Aleppo White Sauce and the Spicy Walnuts.

Prepare a grill for direct heat cooking, and preheat to 300°F.

Place the apple wedges in a bowl with enough cold water to cover and add the lemon juice. Set aside until ready to use.

Lightly brush the broccoli quarters, onion, and the cut sides of the orange halves with 1 teaspoon olive oil, and season with salt and pepper.

Grill the broccoli and onion, cut-side down, for 3 minutes. Flip and grill for an additional 3 minutes, then set aside to cool. When cool enough to handle, cut the broccoli into florets and julienne the onion.

Char the orange halves, cut-side down, for 3 minutes. Rotate the orange 45 degrees and char for an additional 3 minutes, then set aside to cool. When cool enough to handle, section the orange halves and remove the peel.

In a small bowl, lightly toss the grapes with ¼ cup olive oil, and season with salt and pepper. Place the grapes in a grill basket on the grill and cook for 3 to 4 minutes, or until they begin to blister. Set aside.

In a large stockpot, bring 4 to 6 quarts water with the salt to a rapid boil over high heat. Add the orecchiette, stir gently, and return to a boil. Cook for 11 minutes, or until the pasta is not quite al dente. Drain, and rinse the pasta with cold water to halt the cooking process. Drain well again, and toss in a large bowl with the remaining 1 teaspoon olive oil to prevent the pasta from sticking.

Drain the apples and pat them dry. In a large bowl, combine the pasta, apples, broccoli, grapes, onion, orange segments, Spicy Walnuts, Tarragon and Aleppo White Sauce, tarragon leaves, and basil. Toss gently to combine. Season with salt and pepper and serve immediately.

PINEAPPLE HOT DISH

My grandmother Florence served this dish alongside a ham at Easter. We kids felt we were getting away with something because we were able to eat this wonderfully sweet dish for dinner! It pairs well with any smoked meats. I have added some cayenne for a kick.

1 pound 6 ounces fresh pineapple, cut into chunks

1 cup bread crumbs

½ cup sugar

2 large eggs

4 tablespoons (½ stick) unsalted butter, at room temperature

½ teaspoon kosher salt

⅛ teaspoon cayenne pepper

Preheat the oven to 325°F.

In the bowl of a stand mixer fitted with the paddle attachment, combine all the ingredients and mix thoroughly. Transfer to a 9 x 13-inch casserole dish and bake for 40 minutes, rotating the pan after 20 minutes. Set aside to cool for 5 minutes before serving.

CORN PUDDING
WITH POBLANO PEPPERS

MAKES 4 TO 6 SERVINGS

Corn pudding is popular in the South, and often very sweet. While this recipe has a hint of sugar, it's more savory than sweet.

4 tablespoons (½ stick) unsalted butter, melted

1½ teaspoons vegetable oil

1 cup diced onions

1 cup fresh corn kernels (cut from the cob)

½ cup finely diced poblano peppers

¼ cup sugar

⅓ cup plus 2 teaspoons all-purpose flour

¼ cup yellow cornmeal

4 extra-large eggs, beaten

2 egg yolks, beaten

2½ cups canned creamed corn

½ cup sour cream

2½ cups whole milk

1 cup heavy cream

1½ tablespoons kosher salt

1 teaspoon freshly ground black pepper

1 teaspoon granulated garlic

Preheat the oven to 350°F. Grease an 8 x 8 x 2-inch glass baking dish with 1 tablespoon of the melted butter.

In a small skillet, heat the vegetable oil over medium heat. Add the onion, corn kernels, and poblano peppers. Cook, stirring occasionally, for 10 minutes, until the vegetables are softened. Set aside.

In the bowl of a stand mixer fitted with the paddle attachment, combine the sugar, flour, cornmeal, eggs, and egg yolks. Beat on medium speed for 1 minute, until combined. Add the creamed corn and sour cream, and beat on the lowest speed for 1 minute. Add the milk and heavy cream, and beat for 1 minute. Add the remaining 3 tablespoons melted butter, the salt, black pepper, granulated garlic, and the cooked corn mixture, and beat on low speed for 30 seconds.

Transfer the pudding to the prepared baking dish.

Place the baking dish in a shallow pan large enough to fit the baking dish, and fill the pan with enough water to come halfway up the sides of the baking dish. Bake on the lower rack of the oven for 20 minutes, then turn the pan a quarter turn and bake for 20 minutes more. Serve hot.

APPLE COLESLAW

Both coleslaw and apples are traditionally paired with pork. The dressing is a little sweet, but is balanced by the tartness of the green apples and the spiciness of the walnuts.

½ cup Spicy Walnuts (page 73)

1 cup Duke's Mayonnaise, or your favorite brand

¼ cup apple cider vinegar

3 tablespoons sugar

¾ teaspoon caraway seeds

¾ teaspoon kosher salt, plus more as needed

¼ teaspoon freshly ground black pepper, plus more as needed

¾ pound green cabbage, julienned

¾ pound Granny Smith apples, cored and julienned

½ tablespoon chopped fresh flat-leaf parsley

Prepare the Spicy Walnuts.

In a medium bowl, whisk together the mayonnaise, vinegar, sugar, caraway seeds, salt, and pepper. Set aside.

In a large bowl, combine the cabbage, apple, Spicy Walnuts, and parsley. Add the mayonnaise dressing and toss to coat. Season with salt and pepper.

Serve immediately or refrigerate until ready to serve. Toss again before serving.

LOADED BAKED POTATO CASSEROLE

MAKES 6 TO 8 SERVINGS

Inspired by a loaded baked potato, this dish is perfect for potluck dinners.

---

2 pounds Yukon Gold potatoes, peeled and cut into 1-inch cubes

4 tablespoons kosher salt

¾ cup heavy cream

¾ cup whole milk

6 tablespoons (¾ stick) unsalted butter

½ cup sliced scallions

¼ cup minced fresh chives

½ cup sour cream

¾ cup crumbled crispy cooked bacon (from about 9 slices)

1½ cup grated Pepper Jack cheese

Preheat the oven to 375°F.

Place the potatoes in a 6-quart stockpot and add 3 quarts cold water, or enough to cover. Add 3 tablespoons of the salt and bring to a boil over medium-high heat, then reduce the heat to medium and cook for 7 to 9 minutes, or until fork-tender.

Meanwhile, in a 2-quart saucepan, heat the cream, milk, and butter over medium heat just until the butter has melted.

Drain the potatoes and return them to the pot. Without turning on the heat, use a potato masher or a wooden spoon to lightly mash the potatoes. Add the hot cream mixture one-third at a time, mashing the potatoes to incorporate the cream before adding more. Continue to mash until all the cream is used.

In a medium bowl, combine the scallions, chives, and sour cream. Add half this mixture to the mashed potatoes and stir to combine. Add ½ cup of the bacon and ½ cup of the cheese to the potatoes, and stir to combine.

Evenly spread the potato mixture in an 8 x 8 x 2-inch casserole dish. Sprinkle the remaining 1 cup cheese and ¼ cup bacon evenly over the top of the casserole. Bake for 10 minutes, or until the cheese is melted and bubbling. Set aside to cool for 5 minutes before serving. Garnish each serving with a dollop of the remaining sour cream mixture.

SESAME CUCUMBER SALAD

I like cucumber salad in the summer—it pairs well with smoked and grilled meat. Toss just before serving to ensure the cucumbers remain crisp.

¾ cup Cucumber Salad Dressing (recipe follows)

6 cups sliced English cucumbers (halve lengthwise, then slice into ¼-inch-thick half-moons)

1½ teaspoons kosher salt

¾ teaspoon cracked black pepper

Prepare the Cucumber Salad Dressing.

Combine the cucumbers, dressing, salt, and pepper in a medium bowl and toss gently. Serve immediately.

CUCUMBER SALAD DRESSING

MAKES ABOUT 1 CUP

½ cup rice vinegar

¾ cup sugar

¼ teaspoon cayenne pepper

¾ teaspoon sesame seeds

Combine the vinegar and sugar in a small saucepan over low heat, and whisk until the sugar has dissolved. Remove from the heat and set aside to cool completely. Whisk in the cayenne and sesame seeds. The dressing can be kept in an airtight container in the refrigerator for up to 1 week.

FENNEL SAUSAGE STUFFING

12 tablespoons (1½ sticks) salted butter, plus more for greasing

1 cup medium-dice yellow onion

1 cup medium-dice celery

1 cup medium-dice fennel

1 pound Italian sausage, sweet or hot or a mixture, casing removed

10 cups 1-inch cubes stale French bread

1 teaspoon kosher salt

1 teaspoon cracked black pepper

1 teaspoon rubbed sage (available at most groceries)

3 cups chicken stock

Preheat the oven to 350°F. Butter a 9 x 13-inch casserole dish.

In a large, heavy-bottomed sauté pan, melt ½ cup (1 stick) of the butter over medium-high heat. Add the onion, celery, and fennel and cook, stirring often, for 15 minutes, or until the onion is lightly browned and translucent. Transfer the vegetables to a large bowl and set aside.

In the same pan, melt the remaining 4 tablespoons (½ stick) butter over medium-high heat, then add the sausage and cook, breaking up the meat into small pieces with a wooden spoon as it browns, for 5 to 7 minutes, or until the sausage is cooked through. Add the cooked sausage to bowl of vegetables, scraping the pan to incorporate any browned bits.

Add the bread cubes to the bowl and toss gently but thoroughly. Season with the salt, pepper, and sage and toss lightly.

Add the stock and toss until the bread has completely absorbed the liquid.

Transfer the mixture to the prepared casserole and bake for 20 to 30 minutes, or until golden brown and crusty on top. Let the sausage stuffing rest for 5 minutes before serving.

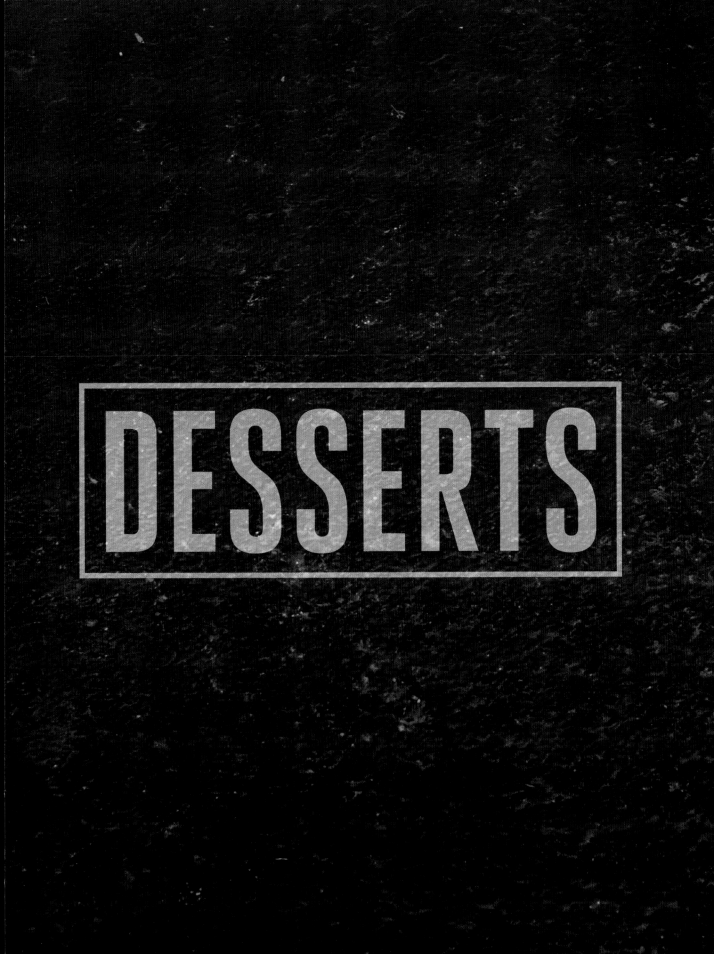

DESSERTS

I THINK OF DESSERTS AS A CONTINUATION OF A GREAT

meal, so in choosing these recipes I considered how they worked as a finish to a meal of grilled or smoked meats. Many of these dishes can be made in advance, making it easier for you to entertain. I've tried to choose a nice balance of desserts to cover everyone from chocoholics and ice cream aficionados to fruit- and berry-based desserts for diners who prefer a lighter finish. For those who reach for the comfort food first, the Banana Pudding with Chocolate Cookie Crumble and Spicy Walnuts (page 258) is a surprisingly different twist on this traditional childhood favorite.

The seasons and the weather played an important part in choosing which desserts to feature. I cook outdoors year-round, as do many people, so we've created a four-season dessert list that will have something for everyone all year. The desserts reflect seasonal ingredient choices, such as Pumpkin Cheesecake with Gingersnap Cookie Crust (page 227), while still offering our creative twist on the beloved desserts of our youth. And some recipes can be adapted to the season, such as the Peach and Blueberry Crisp (page 261): it can be enjoyed in the summer while the fruit is best; then, for the fall or winter, apples can be substituted for peaches and blueberries to create a great seasonal alternative. And, never one to forget the holidays, the Chocolate Whiskey Balls (page 278) are perfect for your Thanksgiving or Christmas table. Enjoy!

SALTED CARAMEL ICE CREAM

MAKES 1½ QUARTS

We love frozen desserts after working over a hot fire—or anytime, really!

If you don't have a candy thermometer to check the heat, you can use a sanitized meat thermometer instead.

1¼ cups sugar

2½ cups heavy cream

½ to ¾ teaspoon kosher salt

1 teaspoon pure vanilla extract

1½ cups whole milk

9 egg yolks

In a 2-quart saucepan, heat 1 cup of the sugar over medium heat, but do not stir as the sugar begins to caramelize and turn an amber color. Cook for 5 to 7 minutes, swirling the pan occasionally to ensure the sugar caramelizes evenly and the sugar is a uniform amber color. Be careful not to burn the sugar.

Add 1¼ cups of the cream (be careful—the mixture will bubble and pop as the cream is added), and cook, stirring, for 2 to 3 minutes, until the cream is thoroughly incorporated. Add the salt and vanilla and stir to combine. Remove from the heat and set aside until ready to use.

In a medium bowl, whisk together the egg yolks and the remaining ¼ cup sugar.

In a separate 2-quart saucepan, bring the milk and the remaining cream just to a simmer over medium-low heat, and remove from the heat. Gradually whisk the hot milk and cream into the egg mixture to temper the egg. Return this mixture to the saucepan and cook over medium heat for 3 to 5 minutes, whisking continuously, until a candy thermometer placed in the pot reads 170°F.

Remove from the heat and strain the mixture through a fine-mesh strainer into the pan with the caramel. Stir to combine, loosely cover, and refrigerate for 1 hour, or until completely cooled.

Pour the cooled ice cream base into an ice cream maker and churn according to the manufacturer's instructions. Transfer the ice cream to an airtight container and freeze until ready to serve.

FROZEN COCONUT LIME PIE

This crust, with grated coconut and graham crackers, is freakin' good. The pie can be made in advance and stored in the freezer, covered, for 1 to 2 weeks.

3 cups broken graham crackers
(½-inch pieces)

1 cup sweetened, shredded coconut

4 tablespoons (½ stick) unsalted butter, melted

2 (8-ounce) packages cream cheese, at room temperature

1 (15-ounce) can Coco Lopez coconut cream (scant 2 cups; available in the Hispanic section of most groceries)

1¾ cups sweetened condensed milk

1 tablespoon lime zest

1 cup fresh lime juice

2 tablespoons coconut extract

1 cup heavy cream

Preheat the oven to 350°F.

In a food processor, pulse the graham crackers and ½ cup of the shredded coconut for 10 seconds, just until the mixture forms coarse crumbs. Add the melted butter and pulse again until just combined. Press the mixture into the bottom of a 9-inch springform pan and bake for 15 to 20 minutes, until golden brown. Set aside to cool completely before adding the filling.

Meanwhile, in the bowl of a stand mixer fitted with the paddle attachment, beat the cream cheese for 3 to 5 minutes, occasionally scraping down the sides of the bowl with a rubber spatula, until smooth. Add the coconut cream, sweetened condensed milk, lime zest, lime juice, and coconut extract and mix until combined. Add the remaining ½ cup shredded coconut and mix until incorporated.

Place a metal bowl in the freezer to chill. When the bowl is chilled, add the heavy cream and whisk just until it holds firm peaks. Gently fold the whipped cream into the cream cheese filling.

Pour the filling into the prepared crust, cover with plastic wrap, and freeze overnight. Remove from the freezer 30 minutes before you plan to slice and serve.

ORANGE AND CREAM ICE CREAM

This ice cream takes me back to my childhood. If you have any leftover Chocolate Shortbread Cookies (page 263), we recommend serving them along with this ice cream.

1 cup whole milk

2 cups heavy cream

1 tablespoon orange zest

¼ cup packed dark brown sugar

1 teaspoon pure vanilla extract

Pinch of kosher salt

9 egg yolks

1 cup granulated sugar

1 cup orange juice, any kind is fine

In a 2-quart saucepan, bring the milk, cream, orange zest, brown sugar, vanilla extract, and salt to a simmer over medium-low heat, then remove from the heat and let cool for 30 minutes at room temperature.

In a large bowl, whisk together the egg yolks and granulated sugar.

Warm the milk and cream mixture over medium heat just until hot, then gradually whisk the milk mixture into the egg yolks to temper them. Return this mixture to the saucepan and cook over medium heat for 3 to 5 minutes, whisking continuously, until a candy thermometer placed in the pot reads 170°F. Stir in the orange juice and set aside to cool slightly. Loosely cover and refrigerate for 1 hour, or until completely cooled.

Remove the ice cream base from the refrigerator and pass it through a fine-mesh strainer.

Pour the strained ice cream base into an ice cream maker and churn according to the manufacturer's instructions. Transfer the ice cream to an airtight container and freeze until ready to serve.

BANANA PUDDING

WITH CHOCOLATE COOKIE CRUMBLE AND SPICY WALNUTS

MAKES 10 TO 12 SERVINGS

The spiciness of the cookies and walnuts brings a savory element to this dessert.

---

14 Chocolate Shortbread Cookies (page 263, or substitute chocolate Nilla wafers), broken into quarters

6 medium bananas, peel on

¾ cup sugar

¼ cup all-purpose flour

4 egg yolks

1 large egg

1 tablespoon pure vanilla extract

4 cups whole milk

4 tablespoons (½ stick) unsalted butter, diced

2 cups Whipped Cream (recipe follows)

1 cup chopped Spicy Walnuts (page 73), or substitute toasted walnuts

½ to ¾ cup Rum Glaze (recipe follows)

Prepare the Chocolate Shortbread Cookies.

Preheat the oven to 350°F. Line a baking sheet with aluminum foil.

Place 4 whole bananas, with the peels on, on the prepared baking sheet and roast for 7 minutes. Set aside to cool completely before peeling. When they have cooled, peel and puree the bananas in a food processor for 1 minute, until smooth; or place them in a large bowl and whisk by hand or with a hand mixer until smooth. Set aside at room temperature until ready to use.

In a medium bowl, whisk together the sugar, flour, egg yolks, egg, and vanilla until thoroughly combined.

In a 2- to 3-quart saucepan, bring the milk to a simmer over medium-low heat. Remove the pot from the heat and gradually whisk the hot milk into the egg mixture to temper the egg. Return this mixture to the saucepan and cook over medium heat for 2 to 3 minutes, whisking continuously, until the mixture comes to a boil. Reduce the heat to medium-low and whisk for 2 to 3 minutes more, or until the pudding thickens. Remove from the heat, add the butter, and stir until it has melted completely. For a smoother consistency, use a rubber spatula or a ladle to press the mixture through a fine-mesh strainer into a large bowl.

Add the pureed bananas to the pudding mixture and stir to combine. Cover the banana pudding with plastic wrap pressed directly against the surface to prevent a skin from forming, and refrigerate for at least 1 hour, or until completely cool.

Prepare the Whipped Cream, Spicy Walnuts, and Rum Glaze.

(continued)

Arrange the broken cookies in a uniform layer in the bottom of a 9 x 13-inch casserole dish and top with the banana pudding. Add a layer of Whipped Cream.

Peel and slice the remaining 2 bananas in ¼-inch-thick rounds.

In a small bowl, gently toss the sliced bananas with the Spicy Walnuts and the Rum Glaze. Arrange the sliced bananas atop the layer of Whipped Cream, cover, and refrigerate for at least 4 hours before serving.

WHIPPED CREAM

MAKES 2 CUPS

1 cup heavy cream
2 tablespoons confectioners' sugar
½ teaspoon vanilla extract

Place a metal bowl in the freezer to chill. When the bowl is chilled, add the cream, sugar, and vanilla. Whisk until the cream holds firm peaks. Cover and refrigerate until ready to use.

RUM GLAZE

MAKES ¾ CUP

½ cup sugar
2 tablespoons dark rum, your favorite brand

In a small saucepan, combine the sugar, rum, and 2 tablespoons water and bring to a boil over medium-high heat. Cook for 2 to 3 minutes, then remove from the heat, cover, and set aside until ready to use. If the sugar crystallizes, rewarm it over low heat.

PEACH AND BLUEBERRY CRISP

I like the crunchiness of this topping, and you can substitute apples for peaches and blueberries in the fall and winter. It's best served warm, not hot, with Whipped Cream (page 260) or Salted Caramel Ice Cream (page 253).

¾ cup plus 1 tablespoon all-purpose flour

1 cup rolled oats

1 cup pecans, coarsely chopped

1 cup packed light brown sugar

8 tablespoons (1 stick) cold unsalted butter, cut into ½-inch pieces, plus 1 tablespoon at room temperature

¼ cup granulated sugar

¼ teaspoon ground cinnamon

⅛ teaspoon freshly grated nutmeg

10 peaches, peeled, pitted, and cut into wedges

2 cups fresh blueberries

Preheat the oven to 350°F.

In a medium bowl, combine ¾ cup of the flour, the oats, pecans, and brown sugar in a medium bowl. Use your fingers to mix the ½-inch pieces of butter into the flour mixture to form fine crumbs. Squeeze the crumbs together to form ½-inch clumps. Cover and refrigerate the crumble until ready to use.

In a small bowl, stir together the granulated sugar, remaining 1 tablespoon flour, the cinnamon, and the nutmeg.

In a large bowl, combine the peaches and blueberries. Add the sugar-spice mixture and toss until the fruit is evenly coated.

Butter a 10-inch cast-iron skillet with the remaining 1 tablespoon butter. Add the fruit to the skillet and spread to form an even layer. Cover the fruit with the crumble topping, maintaining the irregularly shaped clumps.

Bake the crisp for 45 minutes, uncovered, until the crumble is crisp and golden brown. Let cool slightly before serving.

CHOCOLATE SHORTBREAD COOKIES

MAKES 36 TO 48 COOKIES

If you use these cookies for Banana Pudding (page 258) or Chocolate Whiskey Balls (page 278), bake them for an extra 1 to 2 minutes to make them crispier. These cookies may be frozen for up to 3 months.

1½ cups all-purpose flour, plus more for dusting

1½ teaspoons baking powder

¼ teaspoon smoked salt (see Source Guide, page 279) or kosher salt

¾ teaspoon ground cinnamon

½ teaspoon freshly ground black pepper

¼ teaspoon ground cloves

⅛ teaspoon ground chile de árbol (see Source Guide, page 279) or cayenne pepper

¾ cup unsweetened cocoa powder

12 tablespoons (1½ sticks) unsalted butter, at room temperature

1½ teaspoons pure vanilla extract

1 cup sugar

1 large egg

In a small bowl, sift together the flour, baking powder, smoked salt, cinnamon, black pepper, cloves, chile de árbol, and cocoa powder.

In the bowl of a stand mixer fitted with the paddle attachment, cream the butter on medium-high speed for 3 minutes, until fluffy and light in color. Reduce the speed to medium-low, add the vanilla and sugar, and mix until well combined. Add the egg and beat until just combined. Reduce the speed to low, add one-third of the flour mixture, and mix until just combined. Repeat the process, incorporating the remaining two-thirds of the flour mixture, and mix the dough until the dry ingredients are just incorporated. The dough will hold together when squeezed.

Turn the cookie dough out onto a clean, lightly floured work surface and use your hands to shape it into a 12 x 1½- to 2-inch log. Wrap the log in plastic wrap and freeze for at least 1 hour, or until the dough is firm.

Preheat the oven to 375°F. Position an oven rack in the top third of the oven and another rack in the bottom third of the oven. Line two baking sheets with parchment paper or silicone baking mats.

Remove the dough from the freezer and cut it into ¼-inch-thick discs. Arrange the cookies 1 inch apart on the baking sheets, and place one baking sheet on the top oven rack and one on the bottom rack. Bake for 10 to 12 minutes, switching the baking sheets from top to bottom and bottom to top halfway through. Transfer the cookies to a wire rack to cool.

GINGERSNAP COOKIES

If you use these for the Pumpkin Cheesecake crust (page 277), bake them for an extra 1 to 2 minutes for crispier cookies.

1 cup plus 2½ tablespoons all-purpose flour, plus more for dusting

1 teaspoon baking soda

¼ teaspoon kosher salt

1 teaspoon ground ginger

¼ teaspoon ground cloves

1 teaspoon ground cinnamon

6 tablespoons vegetable shortening

½ cup plus 2 tablespoons sugar

2½ tablespoons molasses

1 large egg

In a medium bowl, sift together the flour, baking powder, salt, ginger, cloves, and ½ teaspoon of the cinnamon.

In the bowl of a stand mixer fitted with the paddle attachment, cream the shortening on medium-high speed for 3 minutes, until soft and fluffy. Add ½ cup of the sugar and beat until smooth. Reduce the speed to medium-low and beat in the molasses and egg. Reduce the speed to low, add half the flour mixture, and mix until just combined. Repeat the process, incorporating the remaining flour mixture, and mix the dough until the dry ingredients are just incorporated. The dough will hold together when squeezed.

Turn out the cookie dough onto a clean, lightly floured work surface. Shape dough into a log 1½ to 2 inches in diameter. Wrap in plastic wrap and freeze for at least 1 hour, or until dough is firm.

Preheat the oven to 375°F. Line two baking sheets with parchment paper, or silicone baking mats. Position an oven rack in the top third of the oven, and another rack in the bottom third of the oven.

In a small bowl, combine the remaining 2 tablespoons sugar and ½ teaspoon cinnamon.

Remove the dough from the freezer and cut it into ¼-inch-thick discs. Dip one side of each cookie into the sugar-cinnamon mixture, and place them sugar-side up, 1 inch apart on the baking sheets.

Place one baking sheet on the top oven rack and one sheet on the bottom rack. Bake for 11 to 13 minutes, switching the pans halfway through the baking process from the top to bottom and bottom to top. A longer cooking time will produce crispier cookies. Transfer the cookies to a wire rack to cool.

LEMON CURD
WITH SPONGE CAKE AND BERRIES

MAKES 8 SERVINGS

Leftover lemon curd keeps, refrigerated, for 7 to 10 days. It's great with cookies or on toast.

LEMON CURD

1¼ cups sugar

5 large eggs

1 cup fresh lemon juice

24 tablespoons (3 sticks) unsalted butter, melted

SPONGE CAKE

1 tablespoon unsalted butter, at room temperature

1 cup plus 1 teaspoon all-purpose flour

¾ cup sugar

4 large eggs

6 tablespoons canola oil

⅛ teaspoon pure vanilla extract

⅛ teaspoon kosher salt

2 tablespoons cornstarch

1½ teaspoons baking powder

3 cups seasonal berries

1 teaspoon sugar

Whipped Cream (page 260)

Make the lemon curd: In a small bowl, whisk together the sugar and eggs. Pour 2 inches of water into the bottom of a double boiler and bring to a simmer over medium heat. In the top of the double boiler, stir together the lemon juice and butter. Add the egg mixture and cook for 3 to 5 minutes, stirring continuously, until the curd thickens and a candy thermometer placed in the pot reads 170°F. Remove from the heat and use a spatula or large spoon to press the curd through a fine-mesh strainer into a bowl. Cover the surface of the lemon curd with plastic wrap and refrigerate until completely cool.

Make the sponge cake: Preheat the oven to 350°F. Butter a 9-inch cake pan, then sprinkle with 1 teaspoon of the flour, tapping the sides of the pan and turning it to evenly distribute the flour.

In a small bowl, whisk together the sugar and eggs until smooth. Pour 2 inches of water into the bottom half of a double boiler and bring to a simmer over medium heat. In the top half of the double boiler, put the sugar-egg mixture and whisk continuously for 5 to 7 minutes, until the sugar has dissolved and the batter thickens. Remove the top half of the double boiler from the heat, whisk in the oil and vanilla, and transfer the mixture to a large bowl.

In a separate small bowl, sift together the remaining 1 cup flour, salt, cornstarch, and baking powder. Fold these dry ingredients into the bowl of wet ingredients until well combined. Transfer the batter to the prepared cake pan and bake for 25 minutes, or until a toothpick inserted into the center of the cake comes out clean. Let the cake cool completely in the pan for 1 hour.

To serve, toss the berries with the sugar. Serve each slice of cake with ¼ cup each of the lemon curd and Whipped Cream. Divide the berries equally among the servings.

SPICED PECAN PIE
WITH BOURBON WHIPPED CREAM

MAKES ONE 9-INCH PIE

You might think this is a typical Southern pecan pie, but the addition of the orange zest and chipotle chile powder makes it less cloyingly sweet than the original.

1 recipe Basic Pie Dough (recipe follows)

6 tablespoons (¾ stick) unsalted butter

⅔ cup packed light brown sugar

½ teaspoon kosher salt

1 tablespoon orange zest

½ teaspoon ground cinnamon

¼ teaspoon chipotle chile powder (available in most major groceries)

½ cup light corn syrup

¼ cup molasses

3 tablespoons bourbon

1½ teaspoons pure vanilla extract

3 large eggs

1½ cups chopped toasted pecans

2 cups Cinnamon and Bourbon Whipped Cream (recipe follows)

Prepare the Basic Pie Dough.

Preheat the oven to 400°F.

On a lightly floured surface, roll the chilled dough out to an 11- to 12-inch-diameter circle. Transfer the dough to a 9-inch pie plate and trim it so that the dough is even with the edges of the pie plate. Use the tines of a fork to puncture the bottom of the dough seven times, evenly spacing the punctures.

Cut a piece of parchment paper or aluminum foil just wide enough to cover the dough and press it into the bottom of the pan and over the edges. Arrange pie weights or dry beans evenly over the parchment or foil in the bottom of the pan.

Bake the crust for 15 minutes, then remove from the oven and remove the weights or beans and the parchment or foil. Reduce the oven temperature to 350°F, and bake the crust for 10 minutes more. Transfer to a wire rack to cool completely. Keep the oven on.

In a small saucepan, combine the butter, brown sugar, salt, orange zest, cinnamon, and chipotle powder and cook over medium heat, whisking, for 1 to 2 minutes, until the butter has completely melted and the mixture begins to bubble. Add the corn syrup, molasses, bourbon, and vanilla and whisk to combine. Remove from the heat.

In a large bowl, whisk the eggs. Gradually add half the contents of the saucepan to the eggs, whisking continuously, then return this mixture to the saucepan over medium heat. Bring to a simmer and cook, whisking continuously, for 3 to 4 minutes, until the filling is thick and glossy. Remove from the heat and stir in the pecans. Pour the pie filling into the cooled crust.

Bake 30 to 40 minutes, or until the filling is set and the pie jiggles slightly in the center when gently shaken. Remove from the oven and set aside to cool completely.

Serve each slice with a spoonful of Cinnamon and Bourbon Whipped Cream.

BASIC PIE DOUGH

MAKES ONE 9-INCH SINGLE PIECRUST

2 cups all-purpose flour, plus more for dusting

¾ teaspoon kosher salt

½ teaspoon sugar

12 tablespoons (1½ sticks) cold unsalted butter, diced

2 to 3 tablespoons ice water

Combine the flour, salt, sugar, and butter in a food processor. Pulse the mixture while gradually adding the ice water, until the dough is coarse and the butter has broken down to pieces the size of peas. The dough should be crumbly and hold together when squeezed. Do not overwork the dough.

Roll the dough out on a clean, lightly floured work surface, form it into a disc, and transfer it to a large piece of plastic wrap. Wrap tightly and refrigerate for at least 1 hour, or until the dough is firm. Roll out and bake as directed in the recipe.

CINNAMON AND BOURBON WHIPPED CREAM

MAKES 2 CUPS

1 cup heavy cream

2 tablespoons confectioners' sugar

2 teaspoons bourbon

⅛ teaspoon ground cinnamon

Place a metal bowl in the freezer to chill. When the bowl is chilled, combine the cream, sugar, bourbon, and cinnamon and whisk until the cream holds firm peaks. Cover and refrigerate until ready to use.

UPSIDE-DOWN APPLE TART

MAKES 8 TO 10 SERVINGS

One of the first desserts I learned to make under Chef Alain was tarte tatin. This is basically the same dish. I recommend serving it with Salted Caramel Ice Cream (page 253), or your favorite brand of vanilla ice cream.

1 recipe Basic Pie Dough (page 269)

8 large Granny Smith apples, peeled, quartered, and cored

½ cup sugar

3 tablespoons unsalted butter, at room temperature

Preheat the oven to 350°F.

Prepare the Basic Pie Dough and refrigerate until ready to bake.

In a 10-inch sauté pan or cast-iron skillet, heat the sugar and 2 tablespoons water over medium heat, but do not stir as the sugar begins to caramelize and turn an amber color. Cook for 5 to 7 minutes, swirling the pan occasionally to ensure the sugar caramelizes evenly and the sugar is a uniform amber color. Be careful not to burn the sugar. Remove the pot from the heat and stir in the butter. Set aside to cool slightly before the next step.

When the caramelized sugar has cooled, place 3 or 4 apple quarters in the center of the pan and arrange a layer of apples, curved-side down, in tight concentric circles around the center apples. (It's important to arrange the apples without gaps so the tart inverts easily.) Arrange the remaining apples in an even layer flush with the top of the pan.

On a clean, lightly floured work surface, roll the chilled Basic Pie Dough out to an 11- to 12-inch diameter circle. Drape the dough over the rolling pin to transfer the dough to the pan. Use your fingers to lightly press the dough down to cover the apples. Trim any excess dough from the edges by running a rolling pin over the dough and removing the excess. Tuck the edges of the dough into the outer rim of the pan or skillet.

Return the pan to low heat and cook for 15 to 20 minutes. Transfer the pan to the oven and bake for 30 minutes, or until the crust is golden brown. Remove and set aside to cool for 20 minutes.

To invert the tart, run a sharp knife around the outer edge of the pan. Invert a 12-inch plate or platter atop the crust and, holding the plate and pan together, flip the pan so the tart ends up on the plate. Gently tap the bottom to help release the apples. Let the tart cool for 30 minutes more before slicing and serving.

CHOCOLATE BROWNIES
WITH PEANUT BRITTLE

MAKES ONE 9-INCH SQUARE PAN

These are rich and intense chocolate brownies that give a nod to Virginia peanuts with the addition of crunchy brittle.

1½ cups Peanut Brittle (recipe follows)

16 tablespoons (2 sticks) cold unsalted butter, diced

4 ounces semisweet chocolate

2 cups sugar

1 teaspoon pure vanilla extract

4 large eggs

2 cups all-purpose flour

¼ teaspoon kosher salt

8 ounces bittersweet chocolate

½ cup heavy cream

Prepare the Peanut Brittle.

Preheat the oven to 350°F. Grease a 9-inch square baking pan.

Pour 2 inches of water into the bottom of a double boiler and bring to a simmer over medium-low heat. In the top of the double boiler, melt the butter and chocolate, stirring occasionally, until the mixture is smooth and completely combined. Remove the pot from the heat and set aside to cool slightly.

In a large bowl, gently whisk together the sugar, vanilla, and eggs. Gradually add the chocolate mixture to the egg mixture, stirring to combine.

In a separate bowl, sift together the flour and salt, and gently fold this into the chocolate-and-egg mixture.

Pour the batter into the prepared pan and bake for 28 minutes. Remove from the oven and let cool to room temperature.

While the brownies are cooling, reheat the water in the bottom of the double boiler over medium-low heat and combine the bittersweet chocolate and heavy cream in the top of the double boiler. Cook, stirring occasionally, until the mixture is smooth and melted. Pour this ganache over the cooled brownies. Spread the Peanut Brittle evenly over the ganache and set aside to cool completely before slicing and serving.

PEANUT BRITTLE

½ **cup sugar**

1 cup roasted and salted peanuts, chopped

Line a baking sheet with parchment paper or a silicone baking mat.

In a small saucepan, combine the sugar and 2 tablespoons water over medium heat, but do not stir as the sugar begins to caramelize and turn an amber color. Cook, swirling the pot occasionally, for 5 to 7 minutes, being careful not to burn the sugar, until the sugar is a uniform amber color.

Remove from the heat and quickly stir in the peanuts. Transfer immediately to the prepared baking sheet, spreading the mixture out as quickly and evenly as possible. The brittle will begin to harden immediately. Let cool completely, then transfer the brittle to a heavy-duty, resealable plastic bag and crush to pea-size pieces. Set the peanut brittle aside until ready to use. This will keep for weeks in an airtight container.

PUMPKIN CHEESECAKE
WITH GINGERSNAP COOKIE CRUST

MAKES 16 SERVINGS

Here's a perfect new way to end a fall or winter dinner. The spices, coupled with the gingersnap crust, balance the sweetness of this dessert.

3 cups Gingersnap Cookie pieces (page 264)

8 tablespoons (1 stick) unsalted butter, melted

2 (8-ounce) packages cream cheese, at room temperature

1½ cups confectioners' sugar

1 tablespoon cornstarch

½ cup sour cream

1 cup canned pumpkin puree

1¼ teaspoons ground cinnamon

1¼ teaspoons ground ginger

½ teaspoon freshly grated nutmeg

¼ teaspoon kosher salt

4 large eggs

Prepare the Gingersnap Cookies.

Preheat the oven to 350°F.

Pulse the cookie pieces in a food processor for 15 to 20 seconds, until they have broken down into coarse crumbs. Add the melted butter and pulse until just combined. Use your hands to press this mixture into the bottom and 1 to 1½ inches up the sides of a 9-inch springform pan.

Bake for 10 minutes, then remove from the oven and set aside to cool completely. Lower the oven temperature to 325°F.

Fill a small baking pan with 1 inch of water and place it on the bottom rack of the oven to create steam.

In the bowl of a stand mixer fitted with the paddle attachment, combine the cream cheese, confectioners' sugar, and cornstarch and cream on medium speed for 2 to 3 minutes, until smooth. Add the sour cream and mix until well combined. Add the pumpkin puree, cinnamon, ginger, nutmeg, and salt and mix until smooth. Add the eggs, one at a time, mixing well between additions. Pour the filling into the prepared crust.

Bake for 45 minutes, or until the cheesecake is set and jiggles slightly in the center when gently shaken. Remove from the oven and set aside to cool for 30 minutes. Refrigerate for at least 6 hours or up to overnight before slicing and serving.

CHOCOLATE WHISKEY BALLS

MAKES 15 TO 20 PIECES

Don't let the kids get into these—the whiskey doesn't cook out. These whiskey balls make a great holiday gift.

1 cup Spiced Pecans (page 73)

20 Chocolate Shortbread Cookies (page 263) or chocolate Nilla wafers

1 cup unsweetened cocoa powder

1 cup confectioners' sugar

¼ cup light corn syrup

⅓ cup Jack Daniel's whiskey

All-purpose flour, for dusting

Prepare the Spiced Pecans and the Chocolate Shortbread Cookies.

Put the pecans and cookies in a food processor and pulse until broken down into coarse crumbs.

In a small bowl, combine the cocoa powder and confectioners' sugar.

In a large bowl, combine the cookie crumb mixture with 1⅓ cups of the cocoa-sugar mixture; set aside the remaining cocoa-sugar mixture. Add the corn syrup and whiskey to the bowl and mix until thoroughly incorporated. The dough will be stiff.

On a clean, lightly floured work surface, pinch off enough dough to roll into ¾-inch balls and toss them in the bowl with the remaining cocoa-sugar mixture to coat. The whiskey balls will keep in an airtight container in the refrigerator for up to 1 week.

SOURCE GUIDE

BBQ Guru
Temperature control devices.
bbqguru.com

Big Poppa Smoker's
Barbecue supplies, tools,
and ingredients.
bigpoppasmokers.com

Broken Arrow Ranch
Venison and quail.
brokenarrowranch.com

Butter Pat Industries
Quality cast-iron cookware.
butterpatindustries.com

D'Artagnan
Goose, quail, and duck.
dartagnan.com

Fireboard
Temperature-monitoring
devices.
fireboard.io

Grill Grates
Replacement grill grates
that perform amazingly.
grillgrate.com

Jambo Pits
Quality custom-built
offset stickburner pits.
jambopits.com

JB Prince
Cooking tools.
jbprince.com

The Kansas City BBQ Store
BBQ sauces, seasonings,
smokers, and supplies.
thekansascitybbqstore.com

My Spice Sage
Quality spices.
myspicesage.com

Penzeys Spices
Quality spices.
penzeys.com

Primo Ceramic Grills
Ceramic grills and
accessories.
primogrill.com

Thermo Works
Instant-read thermometers
and other temperature-
monitoring devices.
thermoworks.com

Uline
Bags, gloves, jars, and more.
uline.com

Yeti Coolers
Premium coolers.
yeti.com

ACKNOWLEDGMENTS

I have so many people to thank and will always be grateful to them:

My wife, Leslie, who is my best friend and makes me so much better with her than I am by myself. We have done so much together, and the work and support she has given me and my barbecue life have made this book and so many other things possible. I love you to Alpha Centauri and back.

My son, Sam, who has been so supportive of my work and understanding of when I am gone because of it. You are the best son that I could ever have and I am so proud of who you are.

My mom, Charlotte, who gave me so much love and encouragement and taught me so many lessons in life. Your great love that you had to give is so missed and I wish I could have your fried eggplant one more time.

My dad, George, who I have been so blessed to cook with on the competition circuit. The good fortune we have had as Cool Smoke is amazing, and to share these moments with my father as my teammate is unbelievable.

Danielle Goodreau, you are a rockstar! This book is not mine, but ours! What started off as a request for you to help me with my book turned into collaboration. Developing recipes with you was fun and I am so happy with the dishes we created together. You are a badass chef and one of the most hardworking, brilliant people who I have had the opportunity to work with. You helped make this project so much better than I could have on my own. Thank you for everything!

Elizabeth Moore and Cecelia Strong of Green Olive Media, for introducing me to Janice Shay.

Janice Shay, for helping make this book a reality and for taking my mixed-up writings and helping to bring clarity. You made this project happen, gave guidance, and provided valuable opinions in design and layout. Thank you!

BJ Berti, for being my amazing editor and supporting all of my changes. I was so fortunate to have you as my editor and making this book so great! Thank you!

Libbie Summers, I was so lucky to meet you (thank you, Janice!), and I will always be in awe of your talents! You made our dishes look amazing. I will never forget watching you set the first food shot and knowing that everything was going to be all right! Thank you!

Ken Goodman, after so many years, we did this! You are so talented and these images bring life to this book. When you shared the images from our photo shoot, I was blown away. What is amazing is that these images still have that impact on me after looking at them so many times! Thank you!

Jeff Hayes, for being the great friend that you are and for all the help you give me both in life and at the cooking school.

Josh Loeb, for all of your help with the food preparations for the photo shoot.

David Dempsey, thanks for everything, but especially the jacket.

My publisher, St. Martin's Press, for all of your support and for believing in this project.

David Rotstein and Young Lim, for your work on the cover. Michelle McMillian and Jan Derevjanik, who worked on the interior design, and Eric C. Meyer, my production editor. The entire team at St. Martin's Press is so good! Thanks for sticking with me and helping make this book what it is.

Kelly Alder, for creating the illustrations in this book.

My Grandmother Stone, Florence, for the cookies, pineapple hot dish, sourdough starter, teaching me how to fish, and so much more.

My Grandfather Stone, for teaching me to be humble and for telling me to "marry up" and marry someone that I was better with together than by myself.

Chef Alain Vincey, for the opportunity to learn from you how to be a chef and for being a dear friend.

John Markus, the man who gave me the nickname the "Professor." Thanks for bringing me to the *BBQ Pitmasters* television show and inviting me to travel to Kuwait with you, where we had the honor to cook for thousands of our troops. I owe you so much!

Jamie Geer, for not only building my first Jambo in 2005, which I affectionately call the "Grillvette," but for teaching me so much about cooking barbecue.

Kendall Lamp, who was my first teammate in Cool Smoke and was the guy who first color-coded our spreadsheets for our cooking schedule.

To all the many pitmasters and chefs who have shared so much knowledge with me. This list is long and I apologize to anyone who I may have missed. Many thanks to Steve Farrin, Rod Gray, Johnny Trigg, Myron Mixon, Pat Burke, Melissa Cookston, Mike Mills, Buddy Goodwin, Chris Capel, Joe Amore, Byron Chism, Lee McWright, Gary Sublett, Sterling Ball, Tommy Houston, Mike Davis, David Harmon, Pete Vasquez, Jay Frank, and so many more!

Robert Lerma, for some of the amazing images that you have captured over the years and being willing to share some of your Cool Smoke photos in this book. The feeling that your images provoke always moves me.

Smithfield, for providing me with all of the pork needed for the recipe development for this book. I'm proud to be part of the team.

Primo Ceramic Grills, for making such great products. Most of the recipes were tested over and over, using your grills, which never failed us once.

Yeti Coolers, for getting my competition meats all over the country frosty cold every time.

Snake River Farms, for providing me all the beef needed for the recipe development for this book.

A special thank-you to the Gardner Family, for allowing me to cook and photograph at your beautiful farm, Woodgrove!

INDEX